Jesus Who?

Myth vs. Reality in the Search for the Historical Jesus

Copyright © 2006 Dr. James Gardner

10-Digit ISBN 1-59113-955-4
13-Digit ISBN 978-1-59113-955-3

All rights reserved. No part of this publication may be reproduced, stored in a retrieval system, or transmitted in any form or by any means, electronic, mechanical, recording or otherwise, without the prior written permission of the author.

Printed in the United States of America.

Booklocker.com, Inc.
2006

http://www.JesusWho.net

Jesus Who?

Myth vs. Reality in the Search for the Historical Jesus

Dr. James Gardner

Table of Contents

Table of Contents v
Acknowledgements ix
Introduction xi
About the Gospels 1
   When Were The Gospels Written? 2
   Problems Interpreting the Gospels 8
Who Was Jesus? 41
   Did Jesus Exist? 41
   What Was Jesus' Real Name? 51
   Will the Real Jesus Please Stand Up 52
Birth 57
   When Was Jesus Born? 57
   Was Jesus Born on Christmas? 58
   Born at the Stroke of Midnight? 61
   Born in Bethlehem? 61
   Born in a Manger? 64
   The Magi 65
   Was There a Star? 66
   The Virgin Birth 67
   Was Jesus an Illegitimate Child? 73
   Was Mary a Perpetual Virgin? 77
Family 79
   Who Was Jesus' Father? 79
   Who Was Jesus' Mother? 83
   Did Jesus Have Any Brothers or Sisters? 85
   What Was Jesus' Relationship to His Family? 87
   What Was the Family's Social Status? 89
Childhood 91
   Was Jesus Raised in Nazareth? 91
   Did Jesus Grow up in Qumran? 94
   Did Jesus Live in Egypt? 98
   Did Jesus Live in India? 100
Personal Life 103
   What Education Did Jesus Have? 103

What Was Jesus' Occupation?	105
What Did Jesus Look Like?	105
What Was Jesus' Religion?	110
What Were Jesus' Attitudes Toward Sex?	114
Was Jesus a Homosexual?	116
Was Jesus Married?	117
Did Jesus Have Children?	127
What Was Jesus Like as a Person?	129

Ministry ... 141
- When Did Jesus Preach? ... 141
- How Large Was His Following? ... 144
- Was Jesus a Miracle Worker? ... 149
- Was Jesus an Exorcist? ... 159
- Was Jesus a Prophet? ... 160
- Was Jesus a Zealot? ... 162
- Was Jesus Anti-Gentile? ... 164
- What was Jesus' Relationship With John the Baptist? ... 166
- What Did Jesus Actually Say? ... 174

Death ... 183
- What Was Jesus Accused of? ... 183
- Why Was Jesus Arrested? ... 185
- Was Jesus Beaten? ... 187
- Was Jesus Crucified? ... 189
- When was Jesus Crucified? ... 194
- Was There a Last Supper? ... 199
- How Old Was Jesus When He Died? ... 200
- How Was Jesus Crucified? ... 202
- Did Jesus Die on the Cross? ... 203
- Was Jesus Hung From a Tree? ... 206

Lasting Questions ... 211
- Is The 2nd Coming, Coming? Or Has It Gone? ... 211
- Was Jesus Resurrected? ... 213
- Was Jesus the Old Testament Messiah? ... 222
- Was Jesus the "Suffering Servant? ... 226
- Was Jesus the Son of God? ... 228

Final Thoughts ... 233

Dateline ... 237

Jesus – Myth vs. Reality ... 247

References 251
Index... 261

Acknowledgements

Writing a book is a team effort, even if only one person ends up getting the credit (or blame). Throughout this multi-year project I was graciously supported by my wife, Anne Breuer, and my friends John Devine, Amedeo Scabbia, Alba Souza, Phil Marks, and Henry Chian. Peter Morrison and Michael Holland provided hours of scholarly assistance. Peter Gandy was generous with his time. Norman Cavior and Katie Smith provided excellent suggestions. Jim Quinn, Sheila Levi Strauss, Wade Schlosser, Rebecca McGowen, Richard Dennison, Hoda Anton Culver, Bill Roley and Pam McNeill were great cheerleaders. The Orange County Public Library (especially Catherine Clark) and the Newport Beach Public Library as well as the Orange Coast College Library were instrumental in keeping the costs down, and I thank them for their help. Peter Kirby's website EarlyChristianWritings.com was of enormous assistance, as was Wikipedia.com. I recommend these websites to anyone doing research in this area. Finally, thanks to Angela Hoy, Julie Sartain, and Gregg Porter who helped with the final publishing chores.

Unless otherwise indicated, all quotations from the Bible are from the American Standard Version as displayed on the EarlyChristianWritings website.

Introduction

Are you ready? For the journey of a lifetime, the ultimate search for the pen-ultimate mystery that has captured the imaginations of Freud, Jung, Schweitzer, Voltaire, John Locke, Thomas Jefferson, George Washington, Upton Sinclair, Arthur Canon Doyle, Karl Marx, Tolstoy, Dostoevsky, and more than a billion people for nearly 2000 years? We're going to embark on a momentous journey that starts with the question nearly everyone has asked – "Who was Jesus?" Yet the sheer simplicity of the question hides the awesome complexity of our search. For each person who asks this question, and starts the journey, inquires from their own unique perspective – hence it is a journey with a billion embarkation points and as many different and diverse destinations.

Our time together on this adventure needs to be defined so that your experience is maximized. Our goal is to go looking for Jesus in as empirical and methodological a manner as possible, going wherever the evidence takes us, down any road or back alley, no matter how dark or obscure. Along the way we will encounter the religious Jesus. He will be there, all around us, and the brilliance of his light will obscure the historical Jesus who hides in his shadow. But this challenge is not unique to the quest for Jesus. All great people have two lives, and all true biographers must learn how to separate the public face from the private one, to see where the legend stops and the person begins. The myth versus the reality.

Like any great journey, you'll need to be prepared. Are you ready? Have you done your homework? For the true value of this book lies not solely in what's been prepared, but also in what you bring to the table. Do you have a Bible handy? No? Get one! If this book is to be of any value to you, you're going to want to refer to the Bible often, checking a source, looking at what came before or goes after a given quotation, reasoning yourself that this is what is truly being said. Don't take my word for it. Become a participant, not a passenger.

Are your preconceptions on hold? No? Well, put them aside, for a moment, as difficult as that may be. Don't take this journey if you already know the destination, and unless you put aside your preconceptions, you'll only end up where you started, and wasted both our times. For our time together is going to rock your foundations, if you allow it, but that will only happen if you allow yourself to be open to new possibilities. That doesn't mean you must go forth naked. Let's review what we think we know. Are you ready?

> Jesus Christ was born in the year 0 in a manger in the town of Bethlehem. His mother, Mary, was a virgin and his father, Joseph, was a carpenter. At his birth, three Kings came from the east to worship him, drawn there by a bright star. Shortly after his birth, the family returned to Nazareth where they lived, having come to Bethlehem to participate in the census. Approximately 30 years later, following his baptism by John the Baptist, his cousin, Jesus commenced his ministry, which took place over a period of one to three years, in which he had 12 disciples. He was crucified on the cross, died, and was resurrected three days later.

Sound right? More or less? Well, read it again, because by the time you finish this book, every single thought and concept in this familiar tale will be turned upside down. I promise you, you will never read another thing about the life of Jesus without reflecting back on what we are going to uncover together in this book.

Jesus Who?

But enough is enough. You've signed on for a journey and all this talk is keeping us at the station. It's almost time to take off. Are you ready? One more announcement, and we'll start. All great trips have an itinerary – signposts along the way. Our path will be Jesus' path - his life, from birth to death, each stage considered completely, in order, and without compromise. You should start at the start and stay 'til the finish, but if you're impatient, you can skip around, and visit those times and places which interest you most. Fasten your seat belt. On the way to our first stop, we're going to review some basic information about the sources that provide the foundation for our trip. We'll need this background to see clearly what's ahead. Are you ready?

CHAPTER ONE

About the Gospels

Because so much of what we'll look at depends upon the New Testament, it behooves us to start with a close examination of our main source of information. The New Testament is not like other books that are written by a single author, then published. Even a collection of articles in an edited book has distinct authors and a distinct publishing date. Not so with the New Testament. Not only do we not know who wrote the 27 chapters in this book, we don't know when it was published, or how often it was revised. Indeed, the New Testament as we know it today dates from the mid 4th Century, compiled and canonized more than 200 years after it was written and more than 300 years after Jesus died.

The New Testament opens with four "biographies" of Jesus, referred to as Gospels (derived from "god spell" which means "good news"). His so-called biographers – Mark, Matthew, Luke, and John – are referred to as the evangelists (from the Greek word "*evangelos*" which means "bringing good news"), and for their work each of them earned the status of Saint (from the Latin "*sanctus*" which means "holy"). The first three Gospels are similar and are referred to as the "synoptic Gospels" (from the Greek word meaning "with one eye"); the 4th Gospel (John) is dramatically different. No scholar today believes that the Gospels were actually written by Jesus' disciples, or that a single person wrote them. Nonetheless, by custom we refer to them by their traditional names.

But the Gospels of the New Testament are only the tip of the iceberg. There were many Gospels written in addition to the four that appear in the New Testament, and some of these predate the canonical or official Gospels. For various reasons, these Gospels were destroyed, hidden, declared heretical, and otherwise disappeared from the mainstream of Christian thought. The most famous of these is the *Gospel of Thomas*, discovered in 1945, and authored by Jesus' supposed twin brother.[1]

To the earliest Christians, written works were not important. The oral tradition is what counted. As late as 110 A.D. the *Didakhe*, (or Didache), a manual of Christianity, relied for its main sources on the stories of itinerant evangelists. Even later, in 130 A.D., Papias (c 70-140 A.D.), Bishop of Hierapolis, preferred the oral tradition vs. the written word. Moreover, the very earliest Christian writings were not true writings, but collections of sayings, like the *Gospel of Thomas*, or Papias' *Expositions of the Sayings of the Lord*. Indeed, most scholars believe that the first written words were the so-called Q document (from the German *Quelle* which means "source"), a collection of some 200+ sayings by Jesus that, many believe, were incorporated into the Gospels of Matthew and Luke.

When Were The Gospels Written?

> *"No work of art of any kind has ever been discovered, no painting, or engraving, no sculpture, or other relic of antiquity, which may be*

---

[1] According to the Gospel he authored, his name was Judas Didymos Thomas. According to the Gospels, Jesus did have a brother named Judas. In Hebrew the word Thomas means "twin" and in Greek the work Didymos also means "twin". So the Gospel writer was Judas, the twin twin, and there is, in fact, a disciple of Jesus identified as Thomas the Twin in the *Gospel of John*. In addition, there are several legends about Jesus' twin brother, some of which claim that it was the twin who was crucified. In any event, there is little true evidence for the existence of a twin brother, hence, he is identified here as the "supposed" twin brother.

looked upon as furnishing additional evidence of the existence of these gospels, and which was executed earlier than the latter part of the second century." (Waite, 1992 p. 346)

Methods of Dating Manuscripts

When scholars try to date the Gospels (or any ancient document) they employ a number of methods. One way of dating a document is to determine whether or not actual **historical events** are referred to. If a text discusses the destruction of the 1st Temple, we can assume it was written after 597 B.C. – that's when the Temple was destroyed. Of course, this process is complicated when a document written in 100 B.C. refers to historical events in 500 B.C., a practice that was extremely commonplace among Jewish writers[2]. Thus, while the presence or absence of historical events provides a clue, the method is hardly definitive. It merely gives us a starting point.

Another way of dating a document is to examine the **type of paper** being used. For example, we know that in the 1st Century most documents were written on cheap papyrus and appeared in rolls. By the 2nd Century codices (bound books) appeared, and beginning in the 5th Century, codices of vellum (animal skin[3]) replaced papyrus. In addition to looking at the type of paper, many scholars employ **carbon dating** to establish an historical date. However, carbon dating is not infallible, and at best it gives a range of dates. Moreover, many ancient texts were "erased" and later texts were written over the original, producing an ancient carbon dating for the paper even while the text on the paper dates much later.

A third way of dating a manuscript is called **script analysis**. In the first eight centuries it was common for letters to be printed using only capitals (called "UNCIAL Writing"), and beginning in the 9th Century

---

[2] One reason for this ubiquitous practice was that the writers wanted to express political thoughts but were afraid of repercussions. So attacking the Romans but referring to them as the Babylonians was an effective yet safe method of criticism.

[3] For example, the *Codex Sinaiticus* (mid 4th Century) is written on the skins of 360 young sheep and goats (Wilson, 1984).

upper and lower case letters were used ("Minuscule Writing"). Similarly, 1st Century text lettering is circular, which changed slowly, so that by the 7th Century the letters were more oval shaped. Prior to the 5th Century all letters appeared continuously; starting then the paragraph was introduced. Thus, by looking at the style of the texts inferences can be made for when that text was generated. Though useful, script analysis gives a wide range of dates, because these changes were slow to be adopted and were adopted in different places at different times.

A fourth way of dating a document is by **language analysis**. We know that English English is different from American English, and that our language undergoes changes every few years with the introduction of new words and idioms. While the rate of change in 1st Century Israel was probably not as rapid as it is today, nonetheless there were significant changes that can be dated. For example, the use of the word "synagogue" was relatively rare prior to 70 A.D. (destruction of the 2nd Temple), but following 135 A.D. (expulsion of the Jews from Jerusalem) it became extremely common. Thus, texts in which the word synagogue appears with any frequency are likely to have been written after 100 A.D. In a similar fashion, Jesus' manner of debating mirrors the rabbinical traditions that developed after the destruction of the Temple in 70 A.D[4]. As such, it's unlikely that the Gospels were written before 70 A.D., since they adopt these traditions, and since it took some time for these traditions to seep into the mainstream, the dating is probably much later. Language analysis is useful, but, like many of the other techniques, it can only give an approximate range of dates.

The most difficult and subjective way of dating a document is **content analysis**. For example, Gerald Downing (1992) has shown that there are remarkable similarities between the Gospels and the Cynic Lives of the Philosophers, suggesting a 2nd Century date for the creation of the Gospels as this is the period when the Cynic Lives were most popular. Swedish scholar Alvar Ellegard (1999) has argued that the Gnostic elements in the *Gospel of John* suggest that it was a 2nd Century response to the growing influence of the Gnostics. This

---

[4] See McClymond, 2004, pp. 107-108 for an excellent discussion of this issue.

method of dating is fascinating, but highly subjective, and at best can only provide a guide. The chief problem in this case is that later works can be constructed using the style of the earlier works.

A controversial yet intriguing method of dating documents is by examining **similar or identical text** from documents with known dates of publication. Today we call this practice plagiarism, but at the turn of the millennium, the concepts of authorship were such that plagiarism was not a viable construct. For example, there are many exhortations in the letters of Bishop Ignatius on Antioch that appear in the *Gospel of Matthew*.[5] In Ignatius' letters, these exhortations come from him. In the *Gospel of Matthew*, these same exhortations come from the mouth of Jesus. Since Ignatius' death around 110 A.D. is well known, we can conclude that the *Gospel of Matthew* was written after 110 A.D. because the good bishop, being a devout Christian, would not claim that Jesus' words were his own. The writers of Matthew, on the other hand, were more likely to take these words from such a well known and devout Christian and put them into Jesus' mouth as they did on many occasions. A similar case has been made with regard to the *Gospel of Luke*, where whole passages have been taken from the works of Josephus (e.g., Acharya, 1999; Carrier, 2005; Craveri, 1967; Holding, 2005; Mason, 2003; Massey, 1985.). Since we know that Josephus' works appeared in the very late 1st Century, we can conclude that the *Gospel of Luke* must have been written in the 2nd Century.

The most definitive way of dating a text is from **citations in other texts**. If a Christian scholar in 180 A.D. refers to the Gospels of Mark, Matthew, Luke, and John, we can be pretty sure that those gospels were written before 180 A.D. Of course, this method is not foolproof. We need to know whether or not the Gospels that the writer from 180 A.D. refers to are the same documents we are considering. For example, in 130 A.D. Bishop Papias refers to a "Gospel by Matthew" that consisted of a "book of sayings or oracles". Some scholars are

---

[5] For example, the saying in the *Letter to Ephesus* (14:2) "You know the tree from its fruits" appears in Matthew 12:33; the saying in the *Letter to Polycarp* (2:2) "be in all things wise like the serpent, and always harmless like the dove." appears in Matthew 10:16. etc.

tempted to believe that Papias' mention here means that the *Gospel of Matthew* was written before 130 A.D., yet when we look at the *Gospel of Matthew* it clearly is not a book of sayings. In other words, Papias is referring to a different document, even though the name is identical.

Ideally, good scholarship requires that we examine a text from every aspect (historical events, paper, script, language, content, and citation) and hopefully each method provides an equivalent date. Obviously there is room for error regardless of which method is used, and it should come as no surprise that many scholars differ when they date ancient texts.

The Gospel of Judas

Released in 2006, studies of the *Gospel of Judas* demonstrate how ancient manuscripts should be evaluated by a multi-disciplinary approach. Carbon 14 dating of the paper done at the University of Arizona (the same lab that analyzed the Dead Sea Scrolls) indicated origins between 220 and 340 A.D. Chemical analysis of the ink by transmission electron microscopy and Raman spectroscopy analysis showed a similar 3rd to 4th Century origin. Text analysis and linguistic structure and style found the document to be similar to Gnostic writings from this same period. Handwriting and script analysis performed by Stephen Emmel, Professor of Coptic Studies at Germany's University of Munster, demonstrated a similar pattern.

Dating Early Christian Writings

The earliest known Christian writings are the letters of the Apostle Paul, dated sometime between 48 and 58 A.D.; but there are no copies of these original documents[6], and there are many questions

---

[6] The oldest copy of a letter from Paul (Galatians) is dated at approximately 200 A.D. (Ehrman, 2005, p. 60).

about their authenticity[7]. Some people believe that the earliest versions of the four Gospels were written between 60 A.D. (Mark) and 100 A.D. (John), but there is no proof of these early dates, and some scholars believe that all the Gospels were written after 100 A.D. (e.g., Acharya, 1999; Ellegard, 1999; Keeler, 1965; Koester, 1980; Wheless, 1990). Indeed, the first epistle of Clement of Rome (c 64-96 A.D.), which is reasonably dated to 95 A.D., makes no mention of any of the Gospels although it does mention the epistles of Paul. The *Gospel of Luke* borrows heavily from material in Josephus' (37–100 A.D.) later works[8], especially *Life* and *Against Apion*, implying that the *Gospel of Luke* was not composed (much less published) until after 100 A.D., since Josephus' later works weren't published before 95 A.D. Nor are any of the Gospels mentioned in the letters of Ignatius, Bishop of Antioch, which can be dated from 110 A.D. Archeologically, the earliest dated portion of any Gospel is a tiny fragment consisting of a few words from what could be the *Gospel of John*, and this dates to 125 AD (Funk & Hoover, 1993, p. 9).

The earliest allusion to any of the Gospels is from about 130 A.D. in the works of Bishop Papias, who refers to a collection of Jesus' sayings/oracles in a Hebrew book whose author is said to be the disciple Matthew[9]. This book of sayings may refer to the lost document Q, but it obviously does not refer to the *Gospel of Matthew*, as we know it. Papias also mentions recollections of the disciple Peter, recorded by his secretary Mark. Though neither of these references is to what we now know as the Gospels of Mark or Matthew, they begin to suggest that some things resembling these Gospels were in circulation after 130 A.D. Yet they were certainly not very well known since other prominent Christian writings from this period do not refer to them (e.g., Polycarp, the Epistle of Barnabas, the Exigetica, and The Book of Hermas).

---

[7] "Of the 13 letters of Paul in the New Testament, seven are accepted as largely authentic (Freke & Gandy, 2001, p. 233)."
[8] Schonfield (1974), pp. 36-43. See also Perkins (1988), p. 229.
[9] "Matthew compiled the Sayings in the Aramaic language, and everyone translated them as well as he could (Quoted in Wilson, 1984, p. 44)."

The first mention of the Gospels, as we know them, comes around 140 A.D. in the work of Aristides of Athens who refers to "the holy Gospel writing". Shortly thereafter, a Christian reformer named Marcion (110–160 A.D.) broke with the traditional church over the issue of Jesus' divinity, and set up his own church, including in its writings a stripped down version of the *Gospel of Luke*. In 150 A.D. Justin Martyr (c 100-163 A.D.) of Rome composed the first of his two *Apologies*, in which he specifically referred to the writings of Luke, Matthew, and Mark as "memoirs" (in the tradition of Papias 20 years earlier), but clearly not in the form of the Gospels as we know them (Waite, 1992). About 10 years later, Justin's student, Tatian (c 110-185 A.D.), brought together the four Gospels and combined them into one harmonized book which he called the *Diatessaron*, written in Tatian's native language of Syric. And by 180 A.D. Irenaeus (c 130-202 A.D.) wrote in his principal work, *Against Heresies*, that: "The Gospels could not possibly be either more or less in number than they are. Since there are four zones of the world in which we live, and four principal winds...Now the Gospels, in which Christ is enthroned, are like these... (3.11.7-8)."

To summarize – Evidence from carbon dating, language analysis, and citation show that the Gospels were written in the 2nd Century. By 160 A.D. we know, without question, that all four gospels were in circulation, and by 180 A.D. they were considered authoritative. Yet this is more than 100 years after Jesus' death[10].

Problems Interpreting the Gospels

"...not all true things are the truth." Clement of Alexandria

The use of historical data from the New Testament is limited not only because of the lateness of its origins, but also because of other factors, including the official and unofficial changes to the text, translation errors, writer bias, the use of symbolism and metaphor, tendencies to exaggerate and enhance the original text, and the so-

---

[10] Many orthodox scholars still stick stubbornly to the traditional earlier dates, however, there is an increasing number of scholars who believe the later dates are more accurate (e.g., Koester, 1980; Ellegard, 1999; Freke & Gandy, 1999).

called hidden or secret nature of Jesus' words. We are further hampered by a distance of 2000 years between the language, idioms, and customs of that time, and our own. Let's examine some of these issues. Are you ready?

1. Changes to the New Testament

As soon as the Gospels appeared in the mid 2nd Century, people began to change them. Marcion is the first person to be acknowledged to re-write the Gospels to suit his own theological and political viewpoints. In keeping with his thesis that Jesus was not flesh, his *Gospel of Luke* contains none of the nativity scenes, no references to the Old Testament prophecies, etc. The Syrian cleric Tatian, a pupil of Justin Martyr, composed the *Diatessaron* (a harmony of the Gospels referred to as *The Gospel of the Mixed*) in the mid 2nd Century while he was in Rome, and it contained a significant amount of material not found in the later Gospels, suggesting that he too sculpted the Gospels to suit his theological preferences. Indeed, the editing of the original Gospels was so wide spread that Bishop Dionysius of Corinth, around 170 A.D., wrote that "the devil's apostles were...taking away some things and adding others...tamper [ing] even with the word of the Lord himself."[11] About this same time, Tertullian (c 160-220 A.D.), known as the Father of the Latin Church, reported the case of a priest in Asia Minor being removed from office for falsifying a copy of the *Acts of Paul*. As late as the 3rd Century, Origen (185-254 A.D.), a student of Clement (who himself had been a student of Tatian), complained that people "...add or delete as they please, setting themselves up as correctors (Stanton, 1995, p.35)."

These changes to the New Testament may be the origin of the theories about the different versions of the Gospels. For example, there is a theory that there are three versions of Mark – the short one written in Rome, a longer one written in Alexandria (after Peter's death), and a "secret" one written shortly before Mark died. There are also theories about the original Matthew, written in Hebrew (instead of the commonly thought Greek) and discovered in the Far East. There may actually be such different versions, or, in fact, these different

---

[11] Quoted in Eusebius, *History of the Church*, 4:23.

versions may simply be the altered versions, which we now know, were popular at the time.

Changes to the New Testament were not only made by outsiders; at times, the church authorities themselves made changes. Eusebius, Bishop of Caesarea in Palestine (died 339 A.D.), in *Praeparatio Evangelica* (Preparation for the Gospel) blatantly said: "...it is necessary sometimes to use falsehoods as a medicine for those who need such an approach...For falsehood is something even more useful... (12,14)." Indeed, Chapter 32 of that same work is entitled: "How it may be Lawful and Fitting to use Falsehood as a Medicine, and for the Benefit of those who Want to be Deceived." Clement of Alexandria (150-215 A.D.), a leading Christian in the 2nd Century, wrote a letter concerning the *Secret Gospel of Mark* (that contained much material not found in the traditional version of Mark) in which he said: "...For even if they should say something true, one who loves the truth should not, even so, agree with them. For not all true [things] are the truth, nor should that truth which seems true according to human opinions be preferred to the true truth, that according to faith (quoted in Knight & Lomas, 1994, p. 67)." By these words Clement was approving of the fact that whole passages from the *Gospel of Mark* had been deleted, and others modified, to remove certain things that the early Church leaders found embarrassing.

One of the most controversial issues in discussing official changes to the New Testament is the anti-Semitism that is rampant in the Gospels and elsewhere (Harpur, 2004). Often this took an overt form, by placing words in the mouth of Jesus and others that obviously weren't uttered by them, but served the purpose of denigrating the Jews. Other times it took the form of removing phrases (e.g., "forgive them, for they know not what they do."). It has to be remembered that the writers of the Gospels were competing with the Jewish Christians as well as the Jews for their share of the religious marketplace. Thus, they took every opportunity to impugn the character of their rivals.

In a similar vein, passages concerning Jesus' family were edited because the family held a position of extreme importance among the Christians in Jerusalem, and this Sect was in competition with the other Christian sects throughout the region (Butz, 2005; Wilson, 1992).

Jesus Who?

As a result, the Gospel editors and scribes removed almost all traces of the influence of Jesus' own family, lest this lend credence to their existing Sect and drain resources from the competing sects that sponsored the alternative Gospels. How else does one explain the fact that Jesus' brother James, who, outside the Gospels, was better known than Jesus himself, and who succeeded Jesus as the head of the Jerusalem Christians, was almost never mentioned in the Gospels, and when mentioned at all, it was only in a cursory or derogatory manner? Was James a non-believer who was completely uninvolved in Jesus' ministry, yet as soon as Jesus disappeared from the scene, James became the head of the Sect? How is this possible? How does Peter, the disciple who continually disappointed Jesus and who failed to understand even his most simple parables, as well as denying him three times, suddenly emerge as the "rock" upon which Jesus will build his "church", when in fact there was no church in Jesus' time, and if there were, Peter was obviously not the person to choose as its leader?

While no official documents have been found from the early Christian authorities that specifically instruct the writers and translators of the Gospels to edit the contents to exclude the family of Jesus from their prominent place in his life and ministry, it's beyond question that his mother and brothers were involved and that their involvement was minimized (to say the least) in the Gospels even while it survived in the unofficial and non-canonical histories of the times. Referring to James (but equally true of Jesus' entire family), Butz (2005) claims: "James was forgotten, downplayed, and even intentionally suppressed (p. 18)." Indeed, this consistent stylistic omission lies at the heart of the claims that Mary Magdalene was Jesus' wife, and that the couple had children. We'll have a lot more to say about this in Chapter 6.

Noted scholar Bart Ehrman in his excellent best-selling book *Misquoting Jesus* (2005) provides an exhaustive study of changes to the New Testament. In a chapter entitled "Theologically motivated alterations of the text" he provides many examples of the kinds of official changes that misshaped the writings we'll use as our primary sources. For example, in response to the question of whether or not Joseph or God was the true father of Jesus, numerous changes were made to the original texts....

Location	Original	Revised
Luke 2:33	"his father and mother were marveling…"	"Joseph and his mother were marveling…"
Luke 2:43	"his parents did not know about it."	"Joseph and his mother did not know about it."
Luke 2:48	"Your father and I have been looking for you."	"We have been looking for you."

Looking at the Table, it's clear to see that the original (i.e., earliest) copies of the *Gospel of Luke* referred to Joseph as a parent and father, whereas the revised (i.e., later) copies removed all references to his paternity. Thus, "his father and mother" or "his parents" became "Joseph and his mother" implying that Joseph was not the true father.

Ehrman (2005) shows similar trends with respect to anti-Semitism, competing philosophies, and the role of women. This latter point is of contemporary interest, so some notable examples are called for:

Location	Original	Revised
1 Cor. 33		"…let the women keep silent. For it is not permitted for them to speak…"
Romans 16	"Greet Andronicus and Junia [a woman], my relatives and fellow prisoners, who are foremost among the apostles."	"Greet Andronicus and Junia, my relatives, and also greet my fellow prisoners who are foremost among the apostles."
Acts 17:4	"…along with a large number of prominent women."	"…along with a large number of wives of prominent men."

Looking at this Table, we see that active steps were taken to denigrate women (1 Cor. 33) and changes were made so that "prominent women" become "wives" (Acts 17:4) and female "foremost" apostles become merely "relatives" (Romans 16).

In summary, the fact that official and unofficial changes were made to the New Testament during the first 200 years of its existence means that our ability to use this text as an authoritative historical record is a challenging task. Fortunately there is a trail we can follow that suggests, in many cases, what types of changes were made, so we can try to reconstruct what was and what wasn't a part of the original record. Of course, being "a part of the original record" does not guarantee historical accuracy either, for reasons we take up now.

2. Translation/Transcription Problems

Changes to the New Testament also came about through translation errors that were easy to make[12]. Both the Hebrew and Greek works were difficult to read, almost always without spaces between words (*scriptio continua*), all capitalized, and the characters were such that even minor changes in the length of a stroke could indicate another letter. For example, the phrase GODISNOWHERE, that is the standard Greek 12 letter column, can be translated as "God is nowhere" or as "God is Now Here". These are dramatically different meanings, yet they are generated from the same exact sentence. Multiply this by thousands of 12 character lines in thousands of columns, and the potential for varying translations is enormous.

Ehrman (2005) relates an interesting story about research in 1715 by Swiss scholar Johann Wettstein who was living in England. The example comes from 1 Timothy 3:16 which refers to Jesus as "God made manifest in the flesh, and justified in the Spirit." It's one of the rare occasions in the New Testament where Jesus was identified specifically as God, and thus was of tremendous theological import. Wettstein's research showed that the original translation had been incorrect, because the Greek letter Omicron O had been mistaken for the Greek letter Theta Θ and as a result the word "who" (Omicron +

---

[12] Patzia (1995) estimates that "unintentional errors account for about 95 percent of the variants that are found in the New Testament (p. 138)." See Ehrman (2005) for an excellent discussion of the issues.

Sigma or ΟΣ) was mistaken for the abbreviation of the word "God" (Theta + Sigma or ΘΣ). Thus, 1 Timothy 3:16 should read – "who was made manifest in the flesh..." instead of "God made manifest in the flesh", which radically changes the meaning. How did this occur? Because the ink from a previous page had bled onto the page in question, adding the extra line in the circle which changed Ο to Θ. Even today, the King James Version of the Bible still has this mistranslation.[13]

Other well-known examples of translation errors include:

- Jesus "the Nazarene" (*Nazareneus*) is mistakenly translated as Jesus "of Nazareth" (*Nazarethenos*)
- Mary "the young woman" (*almah*) is mistakenly translated as Mary "the virgin" (*parthenos*)
- Joseph the "builder/general contractor" is mistakenly translated as Joseph "the carpenter"
- Jesus being "protected by God" (*hyos Theou*) is mistakenly translated as Jesus the "Son of God" (*ho hyos Theou*)[14]
- Jesus the "slave of God" (*pais Theou*) is mistakenly translated as Jesus the "Son of God" (*ho hyos Theou*)[15]

You can see, these are not minor points.

In addition to <u>errors</u> of translation, there are also <u>differences</u> in translation that make it difficult to interpret the New Testament. Butz (2005) demonstrates how these differences in translation can alter significantly the content and meaning of passages, using Mark 3:21 as his model. The usual translation of Mark 3:21 is as follows:

> "And when his family heard it, they went out to seize him, for people were saying 'He is beside himself.'"

---

[13] The error is not present in *American Standard Bible* or the *New International Version*, but it is present in the *World English Bible*.
[14] Craveri, 1967, p. 83
[15] Craveri, 1967, p. 326

Jesus Who?

This passage is extremely important and is used by almost every scholar to make the point that Jesus' relationship with his family was less than ideal. Now look at some of the other translations of this very same passage:

RSV 2nd Edition	RSV 1st Edition	World Biblical Commentary	Anchor Bible
"And when his *family* heard it, they went out to seize him, for people were saying '*He is beside himself*.'"	"And when his *friends* heard it, they went out to seize him, for they said '*He is beside himself*.'"	"When his **people** heard, they set out to take him into their custody, For they said, '*He was out of his mind*.'"	On hearing this, his *family* set out to take charge of him, for **people were saying** that he was out of his mind

Notice how the various translations identify the main subjects as (alternately) his family, or friends, or people, and there are still other variations that use the word "relatives" (*New American Bible*) and "disciples" (Painter, 1999). Not only are the main subjects varied, the belief about Jesus' state of mind varies from "beside himself" to "out of his mind" and the believers vary from his relatives (family) to the general crowd. So, we have radically different versions of the same story – in one case, Jesus' family is rescuing him from people who think he is out of his mind, and in another case, the disciples are trying to restrain him because they believe he is beside himself. How does this happen? Let's look at the exact translation from the Greek, provided by Butz:

> "And hearing [it], the *ones with him* went forth to seize him; for they said that he is beside himself (Butz, 2005 p. 26)." (italics added)

Obviously, translators have wide latitude in how a specific word or phrase is translated, and for this reason, the number of possible variations is extremely large. The "ones with him" can be his disciples or his followers/people/friends, or it can be his family. Under such circumstances, the biases or predilections of the translator are likely to play a substantial part in determining the outcome. Because of this, it's difficult to determine what is historical and what is literary license. In this particular case, it seems more logical that "the ones with him" refers to his disciples, and not his family who do not show up until much later (10 more verses). Yet almost every "official" translation uses "family" instead of "disciples."

These many translation errors and biases mean that a careful study of the New Testament requires that we test every assumption and check every reference. It is not sufficient to accept the Gospel writers' assertion that this or that phrase has such-and-such a meaning. We need to explore the translation itself and the context in which it occurs.

3. Writer Orientation

> *"The evangelists were fiction writers – not observers or eyewitnesses of the life of Jesus."*
> (Porphyry, *Against the Christians*, 2:12)

Far from being the word of God, the Gospels that finally emerge tell us far more about the people who wrote them than they do about the subject matter. Wilson (1992) writes: "The Gospel writers did not go to a modern research library and spread out all the 'facts' in order to tell a dispassionate story. They started with a set of theological beliefs about Jesus, and they fitted their narratives into these beliefs... (p. 53)." Grant and Freedman (1993) are more to the point: referring to the Gospels, they say: "Ultimately it testifies not to what Jesus said but to what men wished he had said (p. 20)." Even when they weren't consciously inserting themselves into the text, the writers of the Gospels suffered from the "natural tendency ...to transplant situations of their own experience, and personalities of their own knowledge, into that comparatively distant past in which the events which they describe had taken place (Cohn, 1963, p. xvii)."

Each Gospel has its own personality and shape. For example, Mark is the shortest (661 verses), while both Matthew (1068) and Luke (1149) are nearly twice as long. Yet while Matthew absorbs 90% of Mark's content, Luke reflects only 57%. Matthew's Gospel goes on endlessly about the Hebrew prophecies that foreshadowed Jesus' behavior, and makes careful distinctions between the types of Jews with whom Jesus came into contact (e.g., Pharisees, Sadducees, Scribes, Sanhedrin, etc), whereas Luke lumps all Hebrews into one category, "the Jews". On more than a dozen occasions in Matthew's text he interrupts the flow of the narrative to refer to the life of Jesus fulfilling Old Testament prophecy. However, he makes many errors in his references to the Old Testament; for example, confusing Jeremiah with Zachariah (27: 6-10), confusing Rachel with Leah (2:18), confusing one animal with two (21:7), misidentifying the location of Capernaum (4:13), mistranslating Nazarite for Nazareth (2:23), mistaking a nation for a person (2:15), combining two sayings into one (21:4-5), etc[16]. If Matthew is woefully defective in his ability to translate the Old Testament, Mark is equally defective in describing the geography of Jerusalem. For example, Mark places the city of Sidon on the road between the Sea of Galilee and the city of Tyre, when in fact it is in the opposite direction. Mark places Gerasenes to the immediate east of the Sea of Galilee, when in fact it's more than 30 miles to the southeast, a considerable distance in those days.

Mark has another subtext that is characteristic of his Gospel, that Carrier (2005) has labeled "reversal of expectations". Carrier notes:

> "James and John, who ask to sit at the right and left of Jesus in his glory (10:35-40), are replaced by two thieves[17] at his crucifixion (15:27); Simon Peter, Christ's right-hand man who was told he had to 'deny himself and take up his cross and follow' (8:34), is replaced by Simon of Cyrene (a foreigner, from the opposite side of Egypt, a symbol of death) when it comes time to truly bear the cross (15:21); instead of his family as would be expected, his enemies come to bury him (15:43);

---

[16] One scholar wryly notes: "Matthew would seemingly rather make up his own prophecy than recount events not foretold by the prophets (Galambush, 2005, p. 76)."

[17] The word *leste* is commonly translated as "thieves" but Gardner (2001) claims it's better translated as "outlaws" and Baigent (2006) translates it as "Zealots."

> Pilate's expectation that Jesus should still be alive is confounded (15:44); contrary to all expectation, the Jews, mock their own savior (15:29-32) while, it is a Gentile officer of Rome who recognizes his divinity (15:39); likewise, the very disciples are the ones who abandon Christ (14:50 and 66-72 versus 14:31), while it is mere lowly women who attend his death and burial, who truly 'followed him', and continue to seek him thereafter (15:40-41, 15:47, 16:1)...(p. 164)."

Carrier links these reversals with Jesus' own Cynic style of using parables that disarm the reader and offer the unexpected (e.g., turning the other cheek). The adoption of a literary style does not negate the fact that Jesus may have done this or that, or said this or that, but the overwhelming number of instances "begs credulity" as a true historical account. In other words, was Jesus the Cynic or did Mark adopt Jesus' sayings to fit Mark's own Cynic style. We're tempted to vote for the latter, since Mark was writing in a time when the Cynic philosophy and writing style were extremely popular, whereas at the time of Jesus, this was not the case.

Even the structure of the Gospels reflects the concerns of the authors, rather than history itself. Matthew is concerned with showing that Jesus fulfilled the prophecies of the Old Testament, so he arranges Jesus' major sermons/teachings into five events (5:1 to 7:27, 10.5 to 10.42, 13.1 to 13.52, 18.1 to 18.35, and 21.28 to 25.46) to mirror the five books of the Torah. He introduces many elements that mirror Moses' history (e.g., the slaughter of the infants, the Sermon on the Mount, the exodus out of Egypt) - elements that are unique to Matthew's Gospel, and therefore suspect.

Mark's structure is completely different. He uses the various crossings of the Sea of Galilee to juxtapose miracles/exorcisms for the Jews with the Gentiles. Jesus begins exorcising on the Western shores or Jewish side (1:21), then crosses the Sea (4:35) and performs an exorcism on the Eastern shore or Gentile side (5:1), then re-crosses (5:21) and heals the Jews (5:21 to 6:43), then crosses again (6:45) and heals the Gentiles (6:53 to 8:8) before making the final crossing (8:13). Just as Matthew's structure is trying to say - "Jesus is the new Moses, foretold

Jesus Who?

in the Old Testament", Mark's structure shouts – "Jesus came for the Jews <u>and</u> the Gentiles."

Luke has a very different agenda. He seeks to show that women were an integral part of Jesus' ministry, so he adds, unique to his Gospel, parallel stories for the females. For Luke,

- Jesus has male disciples (6:12) and female followers (8:1).
- Jesus raises the widow's son (7:11) but also Jairus' daughter (8:49)[18].
- Jesus straightens a man's hand (6.6), then straightens an old woman's back (13:10).
- The Shepherd looking for his lost sheep (15.3) is paralleled by the woman looking for her lost coin (15:8).
- Simeon the prophet (2:25) is matched by Anna the prophetess (2:36).

In each case, Luke makes sure to introduce the male version first, and later (sometimes, much later) shows the feminine parallel. But almost none of these female-oriented events chronicled by the writers of Luke are in the other Gospels, suggesting either Luke invented them or else he chose to include them from a wider collection that, for whatever reason, the other Gospel writers chose to ignore.

Another characteristic of the *Gospel of Luke* is that it draws heavily on other documents, to such an extent that some scholars go so far as to accuse the writers of Luke of plagiarism (e.g., Acharya, 1999; Carrier, 2005; Grant, 1990; Holding, 2005; Mason, 2003; Massey, 1985; Schonfield, 1965)[19]. Ellegard (1999) is slightly kinder – he calls Luke "a

---

[18] It can be argued with some veracity that Jairus' daughter is not really raised, since Jesus proclaims that she is only sleeping, and then proceeds to awaken her.

[19] Sections of the *Gospel of Luke* that have been identified as probable copies from other sources include the opening address (from Josephus), the annunciation (compare to Judges 13:2-25), Jesus' childhood (1 Samuel 2:26), the story of Jesus in the Temple at age 12 (Josephus), the response to John's emissaries (Isaiah 35: 5-6), Mary's Magnificat (1 Samuel 2:1-10), the

rather careless writer" (p. 229) and Craveri (1967) refers to him as "childish and artless" (p. 126). Of course, our modern concept of authorship is very different from the concept in the early Christian era, but it's striking to see some of these parallels. Because these sections parallel so closely the works of others, one has to ask the question whether or not Luke is historical or literary. Is Luke actually talking about an historical Jesus or is he simply fitting the name of Jesus into well-worn tales and stories ascribed to others?

As if these problems were not sufficient to stymie the most diligent researcher, the dramatic differences between the synoptic authors and the authors of the *Gospel of John* are such that one suspects they were talking about a different person entirely. Here are just a few of the differences:

	Synoptic Gospels	**Gospel of John**
Birth and childhood	Detailed in Matthew and Luke	Never mentioned
Baptism by John	Detailed	Never mentioned
Exorcisms	Many and detailed	Never mentioned
Miracles	Many and detailed	Only 7 "signs"
Jesus' speaking style	Parables and aphorisms	Long involved speeches
Concern with the poor	High	Barely mentioned
Length of ministry	One year	At least 3 years
Temple incident	End of his career	Start of his career
Last supper	On Passover	Before Passover

Yet one doesn't have to compare the synoptic gospels with the *Gospel of John* to come up with radically different pictures. Ehrman (2005) provides a thorough analysis of the Gospels of Mark vs. Luke with respect to their portrait of Jesus. He notes:

---

resurrection of Lazarus (1 Kings 17), and the plea by Joseph of Arimathea for Jesus' body (Josephus).

> "Mark...portrays Jesus as in deep agony in the face of death, telling his disciples that his soul was 'sorrowful unto death', falling on his face in prayer, and beseeching God three times to take away the cup of his suffering; on his way to be crucified he is silent the entire time, and he says nothing on the cross when mocked by everyone, including both robbers, until the very end when he calls out in anguish, 'My God, my God, why have you forsaken me?' He then utters a loud cry and dies. Luke has this version...but he modified it significantly. He removed Mark's comments that Jesus was highly distraught, as well as Jesus' own comments that he was sorrowful to death. Rather than falling on his face, Jesus simply kneels, and instead of pleading three times to have the cup removed, he asks only once, prefacing his prayer with 'if it be your will'. He is not at all silent on the way to his crucifixion but speaks to a group of weeping women, telling them to grieve not for him but for the fate to befall themselves. While being crucified he is not silent but asks God to forgive those responsible...(p. 213)."

The bottom line is that the real story of Jesus is hidden within the literary devices that the writers of the Gospels chose, and we must learn how to see through the strokes of their writing to the historical Jesus.

4. The Use of Symbolism

To the problems already noted, we can add the fact that much of what passes for history in the New Testament is so laced with symbolism, that when the two conflict, the authors invariably voted for symbolism[20]. Harpur (2004) notes: "What was preserved in the amber of allegory, [the Church] misrepresented as plodding fact (p. 2)." Duquesne (1994) refers to this as "theologoumenon", which he defines as "...a kind of image that helps us understand an aspect of faith...we are not dealing with historical truth, but with a symbol...(p.38)." For

---

[20] Spoto (1998) makes the point that religious texts are not the only forms of writing that rely on symbolism – "Every written human text, from ancient poetry in a half-forgotten language to next year's tax forms, is a symbolic rendering of experience... (p. 51)."

example, the *Gospel of Matthew* starts with a list of the generations prior to Jesus, establishing his descent from David. The Gospel notes that the generations are 14, yet a careful counting shows that the final set is only 13. Never mind! - 14 is the choice, because 14 is a magical number (it is two times the magical number 7; and it's half a lunar month, the moon being the symbol for Israel). The number 14 had an additional meaning because the Hebrew letters that spell David (e.g., *daleth, waw*) when given their numerical values (2 daleths + 1 waw = 8 + 6 = 14) added up to 14.[21]

Look closely at the 49th person listed in that very long list of Luke (who goes all the way back to Adam). It is Jesus himself. Why? Because 49 is the most magical of all numbers (magic 7 times magic 7) and hence could only belong to Jesus, whether he had been born yet or not.

Another example where symbol and fact clash is the list of Jesus' disciples. There are 12, the same as the number of tribes in Israel. Yet when the Gospels list the names of the disciples, we have as many as 14 listed, and the *Gospel of John* only mentions 10[22].

The names of Jesus' disciples and followers are also symbolic. Many of the names can be traced to Zodiac signs, appropriate for a religion that sought to compete with Mithra, the Sun God. Thomas the Twin is obviously Gemini, and Mary serves the function of being Virgo. Alphaeus comes from the Babylonian word *alpu*, for bull, the symbol of Taurus. The sons of Zebedee, called the Sons of Thunder[23], give us Jupiter, the God of Thunder, whose name in Babylonian is Zalbatanu. John the Baptist is the obvious symbol for Aquarius.

---

[21] Sullivan, 2002, p. 36. The name of this specific use of numbers is "gematria".
[22] Here's the complete list of the 14 named disciples: Andrew, his brother Simon Peter, John, his brother James, Philip, Thomas, and Judas Iscariot appear in all four Gospels and in Acts. Matthew, Luke, Mark, and Acts agree on four more: Matthew (also called Levi), Simon the Zealot, Bartholomew, and James, son of Alphaeus. The remaining three are Thaddaeus (mentioned in Matthew and Mark), Judas (not Iscariot), the son of James (in Luke, Acts, and John), and Nathanael (only in John).
[23] Schonfield (1965) translates *Boanerges* as "The Stormy Ones" rather than the "Sons of Thunder" (p. 83).

Jesus Who?

The idea of 12 disciples originated in the Egyptian religions long before they were written into Christian myth. For the God Horus, the 12 disciples were "saviors of the treasure of light" who accompanied him to Earth for his mission to sow the seeds and reap the divine harvest. Each of these "saviors" represented a stage of growth in individual consciousness, and corresponded to one of the 12 astronomical signs[24]. Just as the Sun journeyed through every sign of the Zodiac, so too the human personality journeyed through each stage on its road to perfection. Other famous groups of 12 include the 12 labors of Hercules, the 12 generals of Ahura-Mazda, the 12 apostles of Mithra, etc. Is it by mere chance that the only episode concerning Jesus' life between infancy and age 30 happens at age 12[25]?

The number 40 also occupies many significant signposts in the Bible. The great flood lasted 40 days (Genesis 7:4). Moses (Deuteronomy 9:9), Elijah (1 Kings 19:8), and Jesus (Mark 1:13) all fasted for 40 days. Jesus appeared to his apostles after 40 days (Acts 1:3). The Hebrews wandered for 40 years (Numbers 14:33) and later suffered for 40 years (Ezekiel 24:11). Saul ruled for 40 years (Acts, 13:21), etc.

Jesus' own name, *Iesous*, in Greek = 888 (I = 10, E = 8, S = 200 0 = 70, U = 400, and S = 200), a scared number to the Greeks whose alphabet, when all the numbers were added together, equaled 888. That same number is the string ratio of the whole tone, which had a similar sacred meaning for the ancient Greeks. Indeed, Freke & Gandy (1999) maintain that the "Greek name *Iesous* is an artificial and forced transliteration of the Hebrew name Joshua, which had been deliberately constructed by the Gospel writers to make sure that it expresses this symbolically significant number (p. 116)." Several other authors agree (e.g., Eisler, 1920; Fidler, 1993).

Thus, in peeking through the fog of all the ancient manuscripts to get a glimpse of the historical Jesus, we need to understand that numbers have a meaning of their own. In looking at a specific event we have to

---

[24] For the Egyptians, the three powers (body, mind, and spirit) combined with the four elements (fire, air, earth, and water) to create the 12 aspects.

[25] This episode that appears only in the *Gospel of Luke* was probably copied from Josephus' account of his own childhood.

differentiate whether or not the author was speaking symbolically or whether or not it was meant to be historically accurate. By knowing the meaning of the numbers and the symbols, we can help make the proper deduction.

5. The Use of Metaphor

Somewhat related to the issue of symbolism is the issue of metaphor. The Bible combines metaphor with history and biography, with a healthy mix of propaganda thrown in. Very few people today really believe that God created the world in six days, and then rested on the seventh. Some choose to believe that the "six days" refers to days of a thousand years, so that six days makes more sense in that context. Such an approach is not without precedence, since the writers of the Bible often used this type of calculation (e.g., 40 days often means 40 weeks, etc). Others choose to focus on the meaning of that expression, which seems to be that even God has to rest, and thus the Sabbath is sacred above all else. In becoming absorbed in the metaphor, one can loose the meaning. Did wise men really journey to Bethlehem to worship the King of Jews? If they were smart enough to know that the King of Jews was being born, how come they didn't know where? And how come they choose to ask his whereabouts from the one man who wanted to kill him? Not very wise, for "wise" men! No, there probably weren't wise men from the East (especially since this scene only appears in Matthew's Gospel), but the point the writers of Matthew were trying to make was that Jesus' birth was a great occasion that was worthy of being attended by visiting potentates.

Depending upon the nature of the metaphor, it's sometimes difficult to separate what is meant as metaphor, what is symbolic, and what is meant as historical fact. Did Israel really experience a solar eclipse when Jesus was crucified? Did earthquakes and other natural disasters accompany it? Did hundreds of dead "saints" walk the streets of Jerusalem? As metaphor, they are pertinent and telling[26], but if

---

[26] Even today we use the term "earth-shattering event" but don't mean that the earth really shattered. We simply mean, by using metaphor, that it was an important event.

these events were meant as historical facts, why is there no corroboration in the contemporary literature and history?

Along these lines, the noted Christian scholar John Dominic Crosson says: "My point...is not that those ancient people told literal stories and we are now smart enough to take them symbolically, but that they told them symbolically and we are now dumb enough to take them literally (Harpur, 2004, p.1)."

6. Acceleration

To our growing list of problems interpreting the New Testament we must add a new element – acceleration. One can see the exponential acceleration in details and majesty from the *Gospel of Mark*, to Luke and Matthew, and then to John. For example, at his baptism, Mark (1:10) indicates that Jesus sees a dove[27] that we assume is a private vision (skeptics would say - "hallucination"). By the time of Luke (3.22) this dove takes "bodily form" so that everyone can see it. In a similar fashion, Mark's baptism commentary is relatively brief, whereas Matthew adds lines of text from John the Baptist to the effect that it is he who should be baptized by Jesus. When we come to Luke, John the Baptist has disappeared from the scene all together! And in John's Gospel, the whole baptism disappears! The historical kernel here probably goes something like this – Jesus told one of his disciples that when John was baptizing him he (Jesus) had a vision of a dove. Does that mean a dove actually appeared? Probably not. Does it mean that throngs of people saw his anointing by the Holy Spirit? Definitely not! But what is happening here is that each successive author feels the need to further clarify Jesus' life. Today we see the same thing all the time. Celebrities were "stars", then "super stars", then "mega stars", etc.

Not to belabor the point, but let's look at another example of acceleration from a different critical period in Jesus' life. Once Jesus is dead and placed in the tomb, Mark tells us that only a young man is

---

[27] In the Jewish tradition, the Holy Ghost was represented by a dove (In Hebrew the word is *ruah*, which is translated best as "breath" or "sign"). Among African witchdoctors the dove has a similar meaning.

left sitting inside. Matthew elevates the young man's status to that of an angel (sitting outside, not in), and John goes one step further by telling us there are two angels (now inside, instead of out). Who was there and where were they? It probably doesn't matter where they were, but it surely matters whether or not they were angels or gardeners. In this case, as in the others noted above, the process of acceleration works to increase the majesty or divinity of Jesus in each successive Gospel, as if each author (or set of authors) is trying to outdo the previous one. What may start as a simple description, close to the historical facts, grows in length, complexity, and majesty in the re-telling.

Jesus' miracles show us acceleration at work in reverse. In this case, less is more. In the *Gospel of Mark,* Jesus' miracles invariably involve touch. He cures Simon's mother-in-law of her fever by taking her by the hand and lifting her up (1:31), he holds a deaf and dumb man, puts spit on his finger and pokes it in the deaf man's ear (7:33), he holds a blind man and puts spit in his eyes (8:23), etc. But the *Gospel of Matthew* eliminates many of these physical cues. Simon's mother-in-law is merely touched, not raised up (8:15), Jesus simply touches the blind man's eyes, without using spit (9:27; 20:34), and the deaf and dumb man is healed by a word, without any need of touch or spit (12:22). The *Gospel of Luke* removes even more of the physical elements. Now Jesus cures by word alone (Simon's mother-in-law, 4:38; the blind man, 18:42; and the dumb man 11:14). Each successive Gospel magnifies Jesus' powers by removing his healing tools until Jesus himself is the cure.

The greatest example of acceleration comes at the start of the individual Gospels. Mark has no genealogy for Jesus, apart from his mother and father. Matthew brings him back to David and Abraham. Not to settle for mere descent from the father of Israel, Luke draws his genealogical chart all the way back to Adam. Think that's far enough? Not for John! His Gospel starts before Adam, back to the start of all time, and even earlier.

Acceleration occurs not only between different books in the New Testament but within a single book over time. For example, the oldest copy of the *1st Epistle of John* says the following about the concept of the trinity:

> "There are three which bear witness, the spirit and the water and the blood, and the three are one."

But by the 4th Century it has been expanded to look like this:

> "There are three which bear witness, the spirit and the water and the blood, and *these* three are one *in Christ Jesus; and there are three who bear witness in heaven, the Father, the Word and the Spirit, and these three are one* (Johnson, 1976, p. 26)." (Italics indicate changes)

Of course, these are literary peccadilloes and not to be taken too seriously as historical events. The process of acceleration distorts history but does not necessarily eliminate it. For our purposes, it does mean that a good knowledge of what has come before helps us sift through the later works. In general, earlier works are probably more trustworthy in this regard.

7. Improvement

Acceleration is closely related to the issue of improvement (sometimes called harmonizing). Not only do later authors accelerate or intensify the majesty of Jesus, they tend to improve or correct the embarrassing moments in the earlier works. For example, Mark (10:35-40) has an awkward passage where the "Sons of Thunder", James and John, ask Jesus to grant them preferred status in heaven, sitting immediately to his right and left. Jesus rebuffs them, but in Matthew (20:20), this embarrassing scene for the two disciples is changed, and it's their mother who makes the awkward request. Similarly, Mark has the women at Jesus' tomb flee in "terror and amazement…and they said nothing to anyone, for they were afraid (16:8)." Matthew improves the telling. No longer silent, amazed, or terrified, the women "left the tomb with fear and great joy, and ran to tell his disciples (28:8)." The case of Joseph of Arimathea also illustrates this practice. He starts off in Mark as "a respected member of the council, who was also waiting expectantly for the kingdom of God (15:42-46)", but this doesn't explain his access to Pilate, so Matthew (27:57-60) turns him into "a rich man...who was also a disciple of Jesus" and John (19:38-42) makes him "a secret one".

Thus, later authors looked upon the earlier works not as the undisputed word of God, but as stories that were capable of being modified, improved, and/or accelerated in order to get their point across. As a result, we must not only look at the Gospels themselves, and other works, for what they say, but we also have to take account of what prior works have been written, and view the later literature in the context of the earlier ones. Swedish scholar Ellegard (1999) very correctly observed: "Historical research is most of the time concerned with minute details. But the researcher must never tire of comparing the various details with each other, in order to see whether hitherto unnoticed patterns will stand out. When they do, the researcher gets his reward (p. 3)."

8. Non-Biographical Format

> *"Wherever the poetry of myth is interpreted as biography, history, or science, it is killed."* (Joseph Campbell, 1949, p. 249)

For our purposes, the use of the Gospels to flush out an "historical Jesus" is fraught with difficulties because the Gospels were not written as biographies, but rather they were what Bloom (2005) calls "conversionary inspiration". Therefore they do not conform to the contents or the structure of typical biographies. They contain snippets of information, sometimes grouped and sometimes not. Sanders (1993) calls them "pericopes" which means, "cut around". Each snippet has a beginning, middle, and an end, self-sufficient unto itself, and they are strung together by the authors, but, with rare exception, could just as easily be lifted from one section and placed in another. For example, the story of the adulteress[28] whom the mob wants to stone, can be found in different sections of the same Gospel over time - In the various versions of the *Gospel of John* it has appeared after verses 7:36, or 7:44, or 7:52 or 21:25, the most common being 7:52. This form

---

[28] BTW, this pericope does not appear in any manuscript before the 4th Century.

of organization made the pericopes relatively easy to modify at the whim of the scribe or translator, and, as we have seen, these Gospels were continuously modified for hundreds of years. These modifications should probably be considered as "updates" to the previous editions, in much the same way as newspapers today update the news of our generation. The many writers who changed the Gospels, over the years, probably did so in a conscientious effort to bring the old story in line with the current interests and philosophies of their readers. In our own time, we see how the stories of various events (e.g., the discovery of America, the conquering of the West) are continually changed as our times change, and there's no reason to assume that the early Christian writers didn't do the same. Needless to say, this complicates any attempt to reconstruct the past when those earlier documents no longer exist.

9. Writing for Believers

The Gospels were intended for an audience of believers, so that many of the claims that an historical researcher would like more information about is missing. The Gospels illustrate the theological story of Jesus for people who already believe. They were never intended to convince non-believers or even to act as recruitment posters. Rather, they supplemented the recruitment efforts of those apostles who preached, and supported those who already believed. Grant and Freedman (1993) note: "The earliest Christians were not reporting historical facts because they were historians. They were concerned with what the facts meant for their faith (p. 23)." As such, trying to gain historical information from them is difficult indeed.

10. Writing for the Future Audience

Although most of the contents of the New Testament appear to be written within their historical context, there is a significant body that is written with the knowledge of the future as it unfolded after Jesus' death. Because the Gospels were written more than a half century after Jesus died, the people who wrote them were able to craft their words in such a way that they reflected contemporaneous events. There was nothing unusual in doing this: it was commonplace among

Old Testament writers. Here are some examples of text that was meant to reflect future events...

Gospel Text	Explanation
"See, I am sending you out like sheep into the midst of wolves; so be wise as serpents and innocent as doves. Beware of them, for they will hand you over to councils and flog you in their synagogues; and you will be dragged before governors and kings because of me, as a testimony to them and the Gentiles (Matthew 10: 16-18)."	Obviously a reference to the persecutions that were going on when the *Gospel of Matthew* was written. In Jesus' time there were no such persecutions, and no reason to expect any.
"As he came out of the temple, one of his disciples said to him, 'Look, Teacher, what large stones and what large buildings [of the Temple in Jerusalem]!' Then Jesus asked him, 'Do you see these great buildings? Not one stone will be left here upon another; all will be thrown down (Mark 13: 1-2)."	Obviously a reference to the destruction of the Temple in 70 A.D.
"And I tell you, you are Peter, and on this rock I will build my church... (Matthew 16:18)."	This is the only use of the word "church" in the Gospels. Jesus never preached the formation of a church, but by the time the *Gospel of Matthew* was written, a church did exist.

11. The Book Burners

The most vexing and frustrating problem in our search for the historical Jesus is that all the evidence which didn't fit the orthodox view was suppressed or destroyed, the greatest "book burning" being accomplished under the authority of the Emperor Constantine (272 - 337 A.D.) in 326 A.D. Conservative estimates are that thousands of volumes were destroyed in this manner (Smith, 1978), though we can never know the full extent of these pious crimes. Harpur (2004) writes:

> "...the Church of the 3rd and 4th Centuries, when challenged by its Pagan critics as to the real sources of its gospels, dogmas, and rites, reacted with fierce hostility, systematically hunting down and eliminating all traces of its Pagan past. It hounded anyone, whether Christian or not, who bore witness to the old truths. It closed down the traditional "Pagan" philosophical schools, persecuted those involved in the...Mystery Religions, burned hundreds of thousands of books, and hurled the charge of heresy...at any who threatened to question the orthodox party line (p. 12)."

Although it probably made sense at the time, the book burnings eliminated almost every reference to Jesus from outside the canonical Gospels. Ironically, centuries later, this dearth of evidence would be used to make the case that Jesus never existed.

12. Jesus' Secret Language

Time and time again, Jesus told his inner circle that his parables had a secret meaning. He noted:

> "The secret of the Kingdom of God is given to you, but to those who are outside everything comes in parables so that they may see and see again, but not perceive; may hear and hear again, but not understand...[29] (Mark 4:10-13)."

> "To you it has been given to know the mysteries of the kingdom of the heavens, but to them it has not been given (Matthew 13:11)."

> "he did not speak to them [the public] except in parables, but he explained everything in private to his disciples (Mark 4:34)."

---

[29] Obviously adopted from Isaiah – "Hear and hear again, but do not understand; see and see again, but do not perceive... (6:9-10)"

Much of the work used in this book derives from our ability in the 21st Century to translate many of the words and expressions used in the Bible. This ability did not exist for previous generations who were not able to avail themselves of the findings from Nag Hammadi, Qumran, and other discoveries in the past hundred years. Much as the Rosetta Stone allowed 20th Century historians to translate Egyptian hieroglyphics, so these new discoveries allow us to translate words and expressions that have been lost for nearly 2000 years. Doing so not only gives us new insights, but it clarifies what, up until recently, appeared to be meaningless, nonsensical, secretive, or purely mythical remarks.

For example, when Jesus says, "leave the dead to bury their dead (Matthew 8:22)", this comment makes little sense, until we realize that Jesus used the words "dead" and alive" to refer to believers or non-believers, which was the traditional use of these words by the Essenes (from the Greek *essenoi* meaning physician), a Sect he most probably belonged to or was associated with (more about this later). Thus, when he said, "leave the dead to bury the dead" he meant that non-believers should take care of each other and not be the concern of believers. Clearly he didn't mean that biologically dead people should rise from their graves and then bury more biologically dead people. In a similar fashion, in the parable of the prodigal son in the *Gospel of Luke*, when the youngest son returns to his father and seeks forgiveness for having "sinned against God and against you", his father remarks: "...this son of mine was dead, and he has come back to life...(15:24)" This isn't a resurrection story! The boy wasn't resuscitated. The use of dead and alive was a metaphor, specific to the Essenes, and meant to walk with God (alive) or not (dead).

Almost the whole of Jesus' beatitudes were not directed at the world at large, but rather were very specific to the Qumran community. For example, when Jesus said: "Blessed are the poor in spirit[30], for theirs is the kingdom of heaven (Matthew 5:3)", he wasn't referring to poor people, but to "the poor" which is how the Qumran people referred to

---

[30] The *Gospel of Luke* says only "the poor", not "the poor in spirit"

themselves[31]. Indeed, it makes no sense for Jesus to bless "the poor in spirit" if he really meant people who were poor in spirit, because these were not the people who should inherit the kingdom of heaven. The inheritors were the people who were rich in spirit, and this was "the poor" or the Qumran people. In a similar fashion, "those who mourn", the "meek", "the persecuted for righteousness' sake", etc., all referred to the Qumran community. Rather than being seen as a collection of general blessings, the Sermon on the Mount should be viewed as a series of recruiting slogans for people to sign up to the Essene Sect. We'll have lots to say about Jesus and the Essenes in a later chapter.

13. The Language and Culture of 2000 Years Ago[32]

"The words we use...embody meaning, but the meaning does not come from the words. Meaning inevitably derives from the general social system of the speakers of a language. What one says and what one means to say can thus often be quite different, especially for persons not sharing the same social system." (Molina, 2001, pp. 1-2)

One of the key points in the New Testament turns on whether or not Jesus was the Son of God (*ho huios tou theou*) or the Son of Man. Again, the confusion can be cleared up by understanding the nature of the language. To us today, the words "Son of God" imply that Jesus is the biological offspring of God. But in Jesus' time, the words "Son of God" could refer to many things, including angels (Gen. 6:2; Daniel 3:25), righteous individuals (Wisdom 2:18), or to any King who took his authority from the Gods. Thus, Psalm 2 celebrating a new King's coronation says: "...the Lord hath said unto me, Thou art my Son... (2:7)." When the prophet Nathan tells King David that God will look

---

[31] The Jerusalem based Jesus Sect that was headed by Jesus' brother James after the crucifixion was called the Ebionites, which translates as "the poor" or "the poor ones" (Freke & Gandy, 2001; Thiering, 1992; Harvey, 1970).

[32] Two of the most illuminating books on the New Testament - Steven Bridge's *Getting the Gospels* (2004) and A. N. Wilson's *Jesus: A life* (1992) - each takes as their point of departure, the knowledge of the language and culture of Jesus' time. Spoto (1998) notes: "Every word pertaining to God in the history of the human race...is necessarily conditioned by the circumstances of its time and the possibilities and limitations of human language (p. 52)."

down upon his descendants (Samuel 7:13-14), he says: "...I will stablish the throne of his [referring to David] kingdom for ever, I will be his father, and he shall be my son..." This doesn't mean that he will biologically father each of David's descendants, in which case they wouldn't be David's descendants anyway.

Another example of the difference in language is given by the word "salt". Today, salt sits with pepper on our tables and may or may not be used to flavor our food. Currently salt is out of fashion, due to its effects on blood pressure. But in Jesus' time, salt was vital to the preservation of food. Indeed, salt was so important that it was sprinkled on religious offerings to make them pure, and taken with bread to witness covenants. Thus, salt in Jesus' time was associated with purity. So, when Jesus said, "You are the salt to the world (Matthew 5:13)" he meant that his followers were the true preservers of the Kingdom. And when he said that salt which has lost its taste "is no longer good for anything, but is thrown out and trampled under foot (15:13)", he wasn't trying to be Martha Stewart - he was warning of the loss of faith and foreshadowing the destruction of the Temple.

The examples cited so far refer to specific language usages, but it's also true that knowing the customs of 1st Century Israel yields a similar harvest in terms of understanding what is not easily comprehensible. When a man came up to Jesus and began his question with the salutation: "Good Teacher..." Jesus appeared upset and responded: "Why do you call me good? No one is good but God alone (Mark 10:17-18)." Was Jesus having a temper tantrum? This was an uncharacteristic response, and seemingly hostile. The prickly point in this case is that the man was complimenting Jesus with the adjective "good", and for 1st Century Jews, compliments were the kiss of death. Molina (2001, p. 93) explains: "To compliment others is to tell them to their face that they are rising above the level that spells security for all and that they may be confronted with sanctions. The denial of compliments given is the denial of cause for anyone to envy the one complimented." Thus, we better understand Jesus' response "Why do you call me good?" when we understand that compliments were regarded negatively because they made someone stand out from the crowd and made it likely that someone else would envy them, and possibly sanction them. Indeed, the Book of Solomon states: "Through the devil's envy, death entered the world (2:24)."

The point at issue here is not a minor one. Most religious scholars preach that it was Jesus' humility (e.g., Mark 1:44; 3:12; 5:43; 7:36) that made him conceal many of his miracles and ask the people who received the benefits of these miracles to remain silent about his role. Looked at from the perspective of 1st Century Jewish culture, it was not humility but self-defense. Mark (15:10) says: "...it was out of envy that the chief priests had handed him over." Jesus' ultimate death comes partly as a result of the envy of the Pharisees. The first time that Jesus' death was contemplated came when Jesus cured the withered hand of a man in a synagogue in Capernaum – "The Pharisees went out and immediately conspired with the Herodians against him, how to destroy him (3:6)." One has to wonder, when first reading this passage, why would anyone want to kill a healer. But within the 1st Century Jewish context, it was Jesus' "celebrity" and his accumulation of fame (Mark 1:45; 2:12; 4:1) that lead to the conspiracy to kill him.

By knowing the language and the customs of the people of the New Testament, we can better explain many of the issues about which people have asked questions for more than two thousand years.

14. Prior Knowledge

The Gospels assumed that the people reading them had prior knowledge of Jewish history, particularly biblical references (McClymond, 2004; Chilton and Evans, 1997). Unfortunately for us in the 21st Century, much of this prior knowledge has been lost. We read these passages in isolation from their Old Testament context, mistaking the Gospel text for unique sayings and/or occurrences, when, in fact, they are shaded images of prior sayings and stories, suggesting that the Gospel sayings and stories themselves may owe their origins to history rather than to biography. Here are some examples of what appear to be the words/stories from the Gospels, but actually refer back to the words and stories of others...

Gospel References	Prior References
"...wise men from the east came...asking, 'Where is the child who has been born king of the Jews? For we observed his star at its rising...(Matthew 2:1-2)."	"When you behold the star, follow it wherever it leads you. Adore the mysterious child, offering him gifts with profound humility, He is indeed the Almighty Word which created the heavens. He is indeed your Lord and everlasting King (Book of Enoch)."
"You are my beloved Son... (Mark 1:10)."	"You are my son; today I have begotten you... (Psalms 2:7)."
"Verily, verily, I say unto you, Before Abraham was, I am (John 8:58)."	"And God said unto Moses...Thus shalt thou say unto the children of Israel, 'I am' hath sent me unto you (Exodus, 3:14)."
"I am the good shepherd (John 10:11)."	"Woe be to the shepherds of Israel that do feed themselves! Should not the shepherds feed the flocks? (Ezekiel 34:2)"
"So when he dipped the piece of bread, he gave it to Judas son of Simon Iscariot... (John 13:26)."	"He who eats bread with me has turned against me (Psalms 41:9)."
"Be ye therefore wise as serpents and harmless as doves (Matthew 10:16)."	"Be in all things wise like the serpent, and always harmless like the dove (Ignatius, Letter to Polycarp, 2:2)."
"the tree is known by its fruit (Matthew 12:33)."	"You know the tree from its fruits (Ignatius, Letter to Ephesus, 14:2)."
"the stone that was rejected by you, the builders; it has become the cornerstone (Acts 4:11)."	"The stone which the builders rejected; this has become the head of the corner (Psalm 118)."

Jesus Who?

Clearly, the writers of the Gospels were well versed in the Old Testament, so the use of traditional sayings and events came naturally to them. Our difficult task is to try to discriminate what is simply old wine in new skins and what is authentic. Obviously, where the story and/or saying can be traced back to Old Testament sources, the authenticity as a true act/saying of Jesus has to be questioned.

In summary - what ultimately emerges more than 300 years after Jesus' birth is not the final product we have before us today, but the end of the process of selecting what would become the Bible we know. After 350 A.D. there would be many more changes to the Bible as a result of political and theological considerations of the powers that ruled at the time. However, that very interesting story is far beyond the scope of this book[33]. The important point being made is that using the New Testament as our major source of information is fraught with difficulties. Yet it's our largest single repository of information about Jesus, and therefore we must go forward.

To overcome the difficulties cited in this chapter (or at the very least, to try to deal with them), we will adopt a schema not unlike those used by others who have previously undertaken this task. The difference in our approach will be to use more criteria in an attempt to separate the historical elements more accurately. Those factors that are being used include the old stand-bys of multiple attestation, similarity/dissimilarity, and embarrassment, all of which have been defined in detail by scholars more qualified than I (e.g., Crosson, 1991; Witherington, 1997). To these we will add the following: non-derivative, non-stylistic, as ancient as possible, minimally motivated, and as unaltered as possible. Let's examine each of these in some detail:

- Non-derivative: to the extent that a passage in the New Testament can be seen to derive from prior legends or myths, or even contemporary events, it is likely to be less historically accurate and more likely to be a work of literature. For example, the fact that so contemptible a character as the Roman emperor Nero was being visited by Magi suggests that

---

[33] See, for example, Arthur Patzia's (1995) *The Making of the New Testament*.

Magi visiting the baby Jesus may be more of a literary event than an historical one.

- Non-stylistic: to the extent that a passage adopts the literary form of another work of literature, it is likely to be less historically accurate and more likely to be a work of literature. For example, the *Gospel of Mark* continuously uses a "reversal of expectation" motif, which has dramatic implications, but may tempt the authors to have an empty tomb not because it existed, but because it wasn't supposed to exist. Or in the *Gospel of Luke*, the additional miracles associated with women may not be factual, but may be part of the author's style of providing a female counterpoint to the male.
- Non-prophetic: events in the New Testament that fulfill prophecies can be suspected to have arisen for the purposes of fulfilling prophesy, rather than the other way around. Thus, it is likely that the *Gospel of Matthew* has Joseph and his family flee to Egypt so that the Old Testament prophesy can be fulfilled, since there is no other evidence for this event, and no rationale for its occurrence.
- Ancient as possible: sources that are as old as possible are less likely to have been subjected to changes. This may be why Bloom (2005) says: "The Marcan Jesus may be as close to 'the real Jesus' as we can get (p. 11)."
- Minimally motivated: Because Paul's entire raison d'etre is to recruit believers in Jesus, we should look skeptically upon his record of events. This is true of the entire New Testament, but it is equally true of sources such as Josephus, who while he wasn't concerned with promoting the Jesus Cult, had his own agenda (Bloom 2005). Archeological findings, on the other hand (e.g., there is no evidence for a town of Nazareth before mid 1st Century A.D.) gives us more confidence, as does correspondence that was not meant for public consumption (e.g., a letter from Eusebius who promotes changing the Gospels for theological reasons).
- Unaltered: sources that have been relatively unaltered are more likely to be closer to the historical reality. Thus, documents which were discovered thousands of years later (e.g., *Dead Sea Scrolls, Gospel of Thomas*) are to be preferred

to the documents that date to the 1st and 2nd Centuries, because those documents that have been around have been altered so many times that their historical accuracy has to be questioned.

Let's begin. Are you ready?

Summary

In this chapter we looked closely at the New Testament and other ancient writings. Despite the traditional belief that the Gospels were written by the disciples under divine guidance, evidence from carbon dating, language analysis, and citation show that the Gospels were written in the 2nd Century. By 160 A.D. we know, without question, that all four gospels were in circulation, and by 180 A.D. they were considered authoritative. Yet this was more than 100 years after Jesus' death. Moreover, we found that for a variety of reasons, the Gospels as they appear today bear only slight resemblance to how they were originally written, and we've found that some changes were random but others were systematic attempts by early Church authorities to distort the facts. Of particular interest, we found that attempts were made to de-emphasize the influence of Jesus' immediate family, to downplay the role of women in his life and ministry, and to dramatically increase the divine aspects as they applied to Jesus. We also found that many of the elements contained in the New Testament were based on early mythic legends and stories contained in the Old Testament as well as the Pagan Mystery Religions. Finally, we learned that many Gospel passages that appear questionable to readers in the 21st Century can be explained to our satisfaction when we view them through the language and customs of their time.

This coin from the 8th Century is the earliest representation of Jesus on a coin.

CHAPTER TWO

Who Was Jesus?

Did Jesus Exist?

"Some writers, a minority it is true, but not an unintelligent minority, have surveyed the historical 'evidence' and concluded that no such person as Jesus ever existed..." (Wilson, 1992, p. 88)

Although millions of people readily believe that Jesus was a living person, there is some debate about whether or not he really existed[34]. The arguments against the existence of Jesus revolve around four main points: (1) the lack of reference to Jesus in contemporaneous historical texts, (2) the non-belief in the Jesus "of the flesh" among so many early Christian thinkers, (3) the similarities between the stories about Jesus and other mythic figures, and (4) the lack of physical evidence for Jesus' existence.

---

[34] "...over 100 [books] in the past 200 years have fervently denied the very existence of Jesus (Van Voorst, 2000, p. 6)."

Lack of Historical References

While Jesus fills the pages of the New Testament, a careful analysis shows that the picture of Jesus painted in the 1st Century texts (e.g., Epistles of Paul, The *Pastor of Hermas*, *Letter to the Hebrews*, *Letter of Barnabas*, the *Didache*) contain very little historical information about Jesus (e.g., where or when he was born, where he lived, when he died). They only concern themselves with the "risen" Jesus who is a spiritual being, not a human one. The conception of this "risen" Jesus is not unlike the other spiritual beings that influenced the Jewish and Greco-Roman peoples of the time. It was only at the end of the 1st Century in the writings of Ignatius of Antioch that "facts" about Jesus' life emerged, and then, subsequently, in the Gospels that were written in the middle of the 2nd Century. Only in the 2nd Century does Jesus take on a human form.

After carefully reviewing this literature, Swedish scholar Alvar Ellegard (1999) concluded that the Jesus of the 1st Century did not exist at all. Rather, it was in the 2nd Century when sufficient interest had been generated about the "risen" Jesus promoted by Paul and others that the Gospel writers were compelled to build a life around this heretofore wholly spiritual being. They found the formula in the life of "the great prophet and founder of the...Essenes...originating in Judea in the 2nd century B.C. (p. 257)." Thus, according to Ellegard, there was no real Jesus living at the turn of the millennium; he was created 100 years later as a composite from stories about the Essene Teacher of Righteousness. Whether or not Ellegard's conclusions are correct, it's clear that the historical Jesus was a creation of the 2nd Century. Had he lived in the early years of the 1st Century, would we not have found traces of his historical life then? Yet we don't. Instead, he only emerges in the 2nd Century with no prior evidence of having lived before.

If the information inside the New Testament is questionable, outside the New Testament, references to Jesus are virtually non-existent. For example, the famous Jewish historian Josephus (37-103 A.D.) who provided a comprehensive history of the life and times of the period

Jesus Who?

made no mention of Jesus[35]. Other 1st Century writers who made no mention of Jesus include, Philo-Judaeus (15 B.C.–50 A.D.), Seneca the Younger (4 B.C.–65 A.D.), Pliny the Elder (23-79 A.D.), Marcus Fabius Quintilian (39–96 A.D.), and Plutarch (49-119 A.D.).[36] Justus of Tiberias, a Jew and a contemporary of Jesus, lived near Capernaum (where Jesus was said to live) and wrote a history of the Jews beginning with Moses and extending into his own times, but never mentioned Jesus. The *Dead Sea Scrolls* that survived in tact from this period contained no references to Jesus. In fact, the only contemporaneous references to Jesus are from the New Testament, which given the fact that the New Testament was written to promote the belief in Jesus, cannot be considered independent support for his existence[37]. Had Jesus been a real person and as influential as the New Testament writers claimed (e.g., Matthew 4:25, 14:1, 26:3; Luke, 19:47, 23:13), surely there would be other mentions of his exploits. But there are none, lending credence to the theory that Jesus was a fictional character created to promote a new religion, much in the same way that other fictional characters (e.g., Santa Claus, the Easter Bunny) are created to promote other events (e.g., Christmas, Easter). Indeed, this theory has been around as a legitimate source of inquiry since the 18th Century and has sponsored many adherents, the most prominent of whom was Bruno Bauer (1809-1882), a German professor whose student, the revolutionary leader Karl Marx, adopted many of Bauer's ideas for his own purposes. More recent advocates of this theory include British scholar and *Dead Sea Scrolls* expert John Marco Allegro (1970), Claremont religious scholar Dennis MacDonald

---

[35] Most scholars agree that the brief mention of Jesus in Josephus was a later addition (Acharya, 1999; Schonfield, 1974) which some ascribe to Eusebius (Taylor, 1977; Wheless, 1990).

[36] For a complete list of the 27 scholars who lived and wrote at this time, but made no mention of Jesus, see Freke & Gandy, 1999, pp. 133-134.

[37] There are references to a Jewish Messiah ("Christ", "Christus" or "Chrestus") in the works of Pliny the Younger (62-113 A.D.), Suetonius (69-140 A.D.), and Tacitus (55-120 A.D.), but none of these mentions Jesus or Joshua or Yeshu as the specific Messiah in question. At this time there were many people who claimed to be a "Messiah" and many attacks on "false messiahs", so that the mention of a Messiah and his followers is commonly accepted, but not proof that someone named Jesus/Joshua was the Messiah.

(2000), and Canadian Professor and investigative journalist Tom Harpur (2004).

Non-belief in a Jesus "of the flesh"

The idea that Jesus was not a real person comes not only from the lack of historical reference to him inside as well as outside the New Testament, but from the many claims that affirmatively denied his existence. For example, many early Christians believed that the body was corrupt, and hence no true "God" could be made to take human form. As a result, it was believed by an early Christian group called the Docetists (from the Greek *dokein*, meaning "to seem") that Jesus had to be an imaginary person, who appeared to be a human being, but who was, in fact, an illusion[38]. This view was shared by Marcion (110-160 A.D.), who compiled the first version of the New Testament as early as 144 A.D., and whose followers, the Marcionites, continued until the 4th Century. And it appeared in Justin Martyr's (c 100-163 A.D.) *Dialogue with Trypho*[39] in which Trypho says: "...Christ – *if indeed he has been born*, and exists anywhere – is unknown... (Van Voorst, p.15)." On the other side, there were early Christian groups (e.g., the 2nd Century Carpocratians) who believed that Jesus was 100% human, and not divine. They shared this view with the Jews and the Gnostics. Porphyry (c 232 – 304 AD) published a 15 volume book *Against the Christians*, calling the Christians a "confused and vicious sect" and denying Jesus had ever lived (Cohn, 1963) – the book does not survive, but counter arguments by Eusebius (c 275-309 AD) do.

The belief that Jesus was not real was so wide spread among early Christians that Polycarp (c 69-155 A.D.), Bishop of Smyrna, lamented that it was the belief of "the great majority" of Christians (quoted in Price, 2000, p. 24). So, counter arguments sprung up. For example...

- The two *Epistles of John* are very specific in condemning anyone who believed that Jesus did not "come in the flesh (1

---

[38] A synonym for Docetism is Illusionism, referring to the fact that the Docets denied Jesus "came in the flesh" and believed that he was an illusion.
[39] When it appeared, *Dialogue with Trypho* was the longest book ever published. It was 142 chapters in length (Freke & Gandy, p. 310).

John 4:2)" and for warning that "...many deceivers have gone out into this world, men who will not acknowledge the coming of Jesus Christ in the flesh...(2 John 7)." These deceivers were called the "antichrist".

- Ignatius, Bishop of Antioch, in 115 A.D. in the *Epistle to Mary*, urged his followers: "Avoid those that deny the passion of Christ, and His birth according to the flesh; and there are many at present who suffer under this disease (Quoted in Acharya, 1999, p. 67)."
- *The Letter of Polycarp to the Philippians* says: "For anyone who does not confess that Jesus Christ has come in the flesh is an antichrist (v. 7)."

Had Jesus been a true historical figure, there would not have been such a large number of prominent people who denied his existence, or an even larger number who defended him. Such controversies never developed over other contemporary religious figures (e.g., John the Baptist, Paul, James the Just, Hillel, Honi the Circledrawer).

Whatever Happened To...?

The Docetists, an early Gnostic sect, eventually died out by the end of the 1st Century, although some of their beliefs were adopted by the Cathars, who were destroyed by the Catholic Church in the 13th Century.

The Marcionites began in mid 2nd Century and funded by their wealthy founder, grew in stature until they rivaled the Catholic Church. Declared heretics and hounded by the Catholic Church, they slowly lost influence, but continued to flourish in the East, eventually being absorbed by the Manichaeists.

The Caprocratians were active from 125 A.D. through the end of the 2nd Century. They were condemned by church leaders for their libertine sex practices. Legends claim they survived in Israel until the end of the 4th Century, although the last known references to them were around 160 A.D.

Jesus and the Ancient Mythic Figures

Many authors have studied the ancient myths and legends that existed for thousands of years before Jesus' era, and they find that virtually every element in Jesus' story can be found in these prior myths. For example,

- John Robertson's 1990 book, *Christianity and Mythology*, argues that Jesus was a pastiche of various leaders of an Israeli cult of the Sun God, the most famous of whom was Jesus ben Pandera who was executed under the reign of Alexander Janneus (106-79 B.C.). We'll hear more about Pandera later.
- Dennis MacDonald's book *The Homeric Epic and the Gospel of Mark* (2000) claims that Jesus never existed, and the *Gospel of Mark* is a re-working of the Odyssey myth, updated for the Roman/Jewish audience.
- Canadian investigative journalist Tom Harpur (2004) goes further back and relates the Jesus story to Egyptian myths. He writes: "...there is nothing the Jesus of the Gospels either said or did – from the Sermon on the Mount to the miracles, from his flight as an infant from Herod to the Resurrection itself – that cannot be shown to have originated thousands of years before, in Egyptian Mystery rites and other sacred liturgies such as the Egyptian Book of the Dead (p. 10)."
- Timothy Freke and Peter Gandy's excellent book, *The Jesus Mysteries* (1999), makes a strong case that Jesus was created from a composite myth based on the cult of Mithra[40]. They offer the following comparisons between the Jesus story and the Mithra cult[41].

---

[40] While the comparisons here are with Mithra, similar comparisons could be made with Buddha, Krishna, Osiris, Horus, Hermes, Orpheus, Adonis, Attis, Hercules, Tammuz, Thor, Beddru, Deva Tat, Zoroaster, etc. (Graves, 1999).

[41] See Harpur (2004) pp. 84-85 for a similar comparison between Jesus and Horus, or Massey (2002) who matches Jesus and Horus on nearly 200 variables. Acharya (1999) identifies 36 different "saviors" who preceded Jesus and about whom there are almost identical legends.

Jesus Who?

	Mithra	**Jesus**
Divinity	Son of God	Son of God
Father	God	God
Mother	Mortal virgin	Mortal virgin
Birthplace	Cave (in a manger)	Cave (in a manger)
Birth date	December 25	December 25
Sanctified by	Morning star, Sirius	Star of Bethlehem
Witnessed by	three shepherds	shepherds
Glorified with	Myrrh, frankincense, & gold	Myrrh, frankincense, & gold
Preaches	Rebirth	Rebirth
Techniques	Baptism	Baptism
Possessions	Shared with community	Shared with community
Disciples	12	12
Gospel	Open, secret meanings	Open, secret meanings
Miracles include	Water into wine, raise the dead	Water into wine, raise the dead
Time of Death	Vernal equinox	Vernal equinox
When captured	No resistance	No resistance
Type of death	Crucified/hung on a tree	Crucified
Accompanied	Two torchbearers	Two thieves
Says to slayers	"You know not what you do"	"They know not what they do."
Purpose	Sacrifice for others' sins	Sacrifice for others' sins
Corpse	Wrapped in linen, anointed with myrrh	Wrapped in linen, anointed with myrrh
Resurrection	After three days	After three days
Discovered by	Three women	Three women
Return	Judgment day	Judgment day
Eucharist	Bread and wine	Bread and wine

These similarities seem uncanny today, but they were well known in Jesus' time. In fact, one of the early church leaders, Quintus Tertullian (c 160-220 A.D.) wrote in *Apology*:

> "...He [Mithra] baptizes his believers and promises forgiveness of sins from the Sacred Fount, and thereby initiates them into

the religion of Mithra. Thus he celebrates the oblation of bread, and brings in the symbol of the resurrection... (1:62)."

Indeed, Tertullian was so aware of the origins of the Christ myth in the mythologies of old that he referred to his own belief in Jesus as a "shameful thing", and his belief in the death and resurrection stories as "monstrously absurd" and "manifestly impossible" (quoted in Doane, 1985, p. 412).

Making the same comparisons, Tertullian's contemporary, Celsus wrote: "In truth there is nothing at all unusual about what the Christians believe...(Quoted in Freke & Gandy, p. 27)" and St. Augustine (354-430 AD) himself said: "That which is known as the Christian religion existed among the ancients, and never did not exist, from the beginning of the human race...(quoted in Jackson, 1985, p. 1)."

Not only are the details of the Jesus story very similar to those of Mithra and the other Mystery religions, Harpur (2004) points out that many of the sayings are similar too, including prohibitions against adultery, the "lust in the heart" comparisons, the parables about the good and bad seeds, the tête-à-tête with Satan, the story of the prodigal son, etc.

While these similarities do not necessarily prove that Jesus was simply an old myth wrapped in new clothing[42], they are, nonetheless, remarkable. Many authors have argued that the ferocity with which the early Catholic church suppressed "heresies" and "paganism" and their extensive book burning frenzies were designed, at least in part, to

---

[42] It should be noted that Jesus is not the only person in the Bible whose historical existence has been questioned. There is a considerable body of thought and evidence that most of the Old Testament (and its major characters, Abraham, David, etc) is fiction (e.g., Harpur, 2004; Lazare, 2002). The main points in this argument center around the lack of archeological and other evidence that these "kingdoms" ever existed, for surely so great a King as David was said to be, should have left some legacy apart from the chronicles that appear in the Old Testament.

eliminate all evidence of these prior myths (aka diabolical mimicry)[43], so that the Jesus myth could stand alone. Of course, the fact that the story of Jesus bears marked resemblance to the stories of other religious leaders, whether real or mythical, does not necessarily invalidate the claim that Jesus' life was real. Indeed, it is possible that the life of the real Jesus provided an opportunity for many of these mythic stories to be appended to it, so that so-called Pagans would be attracted to the new religion. In other words, Jesus himself was real, but did not do many of the things ascribed to him by his marketing savvy chroniclers, who adapted the prevailing myths to expand upon his life and attract a wider following.

Lack of Physical Evidence

When we look for physical evidence for the existence of ancient notables, we look at several sources, the most prominent of which are archeological sites, coins, and artwork. With regard to archeological sites, Wells (1988) notes: "There is not a single existing site in Jerusalem which is mentioned in connection with Christian history before 326, when Helena (Mother of Constantine) saw a cave that had just been excavated, and which was identified with Jesus' tomb (p. 194)." Had Jesus been a real person, and had he done the things ascribed to him, surely there would have been sacred shrines as early as the 1st Century. Yet there were none. Nor is there any mention of any of the apostles (especially the apostle Paul who wrote endlessly about Jesus) visiting these shrines, despite their presence in the area. For example, can you imagine the apostle Paul visiting Jerusalem and never visiting the tomb of Jesus, and then never including this visit in his many letters? Clearly you can't: which implies that there was no tradition of a tomb, because in fact there was no death and burial.

Not only is there an absence of any archeological sites associated with Jesus, neither his name nor his face appeared on any coinage during the first seven centuries. This might be expected, since Christianity was not in a place of dominance. Nonetheless, there is coinage that

---

[43] Authors such as Justin Martyr, Tertullian, and Irenaeus claimed that the Devil (aka "wicked spirits") created these myths prior to Jesus' birth, so that Jesus' critics would have material with which to criticize the Jesus story.

displays the faces of Herod the Great, Herod Antipas, Pontius Pilate and Augustus as well as the First Jewish Revolt, the Roman Subjugation, and the Second Jewish Revolt (Bar Kochba). There is also coinage thought to show Magi (wise men). Yet the oldest coinage bearing Jesus' likeness is from the 8th Century (See page 40). Surely – the theory goes - such an illustrious visage, had Jesus been real, would have found its way into the coinage before then.

While the meaning of the lack of Jesus coinage may be debated, the lack of any artwork depicting the life of Jesus is surprising. The earliest discoveries date to the mid 2nd Century, and there are precious few of these, and what does exist can also be interpreted as referring to others (e.g., Mithra). Indeed, it's only after the 4th Century that images of Jesus began appearing in large numbers. Yet, had Jesus been the major figure that Christians claimed he was, we should have expected far more and far earlier. Indeed, in the late 4th Century St. Augustine (354-430 A.D.) lamented that "we have absolutely no knowledge of His appearance (quoted in Wheless, 1990, p.112)." Had Jesus been a real person, surely more would have been known about his appearance. Summing up, Archarya (1999) says: "Basically, there is no physical evidence for the existence of Jesus Christ (p. 86)."

Thus, when we look at all four indicators of Jesus' existence (or lack of it), we have to admit that a good case can be made that Jesus was a literary device derived from prior myths and developed to be the poster boy for a new religion. As incredulous as this may sound, there is certainly a reasonable body of evidence to support this theory. Yet despite the fact that there is no independent support for the existence of a historical Jesus, it is the thesis of this book that Jesus was a real person. He may not have done all the deeds that the Bible claimed he did, nor are the events ascribed to him necessarily true (e.g., born on December 25th); however, there probably was a real person named Jesus. Needless to say, this conclusion is somewhat self-serving, because if Jesus never existed, this book would have to end here.

What Was Jesus' Real Name?

"The beginning of the good new of Jesus Christ, the Son of God "
(Mark 1:1)

There never was a person named Jesus Christ! His first name wasn't Jesus and his last name wasn't Christ. Would you believe that Jesus' real name in Hebrew was *Ieschova* or *Yeshua* or Joshua? When the Greeks translated the Hebrew name Joshua they came up with Jesus (*Ieschova* became *Iesous* became Jesus), and that name stuck. But his real name in his own language was Joshua (Hebrew) or Yeshu (Aramaic), which was a very good name in the Hebrew tradition. It meant – "Yahweh (God) is savior (helper)". Josephus mentions more than 20 Joshuas, the most famous of whom was the "Son of Nun" (Exodus, 33:11), from the tribe of Ephraim, who was the successor to Moses as the leader of the Israelites. We remember him best as the trumpeter who blew down the walls of Jericho. What is not so well known is that Nun in Hebrew means fish, the symbol of life, especially for Galileans who lived by the Sea of Galilee. Interestingly enough, the symbol of the fish became associated with Jesus[44], as did the fact that the start of the Age of Pisces (symbolized by the fish) represented the start of the "end of times", since Pisces was the last symbol of the Zodiac, and the start of the new age coincided with Jesus' birth. Moreover, the symbol for "Nun" is equivalent in the Jewish gematria[45] to the number 50, which represents freedom and the fullness of life, and Nun is the fourteenth letter of the Hebrew alphabet, the number 14 symbolizing David, the King of Israel. Thus, in many ways the name Joshua was a very holy name and had many connotations that later became associated with Jesus' life (e.g., Jesus was said to be descended from David, was said to be a "fisher of men", preached the "end of times", etc.).

As far as his last name goes, in those days, people didn't have last names. He would have been called Joshua, son of Joseph, son of

---

[44] The fish was also one of the symbol for Horus, a precursor to Jesus, who was also known as a "fisher of men" (Harpur, 2004).

[45] The numerology of the Hebrew language, that involves translating Hebrew characters into numbers, then seeking the meaning of the numbers.

Jacob. Yet many people think his last name was Christ! Not true. He was never called Jesus Christ! Jesus/Joshua was believed, by some, to be the Messiah, which in Hebrew (*moschiach*) means "the anointed one"[46]. The Greek word for the oil used to anoint someone is "*khrisma*", and the person so anointed is "*Khristos*" in Greek, "*Christus*" in Latin, and "Christ" in English. In reality, had he been considered someone deserving of anointing, he would have been called Joshua the Anointed, or Jesus the Christ.

Many people mistakenly believe that because Jesus was the "anointed one" he was the Messiah. Not true: being anointed was not solely reserved for the Messiah. Other people who were anointed were Kings, High Priests, and prophets. Indeed, in special circumstances, sick people would be anointed to help in the healing process (James 5:14).

The person referred to as "Jesus Christ" is best understood, then, to have been "Yehoshua ben Joseph" or "Joshua, son on Joseph, son of Jacob" or "Joshua the Anointed One". No one ever called him Jesus Christ!

Will the Real Jesus Please Stand Up

OK. If we accept that Jesus really did exist, and we now know that the Hebrew name was Joshua, and the name "Jesus Christ" simply means "Joshua, the Anointed", which Jesus are we talking about? That's right! There are several candidates for the position. In an earlier section we talked about the Essene's Teacher of Righteousness. Looking intensely at the New Testament literature, some scholars have argued

---

[46] The Hebrew word, in turn, was derived from the Egyptian word *messeh*, the "holy crocodile", which referred to the practice of the Pharaoh's sister-brides anointing their husbands with the fat of the crocodile. Interestingly enough, it's a woman (with the alabaster jar) who anoints Jesus during his fatal trip to Jerusalem (Mark 14:3). Later Gospels changed this event to hide the fact that a woman anointed Jesus, since this action implied that a woman was a priest, which was anathema to the later Gospel writers who had a definite masculine prejudice.

Jesus Who?

that the case can be made that the historic Jesus didn't exist (Ellegard, 1999; Koester, 1980), but was composed from memories of the Essene "great prophet and founder" who was called, in the *Dead Sea Scrolls*, the Teacher of Righteousness. But there is another Jesus who lived a few generations later than the Essene founder, and many scholars believe that he could be the Jesus of legend. Let's look at the evidence. Are you ready?

According to the Babylonian Talmud and the Tosfeta[47], at the beginning of the 1st Century BC, Alexander Jannaeus, King of Judea, allied with the Sadducees and persecuted the Pharisees, killing thousands. At this time there was a holy man named Joshua ben Perachiah (aka Perahya), who led a religious group called Notzrim that, to all appearances, seems to be very similar, if not identical, to the Nazarenes[48]. One of his disciples was named Yeshu[49] ben Stada[50]. Yeshu's mother was named Mary, but there were questions about his father. Some claimed that he was a Roman soldier who led Mary astray. Because of the disputed paternity, Jesus was not commonly referred to as ben Stada or ben Pandera, but rather as Jesus the Notzrim (an early form of Nazarene). He and his master fled to Egypt to escape Jannaeus' persecution. Here he learned the black arts, which involved cutting the flesh[51]. On their return to Israel, they stopped at an Inn, where he had a conflict with his master. Back in Israel, he started his own sect, and gathered a group of disciples (Matai, Todah, Naqai, Neitzer, Buni)[52]. Eventually he was accused of

---

[47] Both the Talmud and the Tosfeta were based on centuries of oral tradition. The Tosfeta was written down in about 200 A.D. and the Talmud in 400 A.D. They continued to be revised for centuries after first being compiled.
[48] See Ellegard (1999) p. 239 or Schoeps (1948).
[49] Most scholars accept that the word "Yeshu" was used as a substitute for "Yeshua", that was the Hebrew equivalent of Jesus.
[50] Also known as Yeshu ben Pandera. Some scholars argue that these were two different people, but most consider them to be slightly different names for the same person – ben Pandera from the father's name and ben Stada reflecting the fact that the mother "went astray" (in Hebrew *satat da*).
[51] In other versions of the story, the magic secrets are smuggled out of Egypt in a cut in his flesh.
[52] These same five disciples were, in fact, ascribed to Jesus ben Joseph instead of the traditional 12 (Schonfield, 1965, p. 238). The five disciples

idolatry, practicing black magic, deceiving people, enticing them, and leading Israel astray. He was tried, false witnesses were used, and he was hung to death (some claim, stoned[53]) at Lydda (Lod) on the eve of Passover.[54]

Notice the similarities between the life of Jesus ben Stada from around 80 B.C. and the life of our Jesus. Both are from Galilee and born of a mother named Mary. In both cases the paternity is disputed. Both become disciples of prominent religious leaders, and both eventually develop their own following, amongst their disciples are men named Matthew and Thaddeus. Both are called Jesus the Nazarene. Both escape death from an evil King by fleeing from Israel into Egypt, and both have a significant event associated with an Inn. Later, both are accused of practicing magic and leading people astray, and both are betrayed, tried, convicted, and killed on the eve of Passover.

Jesus ben Stada is not the only possible source for the Jesus story. Around the same time there lived another Jesus, **Jesus ben Sirach**, the reputed author of the *Book of Sirach* (part of the Old Testament *Apocrypha*), who combined Jewish "wisdom" literature with Homeric-style heroes. In the 1st Century A.D. there were nearly a dozen Jesus' whose lives had similarities to the life of Jesus. For example...

- **Jesus ben Gamala** was a well known rebel and "peace activist" who was put to death during the 1st Jewish rebellion.
- **Jesus ben Ananias** (Ananius) was known for prophecy (e.g., destruction of the Temple) and preached the "end of times" until his death at Roman hands in 68/69 A.D.
- **Jesus ben Saphat** was a Galilean who led the Zealot revolt in Tiberias. Just before the city fell to Vespasian's Legionnaires he fled north to Tarichea on the Sea of Galilee.

---

listed were believed to correspond to the five books in the *Gospel of Matthew*, which itself mirrored the five books of the Torah. Papias originally spoke of Matthew's Gospel as consisting of five books.

[53] It's most likely that he was stoned to death, and then left to hang (Cohn, 1963).

[54] See Chagigah 4b, B Shabbat 104b, B Sanhedrin 67a, 107b and Sotah 47a. See also Cohn (1963).

Jesus Who?

Is Jesus ben Stada the original Jesus? Were the legends associated with this Jesus incorporated into the stories of the later Jesus? Did the Jews of the 3rd and 5th Centuries invent stories about Jesus ben Stada to undercut the Christian movement? Did the lives of Jesus ben Gamala, Jesus ben Ananias, and Jesus ben Saphat get woven into the tapestry of the New Testament? We can never know. It's certain that the writers of the New Testament did not set pen to paper until the mid 2nd Century, and by this time, the oral stories of all these men named Jesus surely combined in ways that we're unable to ascertain.

Summary

We started this chapter by reviewing the substantial amount of evidence about whether or not Jesus existed. Many scholars question his authenticity due to the lack of historical reference to him outside the New Testament, the close similarities between his life and the lives of Pagan Gods such as Mithra and Dionysus, the early disputes among Christians about his existence "in the flesh", and the absence of any physical evidence (e.g., coins, tomb and birthplace veneration, artwork). We concluded that he probably did exist, although we find that there was a prior Jesus who lived about 100 years before the turn of the Century, and the similarities between the life of this Jesus and the traditional Jesus suggests that he may be the original model that Paul used in developing his religion. Moreover, the lives of many other Jesus figures in the 1st Century undoubtedly came to be woven into the fabric of the Gospels. Finally, we can note that his true name would have been Joshua ben Joseph, and that the person called "Jesus Christ" never existed.

One of the earliest images of Jesus shows him as the Good Shepherd (Luke 15, John 10). Note that Jesus has short hair and is beardless. The painting is from the 3rd Century. It can be found on the ceiling of the Catacomb of St. Callistus.

CHAPTER THREE

Birth

When Was Jesus Born?

"In those days a decree went out from Emperor Augustus that all the world should be registered. This was the first registration and was taken when Quirinius was governor of Syria....While they were there, the time came for her to deliver her child." (Luke, 2:1-6)

Most people think that Jesus was born in the year 0, and everything before that was B.C. (Before Christ) and everything after that was A.D. (Annon Domini or "the year of our lord"). Not true! The New Testament is not exact in dating the birth of Jesus, but about 500 years after the fact, a Roman scholar and Dacian monk named Dionysius Exiguus (470-540 A.D.) calculated that Jesus was born in 753 AUC (or *ab urbe condita,* meaning from the "founding of the city" of Rome). As the Roman dating system gave way to the B.C./A.D. system, later scholars determined that Exiguus had made a slight miscalculation, and if we accept that Jesus was born "in the days of Herod the King (Matthew 2:1)", then he had to be born before 4 B.C. which is the year that Herod died. And in fact he could have been born as early as 37 B.C., when Herod's reign began.

Looking to the *Gospel of Luke* that claims that Jesus was born when Quirinius (51 B.C. – 21 A.D.) was Governor of Syria, we come up with a date of 6 or 7 A.D., which is out of place with Matthew. However, Luke may be mistaking the Essene ceremony of the "second birth" for Jesus' actual birth. It was the custom among the Essenes that when children reached the age of 12, they were separated from their mother, wrapped in linens, and then presented to the world, much like in today's orthodox Bar Mitzvah ceremonies. Assuming that Jesus was born around 6 B.C., he would have been about 12 years old in 6 A.D., thus accounting for Luke's error in mistaking the first birth with the second birth.

All things considered, 6 B.C. is a good date. Some scholars use 4 B.C. since this is the date of Herod's death, however, this practice ignores the story in the *Gospel of Matthew* of the killing of the children by Herod. In that account, the Magi came to worship the "King of Jews", and once Herod learned of this, he had all the children two years of age or younger, killed[55]. Moreover, when the Magi found young Jesus he was a small child, not an infant. Disregarding the story of the killing of the children, which many believe did not happen, the clear implication is that while Herod was still alive, Jesus was a small child. Herod died in 4 B.C., so 6 B.C. is a good date for the birth of Jesus[56].

Was Jesus Born on Christmas?

"In that region there were shepherds living in the fields, keeping watch over the flock by night." (Luke 2:8)

We celebrate the birth of Jesus – Christmas – on December 25th, but what evidence is there that Jesus was born on that day? None! One thing we can be sure of, though, is that he most likely wasn't born in December since the *Gospel of Luke* tell us that shepherds were

---

[55] In reality, Herod had his own sons strangled in 7 B.C. as a result of their plot against him.
[56] Using this same logic, Harvey (1970) concludes: "...Jesus was born not less than two years before [Herod's death in 4 B.C.], but also not much more, say, 7-6 B.C.. (p. 19)."

tending their sheep in the fields when he was born. In Israel at that time, shepherds stayed outside from June until November.

There are various theories about Jesus' birth. Many believed that Jesus was born on January 6th (the birthday of the God Osiris). The rationale for this date was the belief that Jesus was exactly 30 years old when he died and that he died on April 6th. Counting backwards from April 6 exactly 29 years and 3 months gave a birth date of January 6th (Craveri, 1967). This date was adopted by the Eastern Church and called "Epiphany[57]" or "The Appearance."

The African Tertullian (c 160 –220 A.D.) and the Roman Hippolytus (c 170-235 A.D.) believed the date to be March 25th, the spring equinox under the ancient Roman calendar. Clement of Alexandria (c 150-215 A.D.) believed that Jesus was born on May 20th, the 25th day of the Egyptian month of Pachon. None of these theories had any real facts associated with them, but they were popular nonetheless.

A 3rd Century Christian named Sextus Julius Africanus believed that March 25th was Jesus' conception and the day of Earth's creation as well. Using March 25th as the day of conception, he skipped ahead nine months to December 25th as the birth date.

So it's clear that there were a large number of dates competing for the right to be Jesus' birth date, none based on any form of evidence. Now into the fray came a long-standing competition between early Christians and Pagan worshipers of the Sun God. In 274 A.D., Roman emperor Aurelian (214-275 A.D.) made the Pagan cult Sol Invictus the official religion of Rome, building temples and establishing December 25th as the birthday of the Sun.[58] Some 60 years later, the Roman church officially declared December 25th to be Jesus' birth day.

---

[57] The word "epiphany" was corrupted in Italy and became associated with "Befana", the old witch who delivered candy to the good children and a lump of coal to the bad children by coming down the chimney, the forerunner of the Santa Claus tradition. Legend has it that she provided respite for the Magi on their journey, but declined to join them.
[58] This date followed naturally for Sol Invictus, since the original Pagan cult upon which it was based, the Syrian cult of Mithra, also celebrated December 25th as Mithra's birth date.

Hence, December 25th became Jesus' birthday, largely as a Christian attempt to co-opt the existing celebrations that surrounded that date. Because Christianity was often an add-on religion (i.e., people were allowed to keep remnants of their own beliefs as long as they ascribed to the greater power of the Christian beliefs when the two belief systems conflicted), it made sense to co-opt, whenever possible, the symbols of the existing religions or cults. Indeed, in the middle of the 5th Century, Pope Leo I (aka Leo the Great) was still trying to explain away the fact that many Christians were followers of the Sun God, bowing to the Sun as they entered church, and celebrating the joint birthdays of Jesus and Sol Invictus (or Mithra).[59]

According to the Essene customs under which Jesus' father and mother lived, couples had sex in December (when the wheat was planted) so that the child would be born in September (the holy month of Atonement). This would have been the natural course of events, however, Mary conceived during their engagement (See page 71 for a fuller explanation), and thus the expected birth in September did not take place then, but a few months earlier. It was probably sometime between April (when the rains stopped and temperatures first allowed shepherds to tend their sheep in the fields) and September (when Jesus was supposed to be born). The most likely month is June, following the wheat harvest, when sheep were placed in the fields to graze on the remains of the crops (Porter, p. 70), for this was the one month especially associated with shepherds being in the fields with their sheep (Luke 2:8). Today, we say that April brings showers. It doesn't mean that April is the only month in which it rains, but each month has a characteristic that we associate with it (e.g., February is the shortest month, December is the darkest month, October is the harvest month, etc). So too, when Jesus' birth is associated with

---

[59] The close connection between Christianity and the Sun cults is also seen in the use of the halo (which originated at this time and first appeared more like a Sun God head) and the fact that early Christian church entrances faced East (Acharya, 1999) and (according to Tertullian) early Christians faced East when they prayed.

shepherds being in the fields with their sheep, this was equivalent to saying he was born in June[60].

Born at the Stroke of Midnight?

There is very little evidence about what time Jesus was born. The Gospels tell us only that he was born at night. But verses from the *Wisdom of Solomon* (18: 14-15) that spoke of the night "half gone" were taken as prophesy of Jesus' birth, and hence the tradition of the midnight birth, which in turn, gave birth to the midnight mass, still celebrated today. This midnight mass, called Christ's Mass by the 11th Century English Christians, is the origin of the word "Christmas".

Born in Bethlehem?

> *"In the time of King Herod, after Jesus was born in Bethlehem of Judea..."* (Matthew 2:1)

The *Gospel of Mark* tells us nothing about Jesus' birth. It begins with his baptism and then concentrates on the last week of his life. The likely reason for this omission was that devout followers of what was to become Christianity firmly believed that they lived in the "end of times" and that the end of the world was imminent. With civilization in the balance, what mattered was what Jesus said and did, not his biographical information. Thus, the *Gospel of Mark* hit the ground running, with Jesus' baptism and the heavenly pronouncement that he was God's "beloved son".[61] But one problem with Mark's language was that it implied that Jesus set out on his messianic journey only as a result of heavenly insights during his baptism. Many early Christians

---

[60] Bear in mind that the months in the Jewish calendar usually began in the middle of what we call a month. Hence, the month of June began in mid June and extended into mid July.

[61] Starting a biography at adulthood is not an exception, however. *Res Gestae Divi Augusti* (Achievements of the Divine Augustus) begins with Augustus (future Roman Emperor and declared God) at age 19.

held to the position that Jesus was born to be a Messiah, so Mark's position needed to be changed to coincide with the prevailing wisdom. Hence, decades later, both Luke (2:4-7) and Matthew (2:1) spent substantial time clarifying Jesus' birth and his in vitro messianic future.

Both Matthew and Luke claim that Jesus was born in Bethlehem in Judea (there was another Bethlehem in Galilee), but Matthew claims the family lived there while Luke claims they made the trip from Nazareth to participate in a census. The first census in Israel was in A.D. 6-7, so it makes no sense to say that Joseph and Mary traveled to Bethlehem in response to a census in 6 to 7 B.C, when the first census was more than a decade later. In fact, it makes no sense that Joseph would travel to Bethlehem at all because the census was based on the person's residence, not his birthplace (Craveri, 1967; Perkins, 1988). Moreover, his wife was pregnant, and the journey from Galilee to Bethlehem is about 75 miles, which, in those days, would have taken a week or more (Craveri, 1967). The journey would have been perilous, not only because of its length and the difficult terrain, but also because of the presence of thieves. Duquesne (1994) notes: "... travelers had also to make their way across dry, rocky, tortured country, riddled with caves which served as hide-outs for the bandits who terrorized the roads (p.11)." And in any event, even if Joseph went, he would not have been required to bring his pregnant wife, as only men were required to register (Perkins, 1988).

Indeed, the only reason to have Joseph and Mary travel to Bethlehem is to have Jesus fulfill the Old Testament prophecies that the Messiah would be born in Bethlehem:

> "But you, Bethlehem Ephrathah, the least of the clans of Judah, out of you will be born for me the one who is to rule over Israel (Micah 5:2)."
>
> "I am sending you to Jesse of Bethlehem, for I have chosen myself a king among his sons (1 Samuel 16:1)."

In other words, there was no evidence that Jesus was born in Bethlehem, but his "history" was made to fit into the prophecies of the Old Testament. On the other hand, a careful reading of the *Gospel of*

Jesus Who?

John shows that Jesus was not born in Bethlehem. During the Festival of Booths, as Jesus was recruiting new followers, the crowd questioned his credentials. One asked: "How does this man have such learning, when he has never been taught? (7:15)" and Jesus replied in an extended passage to the effect that what he was teaching came from God. But when others asked: "Surely the Messiah does not come from Galilee[62], does he? Has not the scripture said that the Messiah is descended from David and comes from Bethlehem, the village where David lived? (7: 41-42)." To this question, Jesus offered no reply. Given his penchant to reply to even the most oblique questions, his omission here was telling. Had he been born in Bethlehem, Jesus probably would have said something, but he doesn't[63]. In addition, Jesus is never referred to as "Jesus of Bethlehem", but only as "Jesus the Nazarene". Had he been born in Bethlehem, and given the Old Testament prophecies, surely he would have been known by the name "Jesus of Bethlehem".

While Jesus does not specifically deny that he comes from Bethlehem, he does specifically deny that he is the "Son of David", which is the entire basis for placing his birth in Bethlehem[64]. Jesus said: "How can the Scribes say that the Messiah is the son of David?...David himself calls him Lord, so how can he be his son? (Mark 12: 35-37; Matthew 22:45)." In other words, if the Messiah was alive when David was alive, it was impossible for him to be David's son.

In summary, Jesus was probably born in Galilee (possibly in the village of Bethlehem in Galilee). The two Gospels that claim he was born in Bethlehem of Judea have an agenda of proving that Jesus fulfilled the Old Testament prophecies, and for that reason, they misshape the truth to place him there. Jesus himself never claimed to have been

---

[62] This comment has a deeper meaning. To 1st Century Jews, the word Galilean was synonymous with being a zealot (Bultmann, 1925).
[63] One author (Wilson, 1992) interprets this verse as follows: "...the Fourth Gospel very specifically states that Jesus was not born in Bethlehem (p. 75)."
[64] Indeed, this denial of Davidic descent is a major bone of contention between Mark and the later Gospels. It would appear that for Mark, Jesus is neither the Messiah from birth nor the Messiah from the line of David.

born in Bethlehem, even when he was being taunted to so declare. And there is no reason to believe that he was born there.

Born in a Manger?

"And she gave birth to her firstborn son and wrapped him in bands of cloth, and laid him in a manger, because there was no place for them in the inn." (Luke 2:7)

The common conception is that Jesus was born in a stable, but there is no evidence for this in the Gospels (Gardner, 2001). Matthew says he was born in a house (2:11), and still other early Christian texts claim that he was born in a cave (e.g., *Protoevangelium of James*, Origen's *Against Celsus*, *Dialogue with Trypho* by Justin Martyr). In fact, the word "*katalemna*" which is usually translated as "stable" can also be translated as a "temporary shelter" or a "cave". There was a cave outside Bethlehem that, as early as 215 B.C., was identified as Jesus' birthplace, although before Jesus it had been known as the birthplace of Adonis (Craveri, 1967). In the 4th and 5th Centuries Christians built a basilica over the cave where Jesus supposedly was born. However, we know from our previous discussion, that Jesus was not born in Bethlehem, so the cave commemorating his birth there is misplaced. There is another tradition that claims he was born in a cave in Qumran (Gardner, 2001), and this theory may be closer to the truth.

Luke (2:7) claims that Mary "laid him in a manger" which is basically a feeding troth used as a substitute for a cradle. Thiering (1992) claims he was born in a "manger" but the manger was the name of a cave in the Qumran community.

Interestingly enough, the Egyptian and the Persian Gods were said to be born in caves, and both were said to be born at the Winter Solstice. The Egyptian God was even born in a manger inside the cave (Harpur, 2004).

The idea of a manger, mentioned in Luke, may come from the words of Isaiah (1:2-3) who said: "…The ox knows its owner and the donkey its master's manger..." Both these animals were well known to the ancient Egyptians, who featured them in the Cult of Horus. In any event, while there was no ox or donkey noted in Luke's account of Jesus' birth, virtually every nativity scene from the 2nd Century onwards, pictures them among the inhabitants.

In summary, we will never know where Jesus was born, and the evidence for his birth in a house vs. a cave vs. a stable is sketchy. The concept of the cave has a certain metaphorical beauty, suggesting as it does that Jesus came from the womb of the Earth itself. Thus, one finds it hard to resist the symmetry that he was born in a cave and ultimately returned to a cave, the tomb where he was laid to rest.

The Magi

"In the time of King Herod, after Jesus was born in Bethlehem of Judea, wise men from the East came to Jerusalem..." (Matthew 2:1)

The appearance of the Magi is only told in the *Gospel of Matthew*, where the Magi (from *magos*, a Greek word for priests of Ancient Babylon and Persia) from the East, led by a star, go in search of Jesus whom they expect is to be "the King of Jews". They bring him gold, frankincense (used for royal ceremonies and for cleaning white linen), and myrrh (according to John's Gospel, used in embalming Jesus). The gold and frankincense were foretold in Isaiah (60:6), the myrrh appears to be an added bonus, or may come from the *Song of Solomon* (3:6).

Although the common myth is that the Magi came to worship Jesus in his crib, the Gospel has them arrive while Jesus is a child (*pais* in Greek). Indeed, this is the reason that Herod orders the death of all children two years of age or under (not all infants!), since he must reckon that Jesus was born two years before the Magi arrived. Somehow the Magi were transformed into three Kings, although in the *Gospel of Matthew* they were neither Kings nor were there three of them! This idea came much later, in the 5th Century, first appearing in the *Armenian Gospel of the Infancy*, and probably relates to a prophecy in Isaiah (60:3).

Most scholars maintain that the story of the Magi was an invention and not meant to be historical. One of the best arguments against its veracity is the fact that the Magi appear this one time and then never again. Can you imagine these wise men traveling thousands of miles to attend the birth of "the King of the Jews", bringing costly gifts, and then disappearing, never to be heard from again? No subsequent visits? No mention by Mary of this important tribute to her and her son? No, nothing. There abrupt disappearance suggests that they were simply literary devices, inserted into the text to make a point, and then omitted from future references.

The story of the Magi is undoubtedly a metaphor, told by the writers of Matthew to indicate that Jesus deserved recognition from birth. Matthew's authors were probably responding to the claims that Jesus was simply a magician, and having Magi worship him at birth would indicate that he was more than a mere magician.

Was There a Star?

> *"Where is the child who has been born king of the Jews? For we observed his star at its rising..."* (Matthew 2:2)

The idea of a celebrity's birth being announced by celestial events is not original to Jesus. Alexander, Augustus, and Abraham all had stars accompany their births, as did Buddha and Krishna. So why not Jesus? If it were true, Halley's comet was a good candidate for the celestial event, but the comet was seen in that area in 11 to 12 B.C. which is a little too early for Jesus' birth (As we shall see later, this time does correspond to the birth of John the Baptist). A better candidate is the 70+ day supernova observed by Chinese astronomers of the Han Dynasty in 5 B.C., yet we can't be certain that this same star was seen in the region of Galilee. The best candidate was the conjunction of Jupiter and Saturn in Pisces, in 6 B.C., first elaborated by a 16th Century German astronomer, John Kepler in 1603. Apparently the two planets came into conjunction three times during that year: May 27, October 6, and December 1 (Fidler, 1993, p.169). The one that fits our hypothesis best (i.e., shepherds in the fields) is May 27.

The real problem with Jesus and the "Star of Bethlehem" is that mythology has come to associate the star with his birth, but in fact it is clear from Matthew (2: 1-16) that the wise men from the East followed the star two years after Jesus was born. This is why King Herod "killed all the children in and around Bethlehem who were two years or under, according to the time he had learned from the wise men (Matthew 2:16)." This event, while listed in Matthew, has no corresponding mention in any of the histories of that period. Which isn't to say that Herod wasn't capable of such an act, but its omission questions the veracity of Matthew's claim.

In summary, it's unlikely that there was a star heralding Jesus birth, and then hanging around Bethlehem for two years while the Magi sought Jesus out. Our only possible candidate, the conjunction of Jupiter and Saturn in Pisces, did not hang around long enough. In fact, for the writers of the Gospel of Matthew, "...stars were living beings, intelligent and powerful, exercising great impact on lands over which they move (Malina, 2001, p.104)." This means that the writers of Matthew were implying that the Magi were inspired by angels, rather than following an actual physical entity. Thus, our inability to find a physical entity which fulfills the demands of Matthew's description is not a problem, since a physical entity was never truly meant.

The Virgin Birth

"All this took place to fulfill what had been spoken by the Lord through the prophet: 'Look, the virgin shall conceive and bear a son, and they shall name him Emmanuel'..." (Matthew 1:22)

Everyone is familiar with the story of the "virgin birth", but what is not so familiar is the fact that only in the Gospels of Luke and Matthew is the virgin birth postulated. Neither Mark nor John makes any mention of it at all, nor is it referenced in the rest of the New Testament. In addition, apart from its mention at the start of Luke and Matthew, Jesus' virgin birth plays no part in his subsequent life. It is never mentioned by anyone, even though one can imagine that it would have enhanced his image and added support to the theory that he was the Messiah. Indeed, the story of the virgin birth appears as an isolated entry in both Gospels, important unto itself, but then neglected and forgotten.

There are several issues here. Was Jesus' birth a "virgin" birth? Or is it his conception that was virginal? Was Mary a "perpetual" virgin? Let's look at all these issues.

The so-called "virgin birth" is best described as a "virginal conception", for it's the conception that supposedly occurs without sexual contact, not the actual birth[65]. In any event, virgin conceptions or births are not common today, but in ancient times, especially among the famous, they were not unknown. Famous children born of a virgin include: Buddha (China), Krishna (India), Zoroaster (Persia), Adonis (Babylon), and Mithra (Syria). Among the Greeks it was even more common. For example, Alexander the Great was believed to have been conceived from a celestial thunderbolt, or to have been the result of a union between Philip's wife Olympias and the God Jupiter who took the form of a serpent. Perseus, the Greek hero who decapitated Medusa, was born of a virgin named Danae, by the God Zeus who came to her in a golden shower. Even Plato was said to be born of the union of a virgin (Amphictione) and a God (Apollo), and only after his birth did Ariston, Amphictione's husband, have sex with her. More relevant to Jesus' time, Romulus and Remus, the founders of Rome, were born of a Vestal Virgin whose father was the God of War, Mars. The Roman emperor Octavian was born from the union of his mother, Atia, and the God Apollo. The Egyptian Goddess Isis gave birth to Horus despite the fact that her husband, Osiris, had his phallus cut off by his brother

---

[65] In the *Protoevangelium of James*, Mary is said to have an actual virgin birth, in which the baby Jesus is born without any change to Mary's body. This miracle is tested by a friend of the midwife, Salome, who reaches in and certifies that Mary's hymen is still intact, whereupon God withers her hand for having doubted.

Seth[66]. Thus, virgin conceptions were quite popular at the time, although this was only in "Pagan" cultures, not in the Jewish world.

The choice to give Jesus a "virgin birth" like many of the rich and famous of his time appears to be more of a marketing ploy than a historical fact. Not only did it serve the purpose of competing with contemporaneous cults, but also the virgin birth was another in the line of prophecies (e.g., born in Bethlehem, descended from David) which Jesus was said to fulfill. In this case, the prophecy was from Isaiah (7:14) – "The virgin will conceive and give birth to a son, and they will call him Emmanuel."[67] Unfortunately there was a mistranslation here (as in so many other places) and the original Hebrew word *almah* [68](young girl or young woman) had been mistakenly translated into the Greek *parthenos* (virgin)[69], so that the original prophesy did not, in fact, call for a virgin to conceive, but simply for a young woman to conceive[70]. Moreover, Isaiah was talking about an 8th Century B.C. sign that would appear to King Ahab during his reign. Thus, the prophecy was not only the result of an error in translation; it was also 800 years too late.

Even if the translation was correct, which it wasn't, the use of the word "virgin" within the context of Essene marriages had a different meaning than it does today. In those days, the elite of the Essenes who were allowed to procreate (this included descendants of King David and the High Priest Zadok) went through an elaborate procedure to insure that

---

[66] One can easily see that the images of Isis suckling Horus are the prototypes for the Mary/Jesus art that followed.
[67] If we continue to the next verse we can see that this quote has nothing to do with Jesus. It reads – "Butter and honey shall he eat..." As far as we know, this was not Jesus' diet, although it does resemble the diet of John the Baptist and the Essenes.
[68] The Hebrew word for virgin was *bethula*, not *almah*.
[69] The word originates from Parthenis, a Greek virgin who had sex with the God Apollo, giving birth to Pythagoras (ca 569 – 475 B.C.). Some authors believe that the use of the word here is a play on the word "Panthera" which was one of the names of the Roman soldier believed to be the biological father of Jesus (Yeshu, 2006).
[70] Of course, looking at that quote from Isaiah, one has to wonder why they called him Jesus and not Emmanuel.

they kept to strict purity laws even while fulfilling their marital obligations. Gardner (2001) describes it as follows:

> "Three months after a betrothal ceremony, a 'First Marriage' was formalized to begin in the espousal month of September. Physical relations were allowed after that, but only in the first half of December. This was to ensure that any resultant Messianic birth occurred in the Atonement month of September. If the bride did not conceive, intimate relations were suspended until the next December[71], and so on. Once a probationary wife had conceived, a 'Second Marriage' was performed to legalize the wedlock. However, the bride was still regarded as an almah (young woman) until the completion of the Second Marriage which, as qualified by Flavius Josephus, was never celebrated until she was three months pregnant (pp. 30-31)."

In the event that a woman became pregnant before the first marriage, it was said that "a Virgin had conceived", meant as a play on words since the young woman was still legally (if not biologically) a virgin. This early pregnancy may account for the rumors, reflected in *The Gospel of the Hebrews*, that Jesus was in Mary's womb for only seven[72] months. In other words, instead of being born in September as would be expected (nine months after impregnation in December), Jesus was born around June or July, meaning that Joseph and Mary had sex in October, when she was technically a virgin[73].

---

[71] The December mating was meant to mimic the planting of the wheat in December, wheat being the main crop in Israel.

[72] Dionysus was also said to have been born after seven months. The number 7 was sacred not only to the Jews, but even earlier, to the Pythagoreans, who considered seven the number of the virgin, because it was the only one of the prime numbers (1 to 10) which could not be divided evenly into 360 (the number of degrees in a circle). Thus, the rumor that Jesus was born at seven months may not be entirely accurate, and may be another example of the symbolism replete in the Bible. It may be true, however, that he was born earlier than expected (i.e., prior to September).

[73] Having sex prior to the specific time "…was not regarded as a serious sin in Jewish society (Harvey, 1970, p.19)." In fact, it was commonplace among the

Jesus Who?

Joseph was an elite member of the Essenes and Mary, chosen as his wife, was similarly highly esteemed and had been the equivalent of a nun[74] within the Essene circles. These women were referred to as "virgins" in much the same way as the Greeks and Romans referred to "vestal virgins". Thus, for Mary to conceive during this period would mean that, Mary, a virgin (aka a nun) had conceived which she was still a virgin (aka prior to December). There was nothing supernatural about this at all. But there was a danger that the future husband could avoid the marriage, and the child, as a result, would be considered illegitimate. For a future king of the New Israel, the status as an illegitimate child could be problematic, hence the advice to Joseph from a senior member of the Essenes (called an "angel" or "saint" because they were so pious) to go through with the first marriage as if it were the second marriage (the second marriage being one in which the woman was already pregnant)[75]. Years later, after Jesus' death, the ascension of Jacob (aka James), Jesus' brother and the unquestionably legitimate son of Joseph and Mary, was unchallenged.

The fact that the "virgin" birth as described above was not supernatural at all explains why there is no mention of Jesus' birth throughout the Gospels (except the start of Luke and Matthew). Had it been supernatural or divine, the story would have followed Jesus around and been repeated. The fact that we don't find it in the Gospels or anywhere else in the New Testament confirms that we are not dealing with anything supernatural, even if it was beyond the accepted orthodoxy.

As indicated earlier, only Matthew and Luke recorded a virgin conception. The *Gospel of John* has the disciple Philip say that Jesus is the "son of Joseph" (1:45). Paul, describing Jesus' birth, says that "God sent his Son, born of a woman" (Galatians 4:4), using the word *gune* (woman) rather than *parthenos* (virgin). In Romans, Paul specifically states that Jesus came "from the seed of David, according

---

Jews (Craveri, 1967, p. 17); more so in Judea; less common in Galilee (Spoto, 1998, p. 20).
[74] The name Mary was synonymous with "Sister". This practice is continued even today among various sects.
[75] Thiering, 1992, pp. 44-46.

to the flesh (1:3)." Surely Paul, the Christian master of marketing, writing before even Mark, would have promoted Jesus' virgin birth if it had been the case.

Jesus' natural conception is not only supported by the *Gospel of John* and Paul's letters, but also the works of Cerinthus (c 100 A.D.) and Marcion (c 160 A.D.). In addition, Jesus' natural conception is a basic tenet of the Ebionites ("poor ones"), who were the Jerusalem based Jewish Sect that emerged following Jesus' death. James the Just, Jesus' brother, was the head of this Sect until his death, and leadership was then passed on to his brothers and then nephews. If anyone should know the true story of Jesus' conception and birth, it would be these people. Though little survives of their texts, since they valued the oral tradition over the written one, we have extensive quotations from early Christian leaders (Irenaeus of Lyon, Eusebius of Caesarea) who complained about the Ebionites failure to believe in the virgin birth:

> "Their interpretation is false, who dare to explain the Scripture thus: Behold a girl (instead of a virgin) shall conceive and bear a son. This is how the Ebionites say that Jesus is Joseph's natural son. In saying this they destroy God's tremendous plan for salvation...(Irenaeus, *Against Heresies*, III 21.1)."

> "Those who belong to the heresy of the Ebionites affirm that Christ was born of Joseph and Mary and suppose him to be a mere man (Eusebius, *Ecclesiastical History*, XI, 17)."

Thus, the Sect that was founded by and led by Jesus and his family specifically argued against the virgin conception.

There is another problem with the idea of a virginal conception, and this problem occupied tens of thousands of hours of debate among Christian theologians, even to this date. If the Messiah was to be of the line of David – and Joseph was said to be of David's line – but if Jesus was conceived by the Holy Ghost, ipso facto, Jesus would not be of the line of David, and hence, not a true Messiah. Proponents of the orthodox view claim that by marrying Mary, Joseph "adopted" Jesus and thus the child was entitled, by law, to be considered Joseph's son. While this is true in the strict sense, it's obvious that for the purposes of the Old Testament, the kinship was meant to be biological, not legal. A final problem with the idea of the virgin birth/conception is that following the birth, as described in Luke (2:22), Mary undergoes the ritual purification ceremony. Had Jesus' birth been virginal, there would be no need for Mary to be purified. Indeed, as the virgin bride of God, the thought of purification would be anathema.

In summary, there can be no question that Jesus' birth was not the result of an immaculate conception. The original idea of the "virgin birth" came from a mistranslation of an Old Testament prophecy, and all the supporting evidence (e.g., Mary's ritual purification following the birth, Jesus' descent from David through Joseph, the testimony of the Ebionites, etc.) point to a normal birth. Lest the extremely orthodox take offence at this conclusion, we can note the following comment by Pope Benedict XVI:

> "According to the faith of the Church, the Sonship of Jesus does not rest on the fact that Jesus had no human father: the doctrine of Jesus' divinity would not be affected if Jesus had been the product of a normal human marriage...(1969, pp. 274-275)."

Was Jesus an Illegitimate Child?

We would be less than complete without mentioning the alternate theory of Mary's pregnancy, put down in writing as early as 178 CE by Celsus in *The True Word*[76]. Celsus maintained that Mary was a poor country girl who worked as a seamstress, and when she became pregnant by a Roman Legionnaire called Joseph ben Panthera (aka Pandera, Pantera, Pandira)[77], while betrothed to a carpenter named Joseph, was cast out and had an illegitimate son.

---

[76] Unfortunately this ancient work has been lost, and it is only known through Origen's work, *Contra* Celsus, that dates from about 240/248 A.D.
[77] As fate would have it, a tombstone of a Roman bowman called Pantera, who served in the reign of Tiberius, in Galilee, was discovered in Germany in 1859 (Porter, p. 68). Even more curiously, John Robinson's (1990) book,

The Jewish Talmud and the Tosefta share this view: "...Ben Stada [code name for Jesus] is Ben Pantera. Rabbi Hisda said, 'The husband was Stada, the lover was Pantera...The mother was Miriam [Hebrew for Mary] the dresser of woman's hair...' (b Shabbat 104b)." The *Sefer Toledot Yeshu* (Book of the Life of Jesus) is a medieval book based on earlier oral traditions, which offers an alternate view of Jesus' life from the point of view of the Jews. In it, they claimed that "Joseph Pandera" raped Mary[78].

Lest these speculations be dismissed, there are hints of the illegitimate status of Jesus' birth in several places.

- In Matthew's genealogy of Jesus, there were only four women mentioned (Tamar, Rahab, Ruth, and Bathsheba), and each of them was tainted in some way: Tamar's children were born of incest, Rahab was the madam of a brothel, Ruth got her second husband by fornication, and Bathsheba was an adulteress. Is it possible that the writers of Matthew inserted these four names into the genealogy of Jesus as a way of responding to the rumors about Mary? Can Matthew be foreshadowing the criticism of Mary by saying that women of dubious reputations nonetheless, made his illustrious list?
- In the *Gospel of John* (8: 31-42), Jesus had a discussion with "The Jews who had believed in him" and he said that becoming his disciples will set them free. They objected, because as descendants of Abraham they "have never been slaves to anyone". The debate went on, and became rancorous. At one point they said: "We are not illegitimate children..." The clear

---

Christianity and Mythology, claims that an Israeli cult leader named Jesus ben Pandera was executed during the reign of Alexander Janneus (106-79 B.C.), and in the Sanhedrin (106a) there is a Yeshu Ben Pandira who studied under Rabbi Joshua ben Perachya at this time and who "practiced magic and led astray and deceived Israel."

[78] Christian sources were concerned with this rumor that had become part of Roman pantomimes. To combat it, Epiphanius (320 – 403 A.D.), Bishop of Salamis, made Panther the father of Joseph, and John of Damascus (676 – 749 A.D.), known as the last of the Church fathers, made him the Great Grandfather of Mary (Craveri, 1967).

implication here was – Who is Jesus to be speaking about the proper relationship of sons to fathers when he is the illegitimate child and they are not? This was such a hot issue, that a few passages later "they picked up stones to throw at him, but Jesus hid himself and went out of the temple (John 8:59)."

- Was Jesus' highly unusual identification as "son of Mary" (Matthew 6:3) really a taunt, mocking him because his father was not known, and hence "Jesus, son of Joseph" - that would be the accepted way of speaking his name - isn't used since they weren't sure who was his father? Indeed, in Semitic usage, "a man is illegitimate when he is called by his mother's name, for a bastard has no father (quoted in Mitchell, 2002, p. 23)."
- When Jesus was asked to approve the Scribes stoning an adulteress, he asked, "Let whoever of you is sinless be the first to cast a stone at her (John 8:7)." When no one raised his hand, he said: "I don't condemn you either. Go now, and sin no more." Jesus' reply – I don't condemn you either – was extremely uncharacteristic for him. The expected (i.e., usual) response would be "You are forgiven" (e.g., Mark 2:5; Luke 7:48), but instead he said, "I don't condemn you either." Can this be his own attitude toward his mother for her act of adultery?
- Can Jesus be making an allusion to the rumors of his illegitimate birth when he said, in the *Gospel of Thomas*, "He who knows the father and the mother will be called the son of a harlot (v. 105)."
- In the *Gospel of John*, the Pharisees question a formerly blind man about Jesus' cure, and they said "…but as for this man [meaning Jesus], we do not know where he comes from (9.29)." Since they knew who Jesus was, was this question another taunt at his illegitimate status?
- Was Jesus' association with known prostitutes, unusual for his time and status, some form of compensation for his own questionable background?
- Jesus took very few strong stands on issues of moral behavior, but he did have strong views on marriage and divorce. Was this a result of the questionable circumstances of his birth?

- Was Jesus' rebuke of his mother, on several occasions, a reflection of some deep seeded hostility for her conduct in earning him the grief associated with an illegitimate birth?

There seem to be too many hints to be simply ignored.

Of course, regardless of whether you were born of God, or born of the rape/seduction by a Roman Legionnaire, your birth was unusual and undoubtedly known to everyone in your small village. Even if, under the best of circumstances, your conception was out of the accepted timeline, you were going to stand out. The Jews had a word for it – *mamzer*. It meant questionable paternity (Chilton, 2000). Everyone who sees you will think: "There goes that Jesus kid, the one whose mother..." (choose from the following)

- slept with that Roman.
- was raped by that Roman.
- had intercourse when she shouldn't.
- claims she was impregnated from God.

Life would not be easy for such a child. Chilton (2000) notes: "It is hard to exaggerate the isolation and unease the boy would have felt growing up as a mamzer... A mamzer was, in effect, an untouchable... (p. 14)."

Interestingly enough, Edward Edinger (1972), a Jungian Psychiatrist, believes that Jesus exhibited the characteristics of an illegitimate child, and Matthew Besdine (1968), a New York Psychiatrist, characterizes him as a "Jocasta-mothered genius[79]". Regardless, there can be no question that Jesus' birth status put him in an unusual circumstance. The implications of this event on his future development will be discussed at length in a later chapter.

---

[79] Jocasta was the mother of Oedipus.

Was Mary a Perpetual Virgin?

The concept of perpetual virginity appeared for the first time in the 2nd Century, possibly as an offshoot of the *Protoevangelium of James*. It became mainstream orthodoxy by the late 4th Century (Spoto, 1998, p. 32). Catholics, who held the position that Jesus' mother, Mary, was a perpetual virgin, explained away Jesus' brothers and sisters as stepchildren or cousins. However, the Greek and Hebrew languages had specific names for stepchildren and cousins, and these names were never used with respect to Jesus' siblings. Moreover, there was never any mention in the Bible of any previous marriage by Joseph.

Mary's perpetual virginity is called into question by a number of other facts. For example, Luke notes that Jesus was the "first born" son (2:7 or 2:25), implying that there must have been a "second" (third, fourth, etc.) son as well, otherwise it would be ridiculous to use the word "first born" instead of "only" or "sole". Luke also says that "the time came for her [Mary] to deliver her first child (2:6)", implying that not only was Jesus the first-born son, but there would be daughters born as well. Moreover, Matthew states that Joseph "knew her not until she had borne a son (1:25)" which clearly implies that they had marital relations after Jesus was born.

In summary, most of what we are told about the birth of Jesus cannot be confirmed for a variety of reasons. There are only two accounts of his birth (Matthew and Luke), and these two accounts differ substantially (e.g., Matthew has the family living in Bethlehem, Luke has them driven there for the census). Not only do the accounts differ, but also whenever we apply external standards (e.g., the census Luke talks about is in 6 A.D. while Jesus' birth is in 6 B.C.), we find that the accounts in the Gospels do not correspond. In addition, many of the issues raised in the birth narratives appear to be purposefully sculpted to fulfill Old Testament prophecies, rather than reflecting a historical reality. And even here we find that the Old Testament prophecies were mistranslated, and then Jesus' life was written to fit exactly into the faulty translations (e.g., the original Isaiah prophecy indicates that a child is born of a "young woman", not a virgin).

What can we say about Jesus' birth? He was probably born in Galilee, not in Bethlehem. It was probably a cave, not a stable. He was the first-born son of Mary and Joseph, not the result of the union between the Holy Spirit and a virgin. The year was not 0 A.D.; it was no earlier than 4 B.C., and possibly as late as 7 B.C., but most likely 6 B.C. The month was sometime between March and July, probably June; it certainly wasn't December. Mary's conception occurred during her engagement to Joseph, which was undoubtedly embarrassing to the young couple, and undoubtedly caused some later distress to Jesus.

Summary

The traditional belief is that Jesus was born at the turn of the millennium, on Christmas day, conceived of a virgin who later married Joseph, a carpenter. The family was on its way to Bethlehem, stopped at an Inn, were turned away, and the young child was born in a manger in a stable. While shepherds watched their sheep, three wise men from the East, led by a star, came to worship the newly born King of the Jews. Alerted to his existence, King Herod had all the young male children killed, so the family fled to Egypt to escape persecution. We now know that most of these ideas are mythic, used by the early Gospel writers to glorify Jesus' birth and conform his life to the prophecies of the Old Testament. In all probability, Jesus was born in Galilee in June/July of the year 6 B.C. His mother was a young woman who became pregnant during her "engagement" to Joseph, which was considered scandalous among the devoutly religious Essene group to whom they belonged, and which earned Jesus the lifetime reputation as a "mamzer" or bastard.

CHAPTER FOUR

Family

Who Was Jesus' Father?

"When his mother Mary had been engaged to Joseph, but before they lived together, she was found to be with child from the Holy Spirit. Her husband, Joseph, being a righteous man..." (Matthew 1:18-19)

Jesus' father was called Joseph (Yosef in Hebrew). In Israel at that time, Joseph was the second most popular name for a male (Shanks & Witherington, 2003). According to the *Gospel of Matthew*, Joseph was descended from King David who ruled in about 1000 B.C., and who was responsible for Israel's "golden age." This genealogy is important because it was prophesized in the Old Testament that the Messiah would come from the line of David.

Joseph had a father whose name was Jacob, also called Heli[80]. Jacob and his son Joseph belonged to the Essene Sect that had originally been created as a "court in absentia", devoted to the return of the

---

[80] Heli or Helios is a reference to the Sun, and was probably a nickname.

Davidic line for Israel's Kings and the Zadokite line as High Priests. From the *Dead Sea Scrolls* we learn that Jacob/Heli was part of a group of people, around 35 B.C., who planned with Herod the Great to establish an Israeli kingdom second to none, incorporating even Rome within its boundaries.[81] About 20 B.C. they had a falling out with Herod, and decided to promulgate their own "New Jerusalem".

We know a little about Joseph. He was said to be a "righteous man" (Matthew 1:19). He was obviously a religious person, as reflected in the naming of his sons – James and Joseph were famous patriarchs, and Judas and Simon were Maccabean war heroes. The *Gospel of Luke* says: "Now every year his [Jesus'] parents went to Jerusalem for the festival of the Passover (2:41)." Had he been a normal Jewish male, he would have been engaged at the age of 16. But if he were an Essene, he would have been prohibited from any kind of sexual behavior until he was 20, and not married before 30. According to Essene customs, he would have been 36 years old at the time that Jesus was conceived[82], however, we know that Jesus was conceived outside the normal Essene customs, and hence could have been born when Joseph was younger. The age difference between Joseph and Mary would have been between 15 and 20 years, partially accounting for the fact that most stories about Joseph depict him as an old man.

The devout nature of Joseph suggests that he was more than a normal Jew, who were unaffiliated with the many sects in Israel at that time. Not only did Joseph attend synagogue, journey to Jerusalem for Passover, and name his children after Jewish icons, he was prone to religious dreams which came to him not only during his engagement to Mary but also after the birth of Jesus. In addition, he saw to it that the ritual laws of circumcision and purification were closely adhered to. His devout persona was in keeping with the Essene theology.

The common conception of Joseph is that he was a carpenter (Matthew 13:55), however, this is a mistranslation of the Greek word, *tecton (tekton)*, which more accurately would be called "general contractor", or more provocatively, "Master of the Craft" (Gardner,

---

[81] Thiering, 1992, p. 29
[82] Thiering, 1992, p. 47

2001). In fact, the *Protoevangelium of James*,[83] which concerns the lives of Jesus' parents, specifically identifies Joseph as a general contractor. The difference between a carpenter and a builder is considerable. Indeed, when one looks at the parables that Jesus told, they were often about constructing a building, rather than making an object. This indicates that his experiences along these lines were more architectural than artisan.

Even more provocative is the concept that tecton/tekton is best translated as scholar, since the original Aramaic word is *naggar*, which translates as craftsman or scholar (Wilson, 1992, p. 893). Indeed several notable authors (e.g., Thiering, 1992; Wilson, 1992; Vermes, 1973) believe that Joseph is best understood as a scholar, and it's as the son of a scholar that Jesus is more readily understood, rather than the son of a carpenter. Certainly this image of the scholar is more consistent with Luke's (2:46-47) tale of the 12-year old Jesus in the Temple, where "...all who heard him were amazed at his understanding and his answers."

It's difficult to know when Joseph died, but there are some hints. If Jesus was the eldest of (at least) seven children, and assuming the relatively high infant mortality of those times (Carney, 1975) as well as the Jewish purity rituals (Gardner, 2001), it's reasonable to assume that Joseph lived at least until Jesus was in his early 20s. This would make Joseph in his 50s. How much longer he lived after this is debatable. Throughout the rest of the Gospels, references to Jesus omit his father's name (e.g., Mark 6:3 asks: "Isn't this the Son of Mary[84]..."): those omissions indicate that Joseph must have been dead for more than a few years for all references to him to be eliminated. If Joseph was alive when Jesus was 12, but dead when he was 30, and assuming a respectable time for all mentions of his name to vanish (e.g., at least five years), then Joseph must have died sometime between Jesus' 12th and 25th birthdays, making Joseph about 60

---

[83] Origen (c 185-254 AD), head of the Christian seminary at Caesarea and later at Alexandria, believed that the *Protoevangelium Jacobi* was a true account, on a par with the Gospels.

[84] On the other hand, John (6:42) says: "Is this not Jesus, the son of Joseph, whose father and mother we know..."

years of age at the time of his death. The average life expectancy for a Jewish man in those days was 29[85] (Crosson, p. 23, see also Bagnall & Frier, 1994), indicating that Joseph was a relatively old man when he died.

Although we can never know when Joseph died, we can speculate that depending upon how old Jesus was when Joseph died, his passing may have dramatically impacted Jesus' life. For example, had Joseph died when Jesus was 12 years old, with six younger siblings, Jesus' adolescent life would have taken a certain turn. Were Joseph to have died when Jesus was 25, the impact would have been quite different. In either event, Eisenstadt (1978) has argued that the loss of a parent is a contributing factor in the lives of many eminent individuals, and this may also be true for Jesus.

We are now entering the realm of pure speculation, however, It's interesting to note that Jesus frequently addressed God as *"Abba"*. In Aramaic, *Abba* is the diminutive of *"Ab"* (father), which was used by small children. An English equivalent might be "Pop". This was a very unusual form of address for God, used by no one else in the Old or New Testaments, and may point to the fact that Joseph died while Jesus was still young enough to be using the diminutive form. If Joseph died when Jesus was still a very young teen, this may also explain why Jesus never married (if you believe that he never married – see Chapter Six for a complete discussion of this very controversial issue). Jewish fathers had five principal obligations[86] toward their sons, the last of which was to find him a wife, and if Joseph died while Jesus was still a young teen, he may not have gotten around to this task. Indeed, a teenage Jesus with lots of younger brothers and sisters might have taken on so many responsibilities that finding a wife was the least of his concerns.

The mention of *Abba* raises another issue vis-à-vis Jesus' father and that is his relationship with Joseph. While there is scarcely any

---

[85] This figure is low because of the high infant mortality rate (Spoto, 1998). Factoring infant mortality out, a man who reached the age of 30 would be expected to stay alive until 59, and a 40 year old could expect to live to 63.
[86] Circumcise, redeem, teach the Torah, teach a trade, find a wife.

information about this at all in the Gospels, we can make a few good inferences. For example, *Abba* being a young child's affectionate reference for his father suggests that Jesus' relationship with his father had been affectionate, making him comfortable with using the word. As well, Jesus comment: "No one knows a son except a father, and no one knows a father except a son (Matt 11:27)" is usually attributed to his Godly father, but can just as easily be a reference to his earthly father, implying a good relationship. Miller (1997) says: "Jesus as a child apparently had made a fundamentally successful passage through the important emotional transitions of the oedipal years, and... exemplified a remarkably positive and insightful appreciation and love for "fathers" both personal and divine (p. 43)."

In summary, Joseph was a devoutly religious member of the Essene Sect. He was probably a scholar and/or master craftsman, not a carpenter. He fathered seven children and died when he was about 60 years of age. In all probability he had a good relationship with his eldest son.

Who Was Jesus' Mother?

> *"In the sixth month the angel Gabriel was sent by God to a town in Galilee called Nazareth, to a virgin engaged to a man whose name was Joseph, of the house of David. The virgin's name was Mary."*
> (Luke 1:26-27)

Jesus' mother was called Miriam[87] (Hebrew) but in Aramaic it was Mariam and in Latin it was shortened to Maria and in English became Mary. Just about everybody in the New Testament is called Mary. There's Mary, mother of Jesus, and Mary Magdalene, and Mary the sister of Martha (who may be Mary Magdalene or not), and Mary, the sister-in-law of Mary, and... It was such a popular name probably because it was the name of Moses' sister (Freke & Gandy, 2001).

---

[87] The name Miriam/Mary is not originally a Hebrew word. The name originated in Egypt (Craveri, 1967).

According to the *Gospel of Luke* (and only Luke!), Mary was related to Elizabeth, the mother of John the Baptist. Elizabeth was described as being descended from Aaron (1:5), which implied that Mary, too, was descended from Aaron, which was the priestly line. The *Protoevangelium of James*, however, claims she was descended from David.

While there is nothing in the Gospels about Mary's background, various other sources place her birth in Judea (Jerusalem or nearby Bethany) or Galilee (Nazareth or nearby Sepphoris). The Talmud claims she was "the dresser of women's hair" (b Shabbat 104b) which in Aramaic is *megadela*[88] *neshaya*. Celsus, in 178 A.D., in his book, *The True Works*, claims she was a seamstress[89]. The *Protoevangelium of James*, claims she was one of the seven Temple Virgins in Jerusalem, and had been dedicated to God from the age of three.

Mary was a young girl when she wed. The average age for first time brides in this era was 12[90] (Witherington, 1997), although it was not uncommon for someone to be as old as 16. The *Gospel of Luke* tells us that she was "full of grace" (1:28) which originally meant (*kecharitomene*) "beautiful, comely, pleasing" (Craveri, 1967), but later was changed to imply a divine connection.

At first glance, Jesus' relationship with his mother appears to be strained. He refers to her as "woman"[91] at the Cana wedding and on the cross, and when someone in the crowd calls out a blessing on his mother, he deflects the praise, saying instead - "Blessed are those who have heard the word of the father and have truly kept it. For there will be days when you will say, 'Blessed are the womb which has not

---

[88] Some scholars argue that the word *megadela* was the origin of the second name for Mary Magdalene (Yeshu, 2006), although the accepted theory is that Magdalene came from the name of the city Magdala. We'll have lots more to say about this later.

[89] Perhaps modeled after Penelope, the wife of Odysseus.

[90] Herod the Great's wife, Mariamne, was 12 years old when she wed Herod.

[91] Smith (1978) says: "Any hero who speaks to his mother only twice, and on both occasions addresses her as "Woman", is a difficult figure for sentimental biographers (p.25)."

conceived and the breasts which have not given milk (*Gospel of Thomas*, v. 79)." Many of his teachings deal with the estrangement from family, and he goes so far as to say that - "If any man comes to me without hating his father, mother, wife, children, brothers, sisters, yes and his own life too, he cannot be my disciple (Luke 14:26)." In fact, when one looks at his many parables, there was not a single one in which a mother and child appeared, and is it by chance that the story of the prodigal son refers only to the father's reaction, not the mother's?

Looking at the female characters in the New Testament (e.g., Martha, her sister Mary, Mary Magdalene, the Syro-Phoenician woman, the Samaritan woman, etc), only two (his mother Mary and Jairus's wife) are mothers.

Despite these suggestions, there is nothing concrete that indicates that Jesus and his mother were in conflict, and the fact that she appears relatively infrequently is not unusual since no female character appears very frequently in the canonical Gospels. She is present when he first displays his powers (in the *Gospel of John*, at the Cana wedding) and immediately thereafter she joins his disciples and relatives in a planning conference in Capernaum (John 2:12). She is present at the crucifixion (Mark 15:40) and afterwards (Mark 15:47; 16:1). As Jesus is on the cross, she is the only person he mentions (John 19:26). So it seems clear that despite any tensions that might have existed, his mother was a supporter and their relationship was as close as might be expected.

Did Jesus Have Any Brothers or Sisters?

"Where did this man get this wisdom and these deeds of power? Is not this the carpenter's son? Is not his mother called Mary? Are not his brothers James and Joseph and Simon and Judas? And are not his sisters with us'" (Matthew 13: 54-56)

The average person believes that Jesus was the only child of Mary and Joseph. Yet the *Gospel of John* says "...he went down to Capernaum with his mother, his brothers, and his disciples (John

2:12)." The *Gospel of Matthew* says: "...Is not his mother called Mary? Are not his brothers called James and Joseph and Simon and Judas? And are not all his sisters with us? (13:54-56)."

Some theologians argue that since Mary was a perpetual virgin (*semper virgo*), it was impossible for Jesus to have brothers or sisters. They argue further that the many references in the New Testament to Jesus' brothers and sisters refer to stepchildren and/or cousins. The stepchildren theory was adopted by the Eastern Orthodox Church and is often referred to as the Epipanian view, after the 4th Century Bishop Epipanius. He proposed that Joseph had been previously married (for which there is no evidence) and Jesus' siblings were all half brothers/sisters who were older than he. The cousin theory, adopted by the Roman Catholic Church, and generally referred to as the Hieronymian viewpoint, argues that these children were the children of Mary's sister-in-law, whose name was also Mary, and who was married to Joseph's brother, Clopas. Indeed, her sister-in-law Mary did have two children named James and Joseph[92], but no sisters, nor brothers named Simeon and Judah! Moreover, the Greek text uses the word *adelphoi* which is clearly "brother", not cousin, which would be *anepsioi*.[93]

Previously we discussed the evidence for Mary's perpetual virginity, which is somewhere between slim and none. Indeed, the evidence we have clearly shows that after Jesus was born, the couple continued to have sexual relations, and the six or more siblings of Jesus are the proof of that.

The most famous brother of Jesus was James (*Ya'akov* in Hebrew, *Iacobus* in Greek, *Iacomus* in Latin, *Jacobus* in Germanic, *Jaime* in Spanish) who led the Jerusalem branch of Jewish Christians (or what

---

[92] According to Shanks & Witherington (2003), Joseph/Yosef was the 2nd most common name at that time, and James/Jacob the 12th most common. Jesus/Joshua was the 6th most common name. Simon/Simeon was the most common name (p. 56).

[93] The Bible makes use of both of these words, *anepsios* and *adelphos*, throughout, so there can be no argument that brother is a generic word used for any male relationship. For example, Paul refers to Mark as the cousin of Barnabas (Colossians 4:10).

Jesus Who?

some have called "the Jesus Cult") until his murder[94] in 62 A.D. Known as Jacob (James) the Just, the apostle Paul called him "the Lord's brother" and acknowledged his supremacy in the early Christian movement. Indeed, when Jesus was asked: "Who is to be our leader" when he departs, Jesus said: "Wherever you are, you are to go to James the righteous, for whose sake heaven and earth came into being (*Gospel of Thomas*, v. 12)"[95]. James the Just was so well known that he was mentioned frequently in the books of Josephus (while Jesus was not) and his tomb was well known and venerated by the early Christians.

Jesus' other brothers were Joseph, Simeon, and Judah (Mark 6:3; Matthew 13:55-56). He also had two sisters, but they were never named in the Gospels. The *Protoevangelium of James* claims that their names were Melkha and Eskha. After the death of James the Just in 62 A.D., his brother Simeon stepped in to continue the leadership of the Jesus cult, and following Simeon's death, the sons of Judah[96] continued. Following their death, the leadership of the Jesus Cult passed out of the hands of the family. Shortly after, it disappeared all together.

What Was Jesus' Relationship to His Family?

"After this he went down to Capernaum, he, and his mother, and his brethren, and his disciples: and they continued there not many days"
(John 2:11)

We've already seen that Jesus probably had a good relationship with his father, which undoubtedly was cut short by Joseph's death while

---

[94] The references to James' murder are indirect. He was stoned, and presumed dead, but his death was never certified. This led to the legends that he survived the stoning and went on to evangelize in France and England, dying in Glastonbury in 82 A.D. (Gardner, 2001).
[95] If you accept the theory that Jesus was the "crown prince" but that his birth had been questionable, then his brother James, next in line, would be the undisputed "crown prince", and Jesus' comment here is understandable in that regard.
[96] According to 1 Corinthians (9:5), the "brothers of the Lord" all had wives.

Jesus was still a teenager. In addition, we've discussed his relationship with his mother, which appeared to have been strained. Yet the relationship was not so strained that he did not have contact with her (e.g., the wedding at Cana, visits to see him), and she was present at his crucifixion, at his tomb, and afterwards in Jerusalem with his brothers and disciples (Acts 1:14). Indeed, according to the *Gospel of John*, her well being is one of the last things he mentions before he dies. All things considered, his relationship probably fit within the bounds of normality for those times (maybe even our times too).

The popular belief is that Jesus was at odds with his mother and brothers. Mark 3:21 ("And when his family heard it, they went out to seize him, for people were saying 'He is beside himself.'") is usually cited as an indication of poor relations, however, as discussed earlier (see Chapter One), we can dismiss this passage as an indictment of his family since it evidently suffers from translation problems. Mark 3:31-35 is also cited as an indication of poor family relations (Jesus was told that his family was outside and he said, "Here are my mother and my brothers. Whoever does the will of God is my brother, and sister, and mother"), however, by itself it appears to be relatively benign, reinforcing the unity of the "new" family without overtly rejecting his biological family. Of all the references to his family in the New Testament, only John 7:5 ("For not even his brothers believed in him") appears to cast a jaded view upon his family relations. Yet the use of the parentheses[97] and the disparity between this comment and the preceding comments by his brothers (that are clearly supportive) suggest strongly that John 7:5 is a later insertion. All things considered, and given the problems that can (and do) arise in any family, the case for Jesus' poor family relations is a weak one.

Considering the prominent place that Jesus' family held in the Jewish Christian Sect that emerged following his death, one has to conclude that he had a good relationship with his family. His mother and brothers all worked together to continue his ministry, and after their

---

[97] Used sparingly in the *Gospel of John*, most parenthetical material is explanatory (e.g., 1:38; 1:41; 1:42; 4:2) and they appear to be later editorial insertions designed to explain the text, suggesting that John 7:5 too may not be original.

deaths, the leadership of the Jerusalem church remained in the hands of his grand nephews. Moreover, during his ministry, there are several clues that indicate his family was actively involved prior to his death. For example, his mother Mary initiated the first of Jesus' "acts of power" (turning water into wine) at the Cana wedding (John 2) and his mother and brothers joined Jesus and his disciples for several days in Capernaum (John 2:12). Moreover, it's his brothers who encouraged him to display his miracles in public (John 7:5), and his brother James was considered one of the apostles to whom the risen Jesus appeared (1 Cor. 7; 1 Gal 18). Looking at all the evidence, pro and con, Butz (2005) concludes: "on balance there is more evidence to support a positive role for Jesus' family in his ministry than a negative one (p. 39)."

Wilson (1992) has theorized that the negative relationship between Jesus and his family was placed in the Gospels (especially in the *Gospel of Mark*) to dissuade early Christians from following the Jesus Cult that was administered by Jesus' family. Wilson says: "...it would not be surprising if other parts of the church, particularly the Gentiles, liked telling stories about Jesus as a man who had no sympathy or support from his family (p. 86)." Butz (2005) is more succinct: "...by the time Mark was writing in the late 60s, the Gentile churches outside of Israel were beginning to resent the authority wielded by Jerusalem where James and the apostles were leaders, thus providing the motive for Mark's antifamily stance... (p. 44)." Other prominent scholars agree (e.g., Crosson, 1973; Mack, 1988; Painter. 1999). Conspiracy theorists take note!

What Was the Family's Social Status?

"...because there was no room for them in the inn." (Luke 2:7)

There are a few hints as to the socioeconomic status of Jesus' family. The nature of his birth (no room at the Inn) suggests that they were of limited means. Yet their means were not so limited that they didn't apply to the Inn for a room, nor were they so impoverished that they didn't journey to Jerusalem for the holy days. And, apparently, Joseph made enough money that he had to go to Jerusalem to pay taxes. As indicated earlier, his father, Joseph, was probably a master builder, and the opportunities for a master builder in the bustling area of central Galilee were many. However, the family's devout religious attitude meant that most of Joseph's earnings went to the Essene cult to which they belonged, leaving enough to live on, but little more.

The wedding at Cana, and the participation of Jesus' mother, suggest that they were squarely in the middle class. Moreover, Jesus had many friends and associates from the wealthy class (e.g., Lazarus, Joseph of Arimathea) and many of his stories indicate his familiarity with the issues confronting the landed gentry. Thus, all things considered, Jesus' family was undoubtedly in the middle class.

Summary

Tradition says that Jesus and Joseph were carpenters and his mother was a perpetual virgin. Thus, any other children referred to were cousins or step-brothers of Jesus. As carpenters, the family was poor. Once Jesus started on his ministry, the Gospels tell us that he was estranged from his family. Almost none of this is true. To the best of our understanding, the family was middle class, as evidenced from Jesus' relatively good education and from what is known of the social standing of the family (e.g., the wedding at Cana). Although the word "tekton" can be translated as "carpenter", other translations are "builder", "master craftsman", and/or "scholar." Given the social standing of the family, it is highly unlikely that either Jesus or Joseph was merely a carpenter. The more likely scenario is that the family was a member of the Essene community, a devoutly religious community that existed alongside the Sadducees and the Pharisees. Jesus was the first-born son, and he had four brothers and two sisters, all of whom were involved in the Essene community and were firm supporters of Jesus. After Jesus' death, the family took control of the Jewish Jesus Cult in Jerusalem, and family members headed the group until the 2nd Century when it disappeared from recorded history.

CHAPTER FIVE

Childhood

Was Jesus Raised in Nazareth?

"When they finished everything required by the law of the Lord, they returned to Galilee, to their own town of Nazareth." (Luke 2:39)

Most people believe Jesus was raised in Nazareth. Speaking of Joseph, Matthew (2:23) says: "he made his home in a town called Nazareth, so that what had been spoken through the prophets might be fulfilled, 'He will be called a Nazorean.'" Of course, this sentence makes no sense. How could a child choose to come from Nazareth so that he could fulfill a prophecy, which he undoubtedly knew nothing about? While it's true that, in his later life, Jesus engaged in various behaviors in order to fulfill prophecies (e.g., arranging for a donkey to make the journey into Jerusalem), it begs the question to believe that, as a child, he arranged to live in Nazareth. In fact, a careful reading of this passage reveals that the writers of Matthew are trying to fulfill the prophecy, not Jesus, and in order to fulfill the prophecy that "He will be called a Nazorean", Matthew gives his hometown as Nazareth. But in fact, there is no Old Testament prophecy to the effect that a Messiah will come from a place called

Nazareth (which is another in the long list of errors that the writers of the *Gospel of Matthew* made about Old Testament prophecies). The closest we come to any such description is a passage in Judges (13:5) where Samson's mother is warned: "...the child shall be a Nazarite [*nazirarios* in Greek, *nazir* in Hebrew] unto God from the womb, and he shall begin to deliver Israel; out of the hand of the Philistines." The words *Iesou Nazarene (Nazareneus)* refer to the fact that Jesus was a Nazarene (or Nazarean), not to the fact that he came from Nazareth. To indicate that Jesus came from a place called Nazareth, the correct wording would have been *Nazarethenos* or *Nazarethaios.*

Thus, Nazareth as the home of Joseph and his family has been seriously questioned. In support of this, the town of Nazareth is never mentioned in the Old Testament, or in the works of Jewish historian Josephus nor in any of the Epistles, nor in the Talmud[98]. Nor was there a major road in that area at that time (Sanders, p. 104). In fact, from the archeological evidence available to date (Crosson & Reed, 2001), the town of Nazareth was created after the time of Jesus, partly as a result of a mistranslation. One scholar (Gardner, 2004) dates it from 60 A.D. and Crosson (1991) from 70 A.D. Finegan (1969) provides a thorough discussion of the archeological evidence, and the earliest date he can muster is after the destruction of the Temple in 70 A.D., more than 30 years after Jesus' death.

If Nazareth didn't exist, where did Jesus call home? A careful reading of the *Gospel of Mark* indicates that Jesus' hometown was Capernaum[99], not Nazareth. He notes "When he returned to Capernaum after some days, it was reported that he was at home... (2:1)." Later the Gospel says that "He left that place and came to his hometown, and his disciples followed him. On the Sabbath he began to teach in the synagogue... (6:1)." Given that Nazareth, if it existed at all, was too small to host a synagogue, how could Nazareth have been his hometown? Capernaum, on the other hand, had a "sizable

---

[98] Josephus mentions 45 Galilean towns and the Talmud lists 63 Galilean towns, but neither mentions Nazareth.
[99] Indeed, Jesus rarely addressed the citizenry, but when he did, Capernaum was mentioned (Matthew 11:23) but never Nazareth. Other cities he mentioned included Tyre, Sidon, Chorazin and Bethsaida (Luke 10:13)

synagogue" (Asimov p. 820; Sanders, p. 103), and there is some archeological evidence for that fact (Loffreda, 1985; Wilson, 1992).

Returning to the issue of Jesus the Nazarene, raised by Matthew's mistaken attribution, is it possible that Jesus was a Nazarene? A Nazarene was someone who lived an ascetic life, known as much for what they did (a lot of praying) as for what they didn't do (eat animals, sacrifice animals). Nazarenes were originally called Nazorenes, and they were a prominent Sect in northern Palestine, and according to Epipanius, were also known as Mandaeans. They derived their name from the word "*nasrani*" which referred to a school of small fish. The metaphor to the early Christians is obvious, as is their early symbol, the fish. Famous examples of Nazarenes included John the Baptist, the warrior Samson and the prophet Samuel. It is also likely that Jesus' brother, Jacob (James) the Just, was a Nazarene. All things considered, Jesus' life shared many of the characteristics of a Nazarene, and two of the most prominent people in his life, John the Baptist and his brother James, also were probably Nazarenes.

Some authors treat the word Nazarene and Nazarite (also Nazirite) as if they were the same word; they certainly look the same in English. However, the word Nazarite (*nazir* in Hebrew, meaning consecrated or separated) refers to a type of short-term vow (30 to 100 days), usually made to God to achieve a specific purpose, and then discontinued when the goal was achieved (e.g., I promise not to drink alcohol if I get a new car for Christmas). Nazarite vows are described in Numbers (6: 1-21) and usually involve abstaining from wine, vinegar, grapes, raisins, contact with dead bodies, and cutting the hair on your head. Many people took Nazarite vows, including Samson (Judges 13:5), the prophet Samuel (1 Samuel 1:1), the apostle Paul (Acts 21:20-24), and John the Baptist (Luke: 1:15).

Apart from his birth place, the only reference to Jesus' youth in the Bible occurs in the *Gospel of Luke* which locates Jesus in Jerusalem at the age of 12 preaching in the Temple. This may be an actual event or it may reflect Luke's freedom to borrow heavily from Josephus who tells a similar tale about his own youth. It has been well documented that many of the stories found in Luke can be found, altered slightly, in Josephus' works, which clearly preceded Luke, and it's equally obvious that the people who wrote the *Gospel of Luke* were familiar with these works by Josephus. In any event, whether or not Jesus journeyed to Jerusalem at the age of 12 is generally irrelevant. As a young Jewish male, from a devoutly religious family, it's highly likely that he did.

The bottom line, therefore, is that we have no idea where Jesus grew up, but we can be reasonably certain that he grew up in the countryside, and not in the city, because Jesus used the language of the villages. When Jesus answered questions or when he used parables, almost all his examples came from the simple life of peasants and villagers. For example, he talked about women making bread, men planting trees, people working in the vineyards, etc. Almost all of his talk about wealth was derisive, as was his attitude toward those who promoted themselves and tried to set themselves above others.

Indeed, the Q document, which is a collection of Jesus' sayings (without the editorial comments that accompany them in the Gospels) and the *Gospel of Thomas* (which is also a collection of sayings) are clearly the sayings of a person who has lived most of his life in the countryside and on the road.

Did Jesus Grow up in Qumran?

"And Jesus being full of the Holy Ghost returned from Jordan, and was led by the Spirit into the wilderness," (Luke 4:1)

If Jesus did not grow up in Nazareth, where did he grow up? We can hypothesize that he may have been taken, as a young child, into the care of the Essenes who made a practice of taking young children and rearing them within the framework of their religious teachings[100]. We know that Jesus had an excellent education in the Old Testament, and this would have been impossible had he been brought up in Galilee due to the relative paucity of synagogues in that area, and the distance

---

[100] This theory was first postulated as early as 1800 by K. H. Venturini in his book *A Non-Supernatural History of the Great Prophet of Nazareth*.

from Galilee to Jerusalem. Being raised in Qumran may account for the fact that many of Jesus' teachings were similar/identical to Essene teachings, so much so that some authors believe that Jesus (and John the Baptist) were active members of that religious sect. Indeed, the Essenes have been described as "incubators" that "provided experimental centers" where members could "seize upon some aspect of Essene teaching and practice and develop it in a radically new direction (Johnson, 1976, p.19)", and this is an apt description for the experiences of Jesus and of John the Baptist.

There is further evidence to believe that Jesus had a connection with the Essenes and this comes from Luke's description that Jesus went into the "wilderness" to struggle with the temptations of Satan. While the "wilderness" may be a generic word for the wild and wholly areas in Israel, in fact it was a specific name at that time that referred to the Essene headquarters (Finegan, 1969), which was in Judea, a few miles from the Dead Sea. Legend has it that the site was built to commemorate the place where Joshua/Jesus ben Nun, successor to Moses, crossed the Jordan (Freke & Gandy, 2001). Saying that Jesus went into the wilderness was another way of saying that Jesus went to the Essenes to deal with his struggles, which makes sense under the circumstances.

This might be the proper place to look at the similarities and differences between Jesus and the Qumran community[101]. Both existed at the same time in the same place. Both practiced the daily sacred meal (bread and wine) together. Both used initiation systems, employed baptism, and had different layers of membership. Both despised the wealthy, recommended celibacy (although it was more strongly recommended among the Essenes), and both spoke of themselves using the same names ("The Way", "The New Covenant"). Both were unhappy with the existing Temple administration, though both maintained that the Temple was the sacred cornerstone of the Jewish religion. Moreover, both tended to see themselves and the current times in terms of Old Testament prophecies.

---

[101] For an excellent extended discussion of this topic see John Meier's third volume of *A Marginal Jew* (2001).

Both Jesus and the Essenes preached the sharing of property and both shared an apocalyptic outlook along with the expectation that a Messiah was coming in the end of times, which was their present. In this regard, their concept of what a Messiah would do was very similar. Compare these two passages, one from the *Gospel of Luke* and one from the Qumran documents:

> ",,,he has anointed me to bring good news to the poor. He has sent me to proclaim release to the captives and recovery of sight to the blind, to let the oppressed go free...Luke (4:16-21)."

> "...release the captives, open the eyes of their blind, lifting up those who are oppressed...He shall raise the dead, He shall bring good news to the poor... (4Q521:8-13)."

Both Jesus and the Essenes believed in the resurrection of the body as well as the soul. This was an extremely rare point of view for those times.

It's curious to note that both Jesus and the Essenes used a similar organizational structure. Both relied upon a 12 man circle of disciples or advisers, and in addition, they had a smaller, inner circle. In the Essene case this number was restricted to three, whereas in Jesus' case the number was not so formally cast[102]. Moreover, they both prescribed the same procedures for dealing with disputes within their communities (i.e., individual discussion, discussion with witnesses, and then before the assembly). Indeed, Eusebius (c 275 – 339 A.D.), the Bishop of Caesarea, in *Ecclesiastical History* (Book 2, Chapter 17) that was written about 324 A.D., claimed that the Gospels were mere re-workings of the Essene writings.

As well, to this list can be added government by bishops and the fact that the Essenes and the early Christians both had major centers at Damascus and in Jerusalem.

---

[102] On the other hand, Peter, John, and James do appear to form Jesus' "inner circle" of three, even if they aren't specifically identified as such.

Jesus Who?

Not to over-emphasize the similarities, there were differences. The Essenes were far more legalistic and ritualistic, something which Jesus specifically preached against. Moreover the Essenes tended to be far harsher in their treatment of followers who strayed, even so slightly (e.g., spitting to the right), and far more selective and then demanding of new recruits before they could become full members of the Sect. Moreover, while both used baptism, the Essenes tended to be secretive about the purification rites while Jesus (and John the Baptist) were public in their actions. Another difference between them was that the Essenes expected two Messiahs[103], while Jesus, when he spoke of it (which was rare), only indicated that there would be one Messiah. Moreover, the eschatology of Jesus was in the present (i.e., they were living in the start of the "End Times") while for the Essenes it was soon to be upon us, but had not started yet. Indeed, since we are in the realm of speculation, it may have been this one issue, the start of the Escalon or "End Times" that caused Jesus to break with the mainstream of the Essene movement. While the Essenes were content with preparing for the start of the End Times, Jesus believed that the End Times had already started, the time for preparation was over, and people needed to set their lives in order now for the impending event. Looked at from this point of view, we can see how Jesus was not content to remain in the relative isolation of the Qumran wilderness. He left, probably spurred by John the Baptist's own sense of the start of the Escalon, and went out actively recruiting people for the end that he believed was imminent.

We can see the differences between Jesus' teachings and the Essenes in their discussion of the Sabbath. Jesus preached" "Suppose one of you has only one sheep and it falls into a pit on the sabbath, will you not lay hold of it and lift it out? (Matthew, 12:11-12)." The Qumran document says: "No one should help an animal give birth on the

---

[103] The Jewish Talmud's tractate *Sukkah* also forecasts two messiahs (Klinghoffer, 2005, p. 84), as did the Christian *Testaments of the 12 Patriarchs*: "the Lord will raise up from Levi someone as high priest, and from Judah someone as king (7:1)." Going back even further, the Persian epochal hazar (reign of 1000 years) would end when Dahak (Satan) broke free and was defeated by two prophets, ushering in the final paradise (Renan, 1927).

Sabbath; and if it falls into a well or pit, he may not lift it out on the Sabbath (CD 11.12-14)."

In some very real sense, Jesus represented the left wing of the Essene Sect, while John the Baptist could be said to represent the far right wing. Both of them were rebels against the rules and regulations of the Essene's Sect, but both of them clearly can be located well within the broad reaches of that philosophy. Indeed, Acharya (1999) notes that "In reality, there were several groups of Essenes" (p. 318) and she includes among their diverse branches the Therapeuts[104], Eclectics, Ascetics and Zealots.[105] Whatever differences there were between Jesus' point of view and that of the Essenes were minor when compared to the similarities. Moreover, this degree of relationship can only be found when comparing Jesus to the Essenes. It doesn't exist if the comparison group is the Zealots, the Pharisees, or the Sadducees (see Meier, 2001).

In summary, the facts that there were no records of his childhood, that most of his teachings were similar/identical with Essene teachings, and that it was common practice for Essenes to raise other people's children, do suggest strongly the possibility that he spent his childhood under their tutelage. At the very least, this is the best hypothesis we can generate, and certainly stronger than the infancy tales that circulated during the 2nd and 3rd Centuries.

Did Jesus Live in Egypt?

"Now after they had left, an angel of the Lord appeared to Joseph in a dream and said, 'Get up, take the child and his mother, and flee to Egypt, and remain there until I tell you...Then Joseph got up, took the

---

[104] Freke and Gandy (2001) claim that the Therapeuts and the Essenes were identical and derived from Pythagoras, a belief that Philo and Josephus shared. Ellegard (1999) believes that the Therapeuts were the Essenes living in the Diaspora.
[105] Note that among Jesus' close followers were several known zealots, including Simon the Zealot and Judas the Daggerman. The "Sons of Thunder" may also have been Zealots.

child and his mother by night, and went to Egypt, and remained there until the death of Herod." (Matthew 2:13-14)

The *Gospel of Matthew* claims that following the birth of Jesus, his family fled to Egypt, because King Herod the Great had ordered the slaughter of all children two years of age or younger in order to kill the newly born "King of Jews" whom the Magi prophesized. This event, the slaughter of the children, is not chronicled in any of the histories of the time, nor mentioned in any other Gospel. It does bear a striking resemblance to a similar problem that faced Moses, and for that reason, the writers of Matthew may have introduced it as another of the "Jesus is the new Moses" themes that run through that Gospel. In addition, the story is not dissimilar to the tragic revolt of 7 B.C., led by Herod's two sons, Aristobulus and Alexander, both of whom were his children with Mariamne, his Hasmonean wife. Discovering the plot in time, Herod was able to round up 300 of the accomplices and hand them over to be slaughtered by the mob. His two sons were strangled. The incident was so well known, and the slaughter of his own children so repugnant, that Emperor Augustus was said to have remarked: "It's better to be Herod's pig than his children."

In addition to mirroring the story of Moses and echoing the slaughter of the children of Herod, the story of the escape to Egypt also provided the motivation for moving Jesus from Bethlehem to Egypt. The Egyptian tale is peculiar to Matthew, and undoubtedly reflects the attempt in that Gospel to relate all of Jesus' benchmark events to Old Testament prophecies. Thus, if the Messiah was to "come out of Egypt" (Hosea 11:1) and if Moses came out of Egypt, surely Jesus must have been in Egypt too (Asimov, 1968).

We would be less than complete not to mention the alternative theory of Jesus' childhood, put forward by Celsus in 178 A.D. in his work *The True Word,* Celsus claimed that Jesus was born of an illegitimate union between Mary and a Roman Legionnaire, Pandera, and as a result, he was sent to Egypt where he was a servant. It was here that he learned the magical powers which he later displayed. Although not impossible, this legend may evolve from the appearance, after Jesus' death, of a Messiah who took the name of "The Egyptian" (not to be confused with the terrible Victor Mature movie of the same name).

According to Josephus, in *The Jewish Wars*, around 55 A.D., this new Messiah gathered 30,000 followers and surrounded the city of Jerusalem, hoping that with divine intervention, the walls would come tumbling down. They didn't, many of his followers were slain, and he escaped, never to be heard of again.

There is a variant on the Egyptian story that takes place about 100 years before Jesus was born, involving a magician from Egypt named Jesus ben Pandera, who is put to death by stoning (some versions say hanging). There is scant evidence for the existence of this Jesus (Acharya, 1999; Massey, 1985), while there is some evidence for the existence of the 1st Century "Egyptian". In any event, Morton (1978) believes that it was the stories about The Egyptian which led the writers of the *Gospel of Matthew* to refer to the flight to Egypt after Jesus was born. Jesus and his family's flight into Egypt fulfilled Old Testament prophecies, continued Matthew's theme that Jesus was everything that Moses was and more, and also offered a counter to the stories that Jesus was an Egyptian magician.

It's impossible to know whether or not Jesus ever lived in Egypt. The evidence for this is very slim and highly suspect.

Did Jesus Live in India?

> *"There, in the Land of the Hun, the powerful king saw a man sitting on a mountain, who seemed to promise auspiciousness. His skin was fair and he wore white garments."* (Bhayishya MahaPurana, v. 17)

In 1894 ancient Buddhist scrolls from Tibet were discovered by an aristocratic Russian Jew who had converted to the Greek Orthodox version of Christianity (Notovitch, 1894). The scrolls were said to date from the 2nd or 3rd Century, and revealed the story of Issa/Isa (Jesus' name in the Qur'an), a young boy of 12 or 13, who journeyed from Israel to India and Tibet where he studied Buddhism until he was 29 years old, and then returned home. During his stay, he learned to heal by prayer, to cast out evil spirits, and to study the holy scriptures. It was here that he developed his concern for the poor and

disadvantaged, and as a result he came into conflict with various groups (e.g., the evil Brahmins who kept the peaceful Shudras as slaves, Persian priests who believed in an evil God).
Why did Jesus go to India in the first place? Notovitch (1894) explains:

> "People came from everywhere to listen to him and were amazed at the wisdom that flowed from his youthful lips; the Israelites maintained that the Holy Spirit dwelt in this child. When Isa reached the age of 13, the time at which an Israelite takes a wife, the house in which his parents earned their modest living became a meeting place for the rich and noble who wished to have Isa for a son-in-law, for, owing to his edifying discourses in the name of the Almighty, his fame had spread far and wide. It was at this time that Isa disappeared secretly from his parent's home. He abandoned Jerusalem and set out towards Sind, joining a caravan of merchants...(5:4)."

In other words, Jesus was a "runaway groom."

As strange a tale as this may seem, it does cover a period that the New Testament doesn't address. Lending credence to this theory is the similarity between many of Jesus' preachings and the teachings of Buddhism (Cayce, 2005) as well as the many similarities between the lives of Jesus and Buddha (Graves, 1999; Kaiser, 1977). Cayce (2005) notes: "Many Buddhist parables and legends even sound as if they had been taken right out of the New Testament, but these Buddhist stories and anecdotes predate Christianity. Buddhism was founded in approximately 588 B.C...(p. 61)."

Lending support for the theory that Jesus lived in India is an *Apology* from Melito, the Bishop of Sardia, to Emperor Marcus Antonius, in 170 A.D., in which he claimed that Christianity had "...its high antiquity, as having been imported from countries lying beyond the limits of the Roman empire... (Quoted in Doane, 1985, p. 409)." The strange tale of Jesus in India does not end with his return to Israel. Indeed, there is a rich tradition described in the *Bhayishya MahaPurana* that he escaped from death and returned to India in search of the 10 lost tribes of Israel. Here he was known as *Yuz Asaf* (leader of the healed lepers), married a woman named Maryan, had children, and died at the ripe old age of 120[106].

Higgins (1992) offers a good alternate explanation for the possible origins of these theories. He believes that the Portuguese Christian missionaries who arrived in Southern India mistook the worship of Tammuz for the preachings of Thomas. In turn, they mistook the legends and myths associated with Tammuz with those associated with Jesus, since, as we have already seen, the Jesus myths were nearly identical with those of Tammuz. Linking these two cultures was the tradition of the Mandaeans, an ancient religion that moved from the East into the Middle East and ultimately adopted John the Baptist as its savior.

As appealing as the idea may be, the evidence for Jesus' Indian journeys is scant. It's not impossible; however, it's more likely that he was raised in Qumran.

Summary

Tradition says very little about the childhood of Jesus, except that he lived in Nazareth and at the age of 12 he journeyed to Jerusalem where he separated from his parents and spent time in the synagogue talking with the rabbis. The next thing we know, he is baptized at about age 30. While there is no certainty due to the lack of information, many scholars believe that Jesus grew up in the Essene community at Qumran. This accounts for the many similarities between Jesus' outlook and teachings and the beliefs of the Essenes. It also accounts for Jesus' acquaintance with John the Baptist, who was also an Essene, and furthermore it accounts for the fact that James the Just, Jesus' brother, took control of the Essene movement in Jerusalem following Jesus' death. There are alternate theories about Jesus in Egypt and Jesus in India, but these stories have little supporting evidence.

---

[106] In addition to hosting the grave of Jesus, the Indian subcontinent is also said to host the graves of Moses and the apostle Thomas (Acharya, 1999, p. 82; Kaiser, 1977). Talk about outsourcing!

CHAPTER SIX

Personal Life

What Education Did Jesus Have?

"And he came to Nazareth, where he had been brought up: and, as his custom was, he went into the synagogue on the sabbath day, and stood up for to read." (Luke 4:16)

There is little in the Bible to give us any idea of Jesus' education. The *Gospel of John* recounts an incident wherein Jesus was preaching in a Temple during the Festival of Booths when he was confronted by "Jews" who asked: "How does this man have such learning, when he has never been taught (7:15)." But it isn't clear that the questioners knew who Jesus was, and hence, they would not have been in a position to know what education he had. Moreover, this incident was recorded only in John, so it may be a literary invention of John, and not meant to be a real incident.

As a "young prince" and expected Messiah raised in the Essene Sect, Jesus would have been able to read and write. As the son of a carpenter, living the life of the *am-ha-rez* (people of the country, or despairingly "country bumpkin") in a small village in Galilee, he would have been illiterate, as were 97% of the population (Crosson, 1991, p.

25). What we do know falls on the side of the "crown prince" theory - Luke (4:16-20) has Jesus reading a passage from Isaiah in the Temple and John (8:6-8) has Jesus writing with his finger on the ground on two occasions. Even more striking, Eusebius, Bishop of Caesarea from 313 to 339 A.D., wrote in his *History of the Church*, that he was in possession of a letter written by Jesus to King Agbar V of Edessa in which Jesus promised to send one of his disciples to help cure him[107].

At a minimum then, Jesus could read. One can also conclude that he spoke Greek, because the *Gospel of Mark* (7:24-30) says that Jesus met with a Syro-Phoenician woman from Tyre who was "Greek-speaking" and he had a conversation with her.

Apart from these scant references to any formal skills, it's obvious from the many passages in the New Testament that Jesus was extremely skilled in his verbal abilities as well as his knowledge of the Old Testament. Indeed his verbal sparing abilities were equal to, if not superior to, any of the scholars with whom he debated.

There does appear to be upper limits to Jesus' education. For example, while Jesus probably was able to speak and understand Greek at some level, his primary language was Aramaic. Had he been better educated, his primary language would have been Greek (compare to Paul, for example). In addition, his Aramaic reflects the speech of the common people. In the Synoptic Gospels his sentences are short, his vocabulary limited, and he rarely engages in abstract thinking. In addition, despite his good verbal sparring abilities and rhetorical skills, Jesus apparently never wrote anything down (the "finger writing on the ground" episodes in the *Gospel of John* not withstanding). Moreover, Jesus never attempted a higher level of abstraction.

In summary, Jesus appears to have had an excellent religious education and had above average verbal skills. Apparently he could read and write. Yet he was no theoretician, and there appear to be limits to his language skills.

---

[107] Most scholars debunk this account.

Jesus Who?

What Was Jesus' Occupation?

"Is not this the carpenter, the son of Mary..." (Mark 6:3)

Most people think that Jesus was a carpenter. The *Gospel of Mark* says: "Is not this the carpenter, the son of Mary... (6:3)", although Matthew has a slightly different wording: "Is not this the carpenter's son? Is not his mother called Mary? (13:55)"[108]

Earlier, in our discussion of Joseph (see Chapter Four), we noted that *tekton* should be translated as "builder" or "master craftsman", and not carpenter. It is highly unlikely that Jesus was a carpenter. If we examine the 48 parables that occur in the Gospels, not a single one draws upon the experiences of a carpenter. Three of them refer to buildings (e.g., house divided, foolish builder, unfinished tower), and these may offer support for the idea that Jesus and/or his father was a builder, not a carpenter.[109]

What Did Jesus Look Like?

"...so that I was afraid and cried out, and he, turning about, appeared as a man of small stature..." (Acts of John, v. 90)

Everyone thinks they know what Jesus looked like. Go ahead - Sketch it out. Start with the long flowing white linen robe. Add the long hair and the beard. Give him the face of Max Van Sydow (*Greatest Story Ever Told*, 1965), or Jeffrey Hunter (*King of Kings*, 1961), or even James Caviezel (*Passion of the Christ*, 2004). Think you've got it? Not! The real Jesus looked nothing like that. What did he look like? Are you ready?

---

[108] To complicate matters, Luke (4:22) says: "Is this not Joseph's son?" with no mention of carpentry.
[109] Parable analysis may not be a foolproof way of determining Jesus' occupation or interests. The most common themes (vineyards, slaves, ownership disputes) would dictate that Jesus had been the owner of a large vineyard with serious production problems revolving around personnel.

More than 1500 years ago, St. Augustine (354-430 A.D.) lamented that: "we have absolutely no knowledge of His appearance (quoted in Wheless, 1990, p.112)." One of the problems is that most Jews in Jesus' era shunned the practice of making images of their Gods, specifically forbidden by the *Decalogue of Moses*[110] (v. 2), and this, in turn, generalized to any kinds of images at all (Wilson, 1984). But the good Bishop was mistaken. We have lots of information.

Jesus was Small

One clue to Jesus' appearance comes from the stories about his death. When Mary Magdalene went to the tomb and found it empty, she inquired of the "gardener", where is Jesus? and promised to lift Jesus' body up if he told her where he was. Obviously if Mary were capable of lifting Jesus up, he can't have been very large. In fact, the average male at that time was 5'1" and weighed 110 pounds.

The *Gospel of Luke* (19:3) describes Zaccheus' attempt to see Jesus while he preached in a crowd: "And he sought to see Jesus who he was; and he could not for the crowd, because he was low of stature." Of course, Luke may be referring to Zaccheus rather than Jesus, but the idea that Jesus was slight can be seen again in the *Acts of John*: "...I was afraid and cried out, and he, turning about, appeared as a man of small stature... (v. 90)."

We have another clue to Jesus' appearance in the Qur'an. One night, a winged snow-white beast takes the prophet Muhammad to Jerusalem to the Temple where he meets Moses and Jesus, who is described as being smaller than Moses.

The Slavonic copy of Josephus's *Capture of Jerusalem*, contains the following description of a man wanted by Pontius Pilate for claiming that he was the King of the Jews: "a man of simple appearance, mature age, dark skin, small stature, three cubits high, hunchbacked with a long face, long nose, and meeting eyebrows...with scanty hair

---

[110] "Thou shalt not make thee any graven image, or any likeness of any thing that is in heaven above, or that is in the earth beneath, or that is in the waters beneath the earth..."

with a parting in the middle of his head, after the manner of the Nazarites, and with an undeveloped beard (Quoted in Knight & Lomas, 1996, p. 230)."[111] Thus, from a variety of sources we see that Jesus was small in stature.

Jesus was Physically Unattractive

As noted above, the Slavonic copy of Josephus not only discussed Jesus' stature, it also commented on his physical attractiveness. The picture of Jesus as relatively unattractive comes from many other sources as well. In the *Acts of Peter*, Peter quotes a prophet who described Jesus - "And we saw him and he had no beauty nor comeliness (v. 24)." In the *Acts of John*, John says: "And oft-times he [Jesus] would appear to me as a small man and uncomely (v. 89)." Celsus in *Against Celsus* described Jesus as "...small and ugly and undistinguished (VI, v. 75)." Justin Martyr in *Trypho* declared that Jesus was "made ugly by the sufferings and the humiliation that he endured (v. 88)." Tertullian said: "he would not have been spat upon by the Roman soldiers if his face had not been so ugly as to inspire spitting (v. ix)." The language here suggests that the authors may have been going back to the tradition in Isaiah (53:2-3)[112], which was prominent among the early Christians (Craveri, 1967; Fox 1989). In any event, we have multiple and diverse attestations that Jesus was not attractive in a conventional sense.

Jesus Had Short Hair and was Clean Shaven

Imagine Jesus as your prototypical Marine - short hair, clean-shaven. Hard to imagine, yet that seems to be our best evidence. Freke and Gandy (2001) note: "the earliest representations of Jesus actually portray him beardless, with short hair... (p. 56)." We can see this in our survey of the earliest Christian art on the next page.

---

[111] This description is curiously like that of Paul in the *Acts of Paul and Thecla*: "...a man small in size, bald-headed...with eyebrows meeting, rather hook-nosed... (v. 3)."

[112] "He hath no form nor comeliness; and when we shall see him, there is no beauty that we should desire him..."

Location	Time	Portrait
Fresco, Catacomb of Priscilla (Jesus Preaching)	Rome, mid 2nd Century	Clean shaven, short hair
Fresco, Catacomb of San Callisto, Crypt of Lucina, Fresco (Shepherd)	Rome, 2nd Century	Clean shaven, short hair
Fresco, Catacomb of Priscilla (Last supper)	Rome, 3rd Century	Clean shaven, short hair
Ivory statuette (Shepherd)	Rome, c 300 A.D.	Clean shaven, short hair
Ring seal	3rd Century	Clean shaven
Fresco, Mausoleum of the Julii (Sol Invictus)	Rome, late 3rd Century	Bearded, short hair
Mosaic portrait of Jesus	Hinton St Mary 4th Century	Clean shaven
Catacomb of Sts Peter & Marcellinus (Loaves)	Rome, early 4th Century	Clean shaven, short hair
Fresco, Catacomb Via Latina (Raising Lazarus; at Jacob's Well; Sermon)	Rome, 4th Century	Clean shaven, short hair
Fresco, Catacomb of Domitilla (12 Apostles)	Rome, 4th Century	Clean shaven, short hair
Sarcophagus (Jesus with Adam & Eve)	Rome, 4th Century	Clean shaven, short hair
Santa Costanza (Portrait)	Rome, c 350 A.D.	Clean shaven, short hair
Via Latina Catacomb (Raising Lazarus)	Rome, c 350-400 A.D.	Clean shaven, short hair
Sarcophagus (Jesus rides a Donkey)	Rome, c 359 A.D.	Clean shaven, short hair
Tomb (Resurrection)	Rome, c 400 A.D.	Clean shaven, short hair
Fresco, Catacomb of Praetextatus (Shepherd)	Rome 350 – 450 A.D.	Clean shaven, short hair
Sarcophagus, Catacomb of Praetextatus (Shepherd)	Rome 350 – 450 A.D.	Bearded, short hair

Jesus Who?

Almost all of the early artifacts concerning Jesus picture him as clean-shaven and with short hair (See pages 56 and 140). That should come as no surprise to anyone who has looked at coins, busts or statues of the early Roman emperors. Virtually every one of them had short hair and was clean shaven. The first emperor to sport a beard was Hadrian (117-138 A.D.) and even he had relatively short hair. Long hair would not appear for centuries, until the rise of Byzantium.

Among Jesus' contemporaries, there are very few visages, but what we do have supports the findings among the Roman emperors. For example, coins struck with the faces of Herod the Great's son, King Philip (ruled 4 B.C. to 34 A.D.), Herod's grandson King Agrippa I (ruled 37 to 44 A.D.), and Herod's great grandson, Agrippa II (ruled 44 to 100 A.D.) show them all clean-shaven and with short hair. A Roma bust of Flavius Josephus (right), the Jewish author, shows him clean-shaven with short hair.

This is not to say that some of Jesus' contemporaries were not pictured as having beards and/or long hair. For example, a 3rd Century fresco of the apostle Peter (Hypogeum of the Aurelli, Rome) shows a bearded Peter and a 4th Century diptych of the apostle Paul (Museo Nazionale, Florence) shows him with a beard and long hair. A 5th Century mosaic (Santa Maria in Cosmedin, Ravenna) shows a beardless Jesus but has John the Baptist with a beard and long hair (See page 140). Thus, not only are our earliest depictions of Jesus with short hair and beardless, the depictions of his contemporaries show them with beards and long hair, suggesting that, in fact, Jesus was the prototypical Marine.

Many scholars make the mistake of thinking that Jesus' hair had to be long because he was a Nazorean. In fact, this confuses the Nazoreans with the Nazarite vows. Nazarite vows required that you let your hair grow long during the time of the vow, and once the vow was finished, you shaved your head and offered the hair as a sacrifice. Thus, had Jesus taken Nazarite vows (doubtful, since he seemed to enjoy wine and abstinence was required during the length of the vow), his hair would only be long before he shaved it off. The tradition of the long flowing hair has no support. Indeed, the apostle Paul wrote: "Doth not even nature itself teach you, that, if a man have long hair, it is a dishonor to him (1 Cor. 11:14)."

As far as the beard, the earliest images of Jesus were exclusively clean-shaven. Three events promulgated his much later appearance with a beard: (1) The Holy Mandylion of Edessa, (2) the Shroud of Turin, and (3) the increased influence of Byzantium/Constantinople in the early middle ages. Thus, Freke and Gandy (2001) note that: "The now ubiquitous image of the bearded long-haired Jesus did not become established until the 8th century (p. 56)."

Looking at the bulk of the information about Jesus' appearance, it seems clear that he was small in stature and apparently not attractive in a conventional way for those times. He was probably clean-shaven and didn't have long hair.

What Was Jesus' Religion?

"These are the words which I spake unto you, while I was yet with you, that all things must be fulfilled, which were written in the law of Moses, and in the prophets, and in the psalms..." (Luke 24: 44)

Without question, Jesus was a Jew. His God was YHWH, the God of the Jews. Klinghoffer (2005) notes: "Jesus was a Jew; he was circumcised on the 8th day; he observed Passover, in his lifetime all his followers were Jews, he frequented and taught in synagogues (p. 55)." But what type of a Jew was he, and how did this influence his own behavior and the nature of what he preached? To understand this, we need to know a little bit about Jewish history. At the time of Jesus' birth, it was estimated that there were some 5.5 million Jews in the world, 1 million of whom were in Israel (Johnson, 1976, p. 12; Klinghoffer, 2005 p. 44)[113]. Amongst the Jews in Israel there were various groups (Josephus called them "schools of thought"), differentiated by their political beliefs and religious practices. Johnson (1976, p.15) estimates that there were as many of 24 identifiable sects, and Carrier (2005) puts the number at 30 plus. Most commonly known of these groups were the Pharisees, the Sadducees, and the Zealots, all of whom were mentioned prominently in the Gospels[114]. In addition, pertinent to the study of Jesus, there were the Essenes and the Zardoks, neither of whom were mentioned in the Gospels.

The **Pharisees** (from the Aramaic word "Perishaiya" meaning "separated ones", which became "p'rushim" in Hebrew, "Pharisaios" in Greek and then "Pharisees" in English) were an anti-Hellenistic group which grew from the Hasidim (the "pious ones") which had formed at the time of the Seleucid King, sometime in the 2nd Century B.C. Their chief concern was maintaining the Jewish laws. They relied upon oral traditions to interpret the Bible. This was considered particularly difficult in those times due to the influences of Hellenistic and Roman cultures. The Pharisees were often allied with the **Scribes**, who differed in some ritual areas (e.g., Marek 7:3-4). Opposed to the Pharisees were the **Sadducees** (from the Hebrew word "Zadokim" meaning "followers of Zadok", which became "Saddoukaioi" in Greek and "Sadducees" in English), who were more accommodating to the foreign laws and customs (some authors identify them as Quislings) and who took their influence from the priests and wealthy, among whom were numbered the Hasmonean families. If the Pharisees can be considered the "right wing" and the Sadducees as the "left wing", then the **Essenes** (from the Hebrew word meaning healers) were clearly the ultra right wing. They rejected even the so-called piety of the Pharisees (whom they spoke of as the "seekers of smooth things")

---

[113] Ellegard (1999) is outside this framework, estimating 4 million in the Diaspora and 1.5 million in Israel (p. 6).
[114] Interestingly enough, while the Pharisees appear by name nearly 100 times in the canonical Gospels, their main adversaries, the Sadducees, appear less than a dozen times, and the name of the Essenes never appears

and preached a new organization based on their strict observance of the law. In fact, the Essenes were an off-shoot of the Pharisees, both of whom originally were called the Hasidim.

Josephus described the three groups as follows:

> "...the Pharisees, they say that certain events are the work of Fate, but not all; as to other events, it depends upon ourselves whether they shall take place or not. The sect of the Essenes, however, declares that Fate is the mistress of all things, and that nothing befalls men unless it be in accordance with her decrees. But the Sadducees do away with Fate, holding that there is no such thing and that human actions are not achieved in accordance with her decrees, but that all things lie within our power... (*Antiquities*, 13. 171-173)."

Most Jews were not aligned with any of these movements or schools of thought. Their daily lives were concerned with survival and making a living, in an increasingly hostile and violent world. In addition, recent natural disasters (earthquakes, famine) had further torn away at the fragile cultural bonds which held this diverse community together. The old tribal system had broken down decades earlier, as had the city state system that the Greeks had sought to impose. Now under the new Roman rule, nothing was certain, except that the Jews, as a people, were under severe stress. This was even more true in Galilee than in Jerusalem.

These stresses had given birth to the Fourth Philosophy, which was a loose confederation of groups committed to anti-Roman activities and to the idea that they were living at the "end of times" and that a Messiah would come to put an end to the chaos around them. To this group belonged the **Zealots**[115] (from the Greek word *zelos* meaning jealous or rebellious) who were also known as the **Sicarii** (literally daggerman, but usually referring to any kind of assassin), the **Zardokites**, and to some extent, The Essenes. Amongst the leaders of the "Fourth Philosophy" were John the Baptist and Judas of Galilee.

---

[115] The Term Zealots came into common usage after the rebellion of Judas of Gamala who was better known as Judas the Galilean.

Jesus Who?

Josephus estimated that there were approximately 4000 Essenes, about 200 of whom lived at Qumran, near the Dead Sea. There are no estimates of the numbers of Zealots or Zardokites at the time of Jesus, but apparently there were sufficient numbers to stage various revolts, and eventually, by mid-Century, they were the largest single faction in Israel.

Whatever Happened to...?

The Sadducees drew their support from the collaboration with the Roman authorities. After the destruction of the Temple, their influence waned, and after the Bar Kochba wars they ceased to exist.

The Zealots started the Jewish War of 66 A.D. and most perished in the siege of Jerusalem or later at Masada. They were condemned by the Jewish people for causing the destruction of the Temple, lost their influence, and eventually faded away.

The Essenes who inhabited Qumran were overrun by the Romans in 68 A.D. Apparently there were Essenes at Masada, and they perished in 73 A.D., committing suicide rather than surrendering to the Romans. But thousands of Essenes survived in the Diaspora, among the Ebionites, Therapeuts, Nazarenes, and related groups.

The Pharisees survived the destruction of the Temple. Rabbi Yohanan ben Zakkai was appointed Patriarch, re-established the Sanhedrin, and began the reform of Judaism and the start of the rabbinical and synagogue systems that continue today.

James M. Gardner

What Were Jesus' Attitudes Toward Sex?

"His disciples said: On what day will you be revealed to us, and on what day shall we see you? Jesus said: When you unclothe yourselves and are not ashamed, and take your garments and lay them beneath your feet like the little children (and) trample on them, then [you will see] the Son of the Living One, and you will not be afraid."
(Gospel of Thomas, v. 37)

It's interesting to note that none of Jesus' healings or exorcisms dealt with sexual issues (e.g., fertility, venereal disease, impotence) even though we can suspect that many of Jesus' followers suffered from these disabilities. In fact, all things sexual were rarely discussed in the Gospels, suggesting that some devoted scribes may have taken a heavy pen to these sections.

Would Jesus have had a sexual life? If he were human, the answer is almost unequivocal – yes; especially in those times when it was the duty of Jewish men to reproduce. Indeed, the eminent early 20th Century scholar Ernest Renan imagines that in despair in the Garden of Gethsemane, shortly before his death, Jesus thinks back on "the young maidens who, perhaps, would have consented to love him (1927, p. 336)." If he were divine, would he abstain from sexuality? Judging from the accounts of the lives of divine men and other Sons of God (e.g., Apollo), the answer is also unequivocal – no; Gods and Sons of Gods had active sex lives. Even if Jesus himself abstained from sexual behavior, he surely would have commented on sexual matters, yet there is a yawning gap in the Gospels on this issue.

With a little detective work we can uncover some hints at what Jesus' attitudes might have been, although we have to preface this enterprise with the caveat that we may as well be looking at the attitudes of the early church[116] rather than the attitudes of Jesus himself. In any event...

---

[116] Take, for example, Paul's comments - 'It is well for a man not to touch a woman ... I wish that all men were as I myself am (1 Cor. 7)" and "...it is better to marry than to burn (1 Cor. 7:8-9)."

- Jesus expresses a clear preference for virginity (or asexuality) in his references to children and the Kingdom of God (Luke 18:16; Matthew 18:3, 19:14; John 13:33; *Gospel of Thomas* v 21, v. 37)[117] and to the fact that among angels in heaven there is no marriage (Mark 12:25; Luke 20:33-36).
- Asexuality asserts itself again in his admonition to Peter that "every woman who makes herself male will enter the kingdom of heaven (*Gospel of Thomas*, v. 114)."[118] Of course, most scholars attribute the use of male and female in this regard to be symbolic of the earthly vs. the spiritual world.
- We get a third look at asexual comments from Jesus' remark in Matthew that there are "eunuchs for the kingdom of heaven's sake. He that is able to receive it, let him receive it (19:12)."[119]
- Jesus agrees with the Law of Moses that people should not commit adultery (Matthew 5:27; Luke 18:20) and adds that lust for another woman is also adultery (Matthew 5:28) and marriage to a man who divorces his previous wife (except for fornication) is also adultery (Matthew 5:32).[120]
- He believes that divorce is justified only when a wife has fornicated with another man (Matthew 5:31; 19:9)[121]
- He admonishes against masturbation (Matthew 5:30).
- According to the *Gospel of Philip*, Jesus said: "For it is by a kiss that the perfect conceive and give birth. For this reason we also kiss one another.... (v. 35)." With regard to Mary Magdalene Philip said that Jesus "loved her more than all the disciples, and used to kiss her often on her [mouth] (v. 59)."

---

[117] Several authors interpret verse 21 in the *Gospel of Thomas* to refer to sexual non-differentiation, purity, or virginity as Jesus' description of the ideal disciple (Funk & Hoover, 1993, p. 485; Meyer, 1992, p.78).

[118] See also the First Apocalypse of James 41:15-19.

[119] Although castration was popular among Christian followers of the cult of Cybelle, it was definitely forbidden among the Jews, bringing into question the authenticity of this passage as a true saying of Jesus.

[120] The story of the "adulteress" (John 8:1-11) is not included here because this pericope is a later addition and contains historic inaccuracies that don't conform to Jewish law (e.g., Deuteronomy 17, 22).

[121] Bear in mind that in Jesus time only a man could seek a divorce: women had no rights. However, other Gospels indicate that Jesus did not allow divorce for any reason (Mark 10:11-12; Luke 16:18).

Generally speaking, apart from the *Gospel of Philip,* which is a late addition, Jesus' views are conservative. He accepts the Law of Moses about adultery and adds broader definitions. He speaks against masturbation and glorifies the innocence of children. His visions of heaven contain no references to marriage, childbirth, or any type of sexual activity.

Was Jesus a Homosexual?

"The young man looked at him intently and loved him; and he began pleading with him that he might be with him." (Secret Gospel of Mark)

It would have been extremely unusual for anyone of Jesus' age and social status not to be married. Yet there is no mention in the Gospels that he was married, and most people believe that he was unmarried. The main reason put forward for Jesus' single status is that he was celibate as befits the Son of God and the Messiah. Advocates of this position often cite one of Jesus' sayings in the *Gospel of Matthew* - "...there are eunuchs who make themselves that way for the sake of the kingdom of heaven (19:12)" or the *Gospel of Luke* – "...those who are judged worthy of a place in the other world and in the resurrection from the dead do not marry because they can no longer die... (20:35-36)." Yet according to the earliest Gospel, Jesus did not become aware of his special status until after his baptism which occurred after he was 30 years old. To have been 30 years old and unmarried raises questions in some people's minds[122].

As the homosexual movement gained strength in the later part of the 20th Century, it was not a great leap to conclude that eventually the issue would be raised in regards to Jesus. And so it was - in 1967 at Oxford by Anglican Bishop Hugh Montefiore and a few years later in 1973 in John Robinson's *The Human Face of God*. In addition to the argument that he was unmarried, proponents of Jesus' (latent) homosexuality point to the fact that he had many female friends

---

[122] If you accept the theory that Jesus was the "crown price in waiting", then his marriage would have taken place at age 36, and being single at 30 would not have been unusual.

(unusual for those times in which women were reviled), that his "beloved disciple" was a man, and then there was the half naked boy in white linen who keeps popping up in all the wrong places (e.g., Mark 14: 51-52 when Jesus is arrested[123]; Mark 16:5 at Jesus' tomb). As well, there is the "Secret Gospel of Mark", discovered in 1958 by Morton Smith, which contained this unorthodox account of the raising of Lazarus:

> "...Immediately he went in where the young man was, stretched out his hand, and raised him by seizing his hand. The young man looked at him intently and loved him; and he began pleading with him that he might be with him. When they came out of the tomb they went to the young man's house, for he was wealthy. And after six days Jesus gave him a command. And when it was evening the young man came to him, wearing a linen cloth over his naked body. He stayed with him that night... (Quoted in Knight & Lomas, 1994, p. 68-69)."

While the case can be made that Jesus had unusually high regard for women, and that he surrounded himself with men, it is a clear stretch to assume that these characteristics constituted homosexual tendencies, either latent or manifest. Jesus' message of love was for everyone.

Was Jesus Married?

> *"And the companion of the [Savior is] Mary Magdalene. [Christ] loved her more than all the disciples, and used to kiss her often on her [mouth]. The rest of the disciples [were offended by it]. They said to him "Why do you love her more than all of us?" The Savior answered and said to them, "Why do I not love you like her?"*
> *(Gospel of Philip, v. 59)*

At the turn of the millennium, a young Jew who reached the age of 12 was invited to "build his house, plant a vineyard, and finally to marry."

---

[123] Compare to Amos (2:16) – "And he that is courageous among the mighty shall flee away naked in that day."

This was vital to the struggling Jews who were bound by sacred oath to be "fruitful and multiply" (Genesis 9:1). In the Old Testament, unmarried people were "sometimes likened to murderers (Craveri, 1967, p. 266)." And this was Jesus' attitude toward marriage. He said "...a man shall leave his father and mother and be joined to his wife... (Matt 19:5/Mark 10:7)." Almost all Jews were married and had children. The exceptions were notable and rare (e.g., Jeremiah in the 7th Century B.C., John the Baptist in Jesus' time).

Being a member of the Essenes did not restrict Jesus from marrying. Although most Sect members were celibate, the Essenes allowed members of the kingly (Davidic) and priestly (Zardokite) lines to marry and reproduce. The only restrictions were that sexual intercourse was not allowed before a man was 20, and marriage was reserved for those who attained 30, an elderly age for that time and place.

Mary of Magdala

The person most favored to be Jesus' wife is Mary Magdalene[124]. Most scholars believe she was called Magdalene because she came from the city of Magdala, that lay on an important trade route, about 10 miles southwest of Capernaum and two miles north of Tiberius, along the shores of the Sea of Galilee. Magdala, better known as Magadan (Matthew 15:39), was famous for its boat building[125] and fishing industries, especially for processing fish for which large amounts of salt were needed. In fact, the city's ancient name was *Migdal Nunaiya*, which meant "tower of fish". At the time of the first Jewish revolt, Josephus claimed it housed nearly 40,000 people.

---

[124] Indian tradition tells the story that Jesus escaped from Israel and fled to India where he was known as *Yuz Asaf* (leader of the healed lepers) and married a woman named Maryan (Kaiser, 1977).

[125] In 1986, a fishing boat dating back to 40 B.C. was discovered in the muddy lake bottom near Magdala's harbor. The boat is 26 1/2 feet long, 7 1/2 feet wide and 4 1/2 feet high and was meant to hold 15 people. Some scholars speculate that it was on such a boat that Jesus and his disciples crossed the Sea of Galilee.

On the other hand, Magdala meant "tower", and some scholars (e.g., Starbird, 2005) have speculated that Mary was such an important disciple of Jesus that she was referred to as "The Tower", using the same kind of affectionate but pertinent nicknames that Jesus was famous for (e.g., Simon "The Rock", John and James "the Sons of Thunder", Simon "the Zealot", Thomas "The Twin" etc.) Baigent (2006) even says that her nickname was actually "Mary the Great", reasoning that calling her "The Tower" was the same as saying she was "Great". All things considered, it's more likely that Magdala was her nickname rather than her place of origin.

Mary the Prostitute

The most common perception of Mary Magdalene is as a prostitute. Even today French rehabilitation centers for "wayward women" are referred to as *les hospices de Madeleine*. Yet there is no support for this idea in the canonical or the non-canonical Gospels. There are two possible referents in the Gospels that could lead to such a belief. The first is the fact that her name was first mentioned following the mention of a sinner[126] (Luke 7:37), yet there was no inference that Mary too was a sinner (Luke 8:2), and the passage about the sinner was clearly distinct from the one in which Mary and several other women were mentioned. The second referent is the fact that the *Gospel of Luke* (7:37) describes the woman who anointed Jesus as a "sinner" but did not give her a name, while the *Gospel of John* says that the woman who anointed Jesus was named Mary (John 11:2), but didn't call her a sinner, and, in fact, identified her as the sister of Lazarus and Martha, who in John's Gospel was clearly not a sinner.

In addition, the word Magdala was used in a Talmudic expression which meant "curling women's hair" and this expression was associated with being an adulteress. The origins of this association came from the similarity between the words *magdalah* (harlot) and *megaddeleh* (hairdresser) that sound alike and appear similar in Hebrew (Craveri, 1967). Indeed, Rabbis of this era considered

---

[126] As used in that context, being a sinner could refer to questionable paternity, suffering a broken betrothal, or having a meager dowry (Chilton, 2000, p. 144).

hairdressing to be "one step away from prostitution (Chilton, 2000)" in the same way that many today consider a massage parlor to be identical to a brothel. But the jump from this expression to the idea that Mary was a prostitute is clearly too great for rational minds.

One other possibility exists for the origin of the idea that Mary Magdalene was a prostitute, and this lies in the story of Simon Magus, a contemporary of Jesus and a fellow miracle worker. Known as a great magician and sometimes called "the first Gnostic" (Grant, 1990), Simon had a large following who regarded him as the Messiah. Among these followers was Helen, a former prostitute. Simonians worshiped the couple, referring to Simon as Zeus and to Helen as Athena[127]. Constructing the Gospels so many years after the lives of both Jesus and Simon, it's possible that the stories about the one generalized to the other, and Simon's former prostitute became Jesus' companion.

Yet despite the lack of any substantial evidence, the smear campaign against Mary was started in the 6th Century by Pope Gregory the Great (Chilton, 2005). In 591 A.D. he wrote in *Homily 33* that: "She whom Luke calls the sinful woman, whom John calls Mary, we believe to be the Mary from whom seven devils were ejected according to Mark. And what did these seven devils signify, if not all the vices?... It is clear, brothers, that the woman previously used the unguent to perfume her flesh in forbidden acts." By the Middle Ages, homes for reformed prostitutes were routinely named after her, and it was only as recently as 1969 that the Catholic Church officially removed the stain from her memory.

Mary Magdalene in the Canonical Gospels

There is a good deal of confusion about Mary Magdalene because there are so many Marys in the Gospels that you need a scorecard to keep track of them. Apart from direct references to Mary Magdalene (Luke 8:2; Mark 15:40; Matthew 27:56; John 20:1), there are numerous

---

[127] Legends grew about Helen, claiming she was eternal and existed in many previous lifetimes, one of which was as Helen of Troy. But always she was flawed, and it was this flaw during her lifetime with Simon that caused Simon to stumble. The analogy to Eve is obvious.

other references to people named Mary, the most notable being Jesus' mother. However, the other Marys include:

- Mary the sister of Martha and Lazarus (Luke 10:39; John 11:1).
- Mary "the sinner" who anoints Jesus' feet (John 11:2).[128]
- Mary the sister-in-law of Jesus' mother (John 19:25).
- Mary the mother of James the Less and of Joses, and Salome (Mark 15:40; Luke 24:10).
- Unspecified Mary's (Matthew 27:61: 28:1).

Notice that most of the other Marys are named with their familial relationships (sister of, mother of). Only Mary Magdalene and Mary the anointer have no familial relationship specified, and it has often been speculated that Mary Magdalene and the woman who anointed Jesus' feet were one and the same person[129]. In any event, the lack of mention of familial relationship meant, according to the customs of the time, that they were "on their own". It would have been extremely unusual for an adult female to have no family with whom she lived and with whom she was associated. Most likely, then, the familial relationship was deleted, and we can only speculate that there was only one special familial relationship that warranted deletion.

The fact that Mary is presented as a single woman who accompanies Jesus is a curiosity by Jewish standards of the time. First, the fact that she is single is a curiosity, because most women were married. If it's true that she had been possessed of a demon, then her spinster status might be explained by this. But the fact that she accompanied Jesus would have gone against the Mishnah (Rabbinic customs) and been considered more than scandalous[130]. Wilson (1984) says: "...in Jesus' day almost any association with a woman outside one's immediate

---

[128] The woman who anoints Jesus is only identified by name in the Gospel of John (11:2; 12:3), and therein she is the sister of Lazarus. In Luke (7:36) she is called "a woman in the city, who was a sinner", while in Mark (14:3) and Matthew (26:7) she is simply "a woman [with] an alabaster jar".

[129] In addition to Pope Gregory there was St. Bernard, the Cistercian Abbot of Clairvaux (1090-1153 A.D.).

[130] See Sotah 1:2 in the Mishnah, or Sotah 3:4 in the Jerusalem Talmud.

family was frowned upon (p. 94.)." Had it been true (i.e., an unmarried woman accompanying an itinerant preacher), it would (at least) have justified negative comments by the Scribes and the Pharisees. Yet there were none. On the contrary, what we do know is that it was common for early Christians to be accompanied by their wives and/or their sisters (Freke & Gandy, 2001), and we know that Mary Magdalene was not Jesus' sister. Ergo...

Despite the controversies that surround Mary Magdalene (e.g., her supposed life as a prostitute, her marriage to Jesus, her miracle of the egg, etc.), the canonical Gospels actually have little to say about her. Luke introduces her as the woman "from whom seven demons had gone out (8:2)." The number "seven" is a curious one. Mary is the only person out of whom "seven" demons are exorcised. Almost every other exorcism performed by Jesus involved a single spirit, with the notably exception of the "legions" who inhabited the insane man in the cemetery. The legions exorcism, however, was obviously a metaphor for Rome[131], and perhaps should be dismissed as having any historical value. In any event, the number seven was significant to the Jews as well as many earlier cultures, and derived from the work of Pythagoras centuries before. But when used with respect to the exorcism of demons, it may refer back to Jesus' belief that a full and final exorcism could involve as many as seven demons[132] (Luke 11:26), which derived from the Gnostic belief in the seven ladders to heaven, each rung represented by one of the five planets plus the Sun and the Moon. The implication was that Mary was completely healed. The other possible meaning of the "seven" demons refers to a Babylonian

---

[131] The name of the demons is "legion", which is the name of the Roman 6000 man force. The man lives in a cemetery, and the Romans often erected cities on the top of cemeteries (e.g., Tiberius). The confrontation takes place in the Decapolis, where Romans (and other gentiles) live. The man repeatedly self-injures (whips) himself, and Romans were known for committing suicide. They demons are turned into pigs, and the symbol used by the 10th Legion that was stationed in Israel was the boar. Etc.

[132] Note also the concept of seven deadly sins: pride, lust, envy, anger, covetousness, gluttony, and sloth.

Jesus Who?

cult of the Goddess Mari[133], which was popular in Galilee at that time, and involved seven charkas or Maskim.

What little more is said about Mary seems to show that she is omnipresent. She is with Jesus "traveling through the towns and villages" (Mark 15:41; Luke 8:1), one of the few witnesses to the crucifixion (Mark, 15:40; Matthew 27:56; John 19:25), and she is at the empty tomb (Mark 15:47; Matthew 27:61). In some accounts she is the first to see the empty tomb (John 20:1). She is the first person to whom Jesus appears after the crucifixion (John 20: 14). And of course, there is that enigmatic response of Jesus when he first appears to Mary – "Do not touch me..." (John 20:17), made even more curious by the fact that later he lets other disciples touch him.[134] Jesus' comment was so unusual that Centuries later it sparked a legend that he touched her on the forehead to prevent further contact, and the spot on her forehead where the resurrected Jesus touched her never decayed. This legend, in turn, prompted many a Medieval pilgrimage to view bits of aging skin hanging to what many claimed was the skull of Mary Magdalene.

Some scholars (e.g., Wilson 1992) claim that the wedding at Cana (only in the *Gospel of John*) represents Jesus' own marriage, edited to make it appear to be some anonymous persons' wedding. In support of this thesis, we have Jesus in attendance with his mother and his disciples, and his mother apparently feels sufficiently empowered to give orders to the servants. Jewish customs at this time allowed only the Governor of the feast or the bridegroom and his parents to exercise authority (Gardner, 2001); hence, Mary must have been the parent of the bridegroom. In addition, Jesus is uncharacteristically concerned with whether or not there is enough wine for the celebrants. His "miracle" here, turning water into wine, seems the most superficial of all his acts if it was only to make the party better. Moreover, the steward speaks to the "bridegroom" and says "you have kept the good

---

[133] Known to the Egyptians as Mer and to the Babylonians as Mari, she was the Goddess of Water and was symbolized as a giant fish that gave birth to Gods. In some legends she was the consort of Yahweh. Magdala's dependence on fish made it fertile grounds for worship of a water Goddess.
[134] Paulus (Quoted in Craveri, 1967, p. 424) suggests that he asks not to be touched because the resuscitated Jesus was still in agony from his ordeal.

wine until now (2:10)" and the very next verse says: "Jesus did this… (2:11)": clearly, it looks as if Jesus is the bridegroom. Indeed, Jesus is often referred to as a bridegroom (e.g., Matthew 9:15; John 3:29).

The evidence seems overwhelming that the wedding at Cana was Jesus' own wedding. The only arguments against this position are that there is no mention of his other relatives (e.g., brothers and sisters, aunts and uncles) and the wedding is not specifically identified as being his. However, we have already seen that the writers and editors of the Gospels took great pains to distort the image of Jesus' family, so that it would not be impossible to believe that they were up to their same old tricks in this instance.

There are more clues to Mary Magdalene's relationship with Jesus in the canonical Gospels, and they revolve around her identity (in John) as the anointer with the jar of nard. In those days, nard was used by the Rich and Famous as a skin softener and a deodorizer. It was imported from India, and took 150 pounds of the herb to produce a quart of ointment. According to the *Song of Solomon*, the bride lovingly anoints her groom - "While the king sitteth at his table, my spikenard sendeth forth the smell thereof… (1:12)." The description in the *Gospel of John* is nearly identical – "Mary took a pound of costly perfume made of pure nard, anointed Jesus' feet, and wiped them with her hair. The house was filled with the fragrance of the perfume (12:3)." Gardner (2001) says: "Only as the wife of Jesus and as a priestess in her own right could Mary have anointed both his head and his feet with the sacred ointment (p. 49)."

In this same scene, the fact that Mary let down her hair in order to wipe Jesus' feet implies that she is his wife, since only a husband was allowed to see his wife's hair unbound (Haskins, 1993).

Still another clue to Mary's relationship can be found in the *Gospel of John* (11:19-35) when Jesus comes to Bethany to raise Lazarus from the dead. When Martha and Mary heard that Jesus was on his way, Martha "went and met him" but Mary stayed behind. Mary only left when Martha returned and told her "privately" that Jesus "is calling for you". Why would Mary stay behind until instructed to leave by Jesus? Because Jewish customs of the time forbade a bride to make such a journey without the permission of her husband (Baigent & Leigh, 1991).

There is another clue to their relationship in this same passage. When Mary reaches Jesus she is distraught and weeps. "When Jesus saw her weeping...he was greatly disturbed in spirit and deeply moved. He said, 'Where have you laid him?' They said to him, 'Lord, come and see.' Jesus began to weep. So the Jews said, 'See how he loved him!' (John 11: 33-35)." The "Jews" were obviously incorrect when they interpreted Jesus' weeping as a sign of emotion about Lazarus' fate. Jesus knew that Lazarus was not dead. An earlier passage (John 11:4-6) notes – "But when Jesus heard it, he said 'This illness does not lead to death...'" and so "...he stayed two days longer in the place where he was." Thus, there was no reason for Jesus to weep for Lazarus. He knew all along that Lazarus wasn't dead[135]. Why then was Jesus weeping? Because he was "greatly disturbed in spirit and deeply moved" by Mary's distress, not by Lazarus' fate.

Mary Outside the Canonical Gospels

We know more about Mary from outside the canonical Gospels. In *The Gospel of Mary*, Peter says: "Sister, we know the savior loved you more than any other woman (v. 10)", and Levi adds: "Surely the savior knows her well. That is why he has loved her more than us (v. 18)." In the *Gospel of Peter*, he says: "The companion of the [savior] is Mary Magdalene. The [savior loved] her more than [all] the disciples, [and he] kissed her often on the [mouth] (59:63)." In the *Pistis Sophia* (meaning Faith Wisdom), Jesus praises her, saying, "Blessed Mary, you whom I shall complete with all the mysteries on high, speak openly, for you are the one whose heart is set on heaven's kingdom more than all your brothers (36:17)." Later, Jesus adds: "You are more blessed than all women on earth, because you will be the fullness of fullnesses and the completion of completions (36:18)."

---

[135] Lazarus is so not dead that, in the *Secret Gospel of Mark*, he speaks to Jesus "from the tomb" as Jesus approaches. So much for Lazarus being raised from the dead!

In the *1st Letter to the Corinthians*, Paul says: "Do we not have the right to be accompanied by a believing wife, as do the other apostles and the brothers of the Lord and Cephas? (9:5)." Paul, of course, was single and urged single hood on others. But his reference here to the married status of the apostles and Jesus' brothers does not include Jesus himself. Hence, we might infer from this that Paul did not believe that Jesus was married. Of course, we have to bear in mind that Jesus' brother James, was not married, and his implied inclusion here ("the brothers of the Lord") would be an error. What is of significance to us in Paul's question is that men were accompanied by their (believing) wives. Thus, the omnipresence of Mary Magdalene with Jesus, accompanying him, suggests that she was his wife.

Unmarried By Default?

Advocates of the position that Jesus was unmarried point to the absence of any references to his married status in the Bible. However, given that the normal state of affairs was for a Jew to be married, we would more likely expect references to his bachelorhood to be made. Indeed, Jesus is criticized for many reasons throughout the gospel. Here are but a few of them:

- He is too young to have wisdom (John 8:57).
- He comes from Galilee (John 7:41).
- He socializes with sinners (Mark 2:15).
- He works on the Sabbath (Mark 2:24).
- He doesn't control his disciples (Mark 7:2; Matthew 9:14).
- He has no formal education and training (John 7:15).
- He has no authority of forgive sins (Luke 5:21).

But there are no criticisms of his single status, despite the fact that he is constantly talking about family, family values, marriage, etc. Surely it would have been legitimate for someone to say: "Hey, Jesus. How can you talk to us about marriage and family when you, yourself, aren't married?" Yet no one asks this question. Indeed there are no references in either direction, suggesting that any references to Jesus' marital status were deleted from all accounts. Why delete these references? If he were single, there would be no need to delete them, for his failure to be married would suggest he was "married to God", which is in the direction the Catholic Church moved with its priests. So it only makes sense that if deletions were done, they were deletions of his married status, not his unmarried status.

We know from our previous discussion of Jesus' family, that the writers of the Gospels went to great lengths to delete and distort his relationship with his family and the family's role in his ministry. This discovery lends credence to the theory that Mary too was a victim of the censor's knife. Indeed, one wonders how so many stories and legends could have arisen about a person who occupied such a small role in the Gospels. Perhaps her role was much greater, and the oral traditions concerning her gave birth to the many legends that remained strong for thousands of years.

While it's impossible to say for certain that Jesus was married, the fact that marriage would have been expected (one could argue, demanded) of him, the many references in the canonical and (especially) the non-canonical Gospels that strongly suggest marriage, combined with the lack of any mention or criticism of his bachelor status (in light of all the criticisms made of him), and our knowledge of the changes made to alter our knowledge of his family's involvement, all suggest that Jesus was married and the person he was married to was Mary Magdalene.

Did Jesus Have Children?

Just as there are no accounts of Jesus being married, there are no accounts of Jesus having children. The only biblical reference to Jesus having children comes from the Old Testament in Isaiah who indicates that the "suffering servant" will "see offspring (53:10)." Verse 53 from Isaiah was used throughout the Gospels to show that Jesus was the prophesized Messiah, yet this significant section is never referred to. In Isaiah it shows that the suffering servant was the ultimate victor, for he sees his own offspring. If Jesus was the suffering servant and if the suffering servant triumphs because he has offspring, it follows that…

Were there references to Jesus' offspring in the Gospels and were these deleted? Why? Quite frankly, it would have been difficult to know how to deal with the progeny of the "Son of God". If he's a boy, who is the Son of the Son of God? Is the Godly gene hereditary, like the Davidic gene was? If she's a girl, how embarrassing that the Son of God fathers a daughter instead of a Son, given the status of women at that time. In either event, what does one do with the children of the Son of God?

There are two scholars whose research has led them to believe that Jesus had children - Barbara Thiering of the University of Sydney in Australia, and Laurence Gardner, a genealogist and history lecturer from England. Thiering (1992) maintains that the Gospels contain hidden words and that the "Word of God" is a coded message that refers to Jesus. Examples of these words occur more in Luke (3:2; 4:4; 5:1; 8:11; 8:21; 11:28) than in John (10:35) or Mark (7:13), but mostly they occur in Acts (e.g., 4:31; 6:2; 6:7; 8:14; 11:1; 12:24; 13:5; 13:44 etc.). Generally speaking, substituting the word "Jesus" for "the word of God" seems to support Thiering's case, although not to such an extend that the case is irrefutable. For example, Acts 6:14 says:

> "Now when the apostles which were at Jerusalem heard that Samaria had received the word of God, they sent unto them Peter and John."

Substitute the word Jesus and you get:

> "Now when the apostles which were at Jerusalem heard that Samaria had received Jesus, they sent unto him Peter and John."

Either way it makes sense.

With regard to any children that Jesus may have fostered, Thiering maintains that verses such as Acts 6:7 ("the word of God increased") and Acts 12:24 ("But the word of God grew and multiplied") clearly meant that Jesus had children.

Gardner (2001, 2004) agrees with this analysis, although he is probably the only other scholar who does (Dan Brown not withstanding). In addition, he believes that the legends about Mary and the red egg (she gains an audience with Roman emperor Tiberius who claims that the likelihood of Jesus having risen from the dead is the same as a white egg turning red – presto chango, the white egg in Mary's hand turns red) refer to Jesus' children. Further, he believes that the legends about Joseph of Arimathea with his nephews in England refer to Jesus' children.

Needless to say, the speculations by Thiering and Gardner are interesting, but hardly supported by any real evidence. Even less evidentiary are the theories that Jesus' descendants can be found today in India (Kaiser (1977) and France (Baigent, Leigh & Lincoln, 1983). As tantalizing as this may be, there is no evidence that Jesus had any children. It certainly would have been expected, almost required of him, given his status as the Davidic messiah. It certainly would have been expected of him as a God or a Son of God, all of whom were known to be prolific. But the gap between expectation/requirement and reality appears to be too large to fill.

What Was Jesus Like as a Person?

Suppose you knew nothing at all about Jesus except for some sketchy details about his major demographic characteristics? What might you presume from these? Let's try. Are you ready?

Jesus was the first-born son and eldest child, born into a devoutly religious middle class Jewish family at the turn of the 1st Century. Jesus' family was large, and included four brothers and two sisters as well as a paternal uncle and his family that lived nearby. The religious practices of the times required that his father, a master craftsman, contribute a large percentage of his income to the religious authorities. They lived in Galilee, which was an area under a great deal of stress, burdened not only by authoritarian Roman rule but by a rapidly changing economic structure moving from a predominately agricultural to a merchant society. Galilee was the cross roads where many cultures met (Egyptian, Persian, Greek, Roman) and where many languages were spoken. Jews at this time were splintered into more than 30 different factions, many of which were openly hostile to each other. Roman taxes, earthquakes, famines, and continual rebellions made life difficult, especially for the emerging middle classes.

With this basic knowledge, what might we presume? First, we can imagine that the eldest male child would follow in the footsteps of his father. For a Jewish child born into a family descended from David, this would undoubtedly mean a formal education grounded in the Old Testament. Second, he would be expected to be a high achiever, and from his earliest days he would be encouraged to take a leadership role in everything he attempted. He would learn not only how to read and write, but his rhetorical skills would be finely honed. He might have enrolled in a special academy where other preeminent children were trained.

As he grew older, he would be expected to assume more and more responsibilities. Especially with a father who traveled a lot as part of his livelihood, he would take on the role of "the little man of the house" and exercise care and control over his many younger siblings. He would identify with his father, successfully navigate the Oedipal hurdles of early childhood, and set his course on a mature, conservative lifestyle. In time he would marry and have the same type of large family from whence he came.

As the heir apparent to a dynastic regime, he would develop excellent social skills. He would be able to interact with a wide variety of people from all social levels, and he would be seen as a man of influence, who could be looked upon for sound advice. He would rise to a prominent position, probably in a religious or political arena, and would attract a large following.

If we look for equivalents in our own time, John Kennedy Jr. would be a good example. Or young Prince Philip. These two young men were born into a similar environment as the young Jesus. True, it is a different time and a different place, but the analogy seems applicable.

So far, so good. Our preliminary description of Jesus based on the demographics alone presents a picture that matches, in many

Jesus Who?

respects, what we know of Jesus. Unfortunately, the match is not perfect. Indeed, we have drawn a better picture of the life of Jesus' brother James than we have of Jesus himself. This is because, for some people, demographics alone are not sufficient to define their development.

But let's pause at this point, before we go any further, and consider those aspects of our picture that do match the life of Jesus.

> Generally speaking Jesus was **self-assured**. He seemed to know what he was doing and why. While he had occasional periods of doubt (e.g., Mark 15:34; Matthew 26:38-9), they were short-lived and he was able to get back on track. This self-assurance would come from being the first-born son in a patriarchic society.
>
> He had **good organizational skills**, setting out a plan, recruiting others to help, and then following the plan. His followers were organized into layers (the 12 disciples, the 70 who go to Jerusalem, the 500 to whom he appears, etc), and he developed procedures for who did what (e.g., Judas was the Treasurer). In addition, he was able to **plan ahead**. For example, during Passover he said to his disciples: "Go into the city, and a man carrying a jar of water will meet you; follow him, and wherever he enters, say to the owner of the house, 'The Teacher asks, Where is my guest room where I may eat the Passover with my disciples?... (Mark 14:13-14)." As well, prior to his entry into Jerusalem, he said to his disciples: "Go into the village ahead of you, and immediately as you enter it, you will find a colt that has never been ridden; untie it and bring it. If anyone says to you, 'Why are you doing this?' just say this, 'The Lord needs it...(Mark 11:2-3)."
>
> Jesus was **highly controlling and manipulative**. He stage-managed every aspect of his career, including the minutest details. He was also a harsh task **master**, promising his followers that "You will be hated by all men (Matthew 10:22)" and "If any man comes to me without hating his father, mother, wife, children, brothers, sisters, yes and his own life too, he

cannot be my disciple (Luke 14:26)." This trait, as well as the previous trait (organizational skills), is related to his training to assume the role of the Davidic leader, a role that his father and paternal grandfather held before him. In 1st Century Israel, with all the competing Jewish sects and cross-cultural influences, it was essential for a leader to be able to wield power effectively.

Jesus was apparently **well educated in the Bible**, from which he was able to quote ad infinitum. He also appeared to have **great rhetorical skills**, seeming to use the best techniques of the Greek school of cynics (Here we can see the influence of the Gospel writers, who themselves were familiar with the Greek schools, so they may have masked Jesus approach in this manner).

Jesus was an itinerant preacher, and was obviously **comfortable traveling**. That much of his life was spent "on the road" is clearly reflected in the Q document and the *Gospel of Thomas* wherein a good percentage of his sayings relate to traveling advice (e.g., "When you go into any region and walk through the countryside, when people receive you, eat what they serve...", "Do not carry money, or bag, or sandals; and do not greet anyone on the road."). The propensity to travel may come from his formative years, and it may be possible, as Eisler (1931) has argued (in *The Messiah Jesus and John the Baptist*) that Jesus' family plied their trade in the timeless manner of the Sleb[136] of Syria, a still existing band of Bedouins whose ancestry and customs include not only the Essenes but go all the way back to Cain.

Jesus drew **support and friendship from a wide variety of people**. His followers and supporters included fishermen, tax collectors, soldiers, wealthy merchants, etc. He even numbered sinners and the mentally ill among his closest associates.

---

[136] The Sleb were known to be accomplished in carpentry, masonry, building and a whole host of skills, and they fit well within the definitions of *tekton*, the name used to describe Joseph's occupation. They were also known to be healers (Sinclair, 1952).

Jesus Who?

Jesus viewed himself as a **teacher**, and it's as a teacher that he is most often called in the Gospels (more than twice as often as he is called Rabbi, the next most common salutation). But it's obvious that Jesus taught by example, and did not have a comprehensive ideology that he brought to bear on different issues. He taught in bits and pieces, rarely connecting the disparate parables, or trying to create a coherent theology. Both his propensity to teach and his style of teaching undoubtedly came from his role as "the little man" with a hoard of younger siblings to care for and a father whose time and energies were not directed at his home.

All these characteristics we can deduce from the broad nature of his circumstances. Most people born into a similar environment would develop in a similar way. Yet there were many aspects of Jesus' personality that could not have been predicted from the demographics, and it is to these characteristics that we now turn. But before we do, we need to mention in what ways Jesus' background did not match the prototype we outlined above.

While everything we noted earlier is true, we left out one very important variable – the questionable circumstances surrounding Jesus' birth. Since we dealt with this issue at some length in earlier chapters, we need not dwell on the details here. Suffice it to say that regardless of which story you believe (e.g., his father was God, or Joseph, or a Roman Legionnaire, or his parents had sex before they were supposed to), the circumstances of his birth were unusual. Not only were they unusual, but it's obvious that the stigma associated with his unusual birth circumstances stayed with Jesus throughout his life. Later passages refer to him as "the son of Mary", an insult in the Jewish culture, and a constant reminder that his father's paternity was in question.

Lest we dismiss this controversy as being a relatively minor matter, which it might be in certain circles today, in 1st Century Israel it struck to the very core of the society and the purity laws around which it was based. Marcus Borg (1995) notes: "One's purity status depended to some extent on birth. According to one purity map of the time, priests and Levites (both hereditary classes) come first, followed by 'Israelites', followed by 'converts' (Jewish persons who were not Jewish by birth). Further down the list are 'bastards', followed by those with damaged testicles and those without a penis (p. 51)." In other words, instead of being at the top of the list, Jesus' questionable birth circumstances placed him at the bottom, just above people with damaged or castrated testicles. While it is true that through behavior, the pure (by birth) could be made impure (or unclean), it was virtually impossible for the impure by birth to be made pure.

Now, what might have been the impact of this major developmental milestone on the young man whose demographic profile we just examined?

> Jesus was a **fatalist**. He believed that he lived in the "end of times" and that the world, as was known, was coming to a violent end. Moreover, these events were foretold and inevitable. Such a fatalism was not uncommon at that time and place, especially given his time with the Essenes, but Jesus appears to have had an exaggerated version. This may come from the unusual nature of his birth and his inability, no matter what he did, to escape from the label and its implications. This fatalism was reinforced with the birth of his younger brother James, whose birth was "pure" and whose life reflected the type of life Jesus might have had, absent his own questionable birth.
>
> According to the Gospels, Jesus had a **tendency to go off by himself**. He did this in the wilderness after his baptism, then in Capernaum after healing the sick, again on the Mount after feeding 5000 people, and again shortly before his death at Gethsemane (from the Hebrew *gath shemane* meaning "olive press"). He did this when he was 12 and wandered off from his parents while they were in Jerusalem. Not only did Jesus have a tendency to go off by himself, when in the company of others he was **often silent**, which would be highly abnormal for a person whose mission in life was preaching. Both these traits could point to an **incipient depression** that lay beneath the surface and threatened to overwhelm him. These tendencies

may stem, as far as we are able to determine, from his birth circumstances, and are related to the fatalism noted above. Although one can draw strength from an eschatological view of the universe, it's difficult to do, and the greater the belief in the "end of times", the stronger the pull.

A running theme through all the Gospels and even in the Q document is Jesus' **concern for the disadvantaged**. This concern is particularly noteworthy in a time when almost no one sought to help this group. Today we have a well-established *noblese oblige* tradition, but in 1st Century Israel there was no such tradition. We can speculate that Jesus' concern for the disadvantaged came from his own situation. He too was an "outsider", burdened by a cause that was not his doing. In that respect, he resembled the people whom he championed, and undoubtedly had great empathy for their position.

Jesus **enjoyed shocking people**. He ate with sinners, said provocative things (e.g., calling God "pop", saying that the Pharisees worried more about having clean plates than having clean souls, etc.), and did even more provocative things (e.g., rode into Jerusalem on a donkey, allowed his disciples to breech the Sabbath rules, refused to wash his hands before eating, entered a graveyard to help a possessed man, etc.). This trait undoubtedly stems from his own shock at learning of his questionable birth. More so than others, Jesus learned that being shocked was a normal part of life, and he continued to use this technique throughout his ministry.

There is a continual thread in the Gospels, most noticeable in Mark, of the **secret life** of Jesus. He takes Thomas aside and preaches secret wisdom, he takes Mary aside and shares secret wisdom only for her, he goes up on the mountain to be transfigured with only three of his disciples, etc. The recent *Gospel of Judas* continues this theme of Jesus' secret relationship with his disciples. The Gospels continually tell us that what Jesus speaks in parables is only the tip of the iceberg - the truth lies beneath in the hidden meanings. This thread of secrecy undoubtedly comes from the dreaded secret – Jesus' birth status. It's a subject he never raises, nor is it ever raised by anyone else, which seems a curious happening if indeed his birth had been miraculous.

Having considered the formation of some aspects of his personality traits from his basic demographic characteristics and the one developmental milestone we are aware of, we can turn to a deeper consideration of who Jesus was as a person. Throughout the Gospels, the main recurring theme is one of love - Jesus cures and exorcises, preaches love for your neighbor and yourself. If we accept the veracity of these claims and acknowledge that this was the driving force in his personality, we also have to note that this trait is not unchallenged by competing forces. For all his cures, he also denigrates the Samaritans and the Gentiles, even refusing to treat them. For all his teachings and love for his disciples, he constantly berates them. For all the talk of peace, he urges his followers to get swords. For his beliefs in the wisdom and power of God, he appears to be tempted, not only by Satan but also by his own fears. Jesus, in short, is a man in conflict.

Where do we go looking for the origins of this conflict? I believe it lies in the conflict between the demands of his Davidic ancestry and his natural personality. Jesus seems to be no happier than when he is eating and drinking with his friends, or when he is engaged in verbal sparing with whomever challenges him. The heavy demands of the Messianic role must have been a burden to this naturally loving and joyful young man. Jesus had a spiritual essence, yet he was being groomed for a Kingly role. For our closest parallel we can look at the life of Prince Charles, the heir apparent to the British throne. Charles' personal interests in music, non-traditional healing, and the esoteric arts are far removed from the demands of the British monarchy. Yet he tried to bend his own desires to the demands of the position, the most tragic example being his marriage to the late Diana.

So: what might we expect as a result of this conflict between Jesus' basic nature and the demands of the life he was born into?

> According to the Gospels, Jesus **behavior is not easy man to predict**. He continually confounds enemies and friends alike, not only in his remarks but also in his actions. Indeed, he takes pride in this ability, and is quoted in the *Gospel of Thomas* as

saying – "Do not let your left hand know what your right hand is doing (v. 62)." This inability to predict his behavior undoubtedly stems from the continual push and pull of the conflict between his basic personality and the needs and demands of his mission.

Accounts of Jesus indicate that he was often **self-contradictory**. That is, at times he spoke of peace as his mission, and at other times, he implied his mission was war. These self-contradictory feelings are never more at work than in Jesus' use of his powers. At times he uses them for the most capricious of reasons, as when he withers a fig tree that fails to supply ripe figs upon demand (Mark 11, 12-14, 20-25). Or when he turns five loaves and 2 fish into enough to feed 5000 people, rather than have his disciples go to a nearby village to buy food (Mark 6, 30-44). Or at the wedding at Cana when he produces wine from water to feed the guests (John 1:1). Yet at other times he is loath to use his powers or even to have others speak of them. Clearly we see the basic conflict between his spiritual essence and his Kingly duties at work in this area.

Many scholars believe that Jesus is best identified as a **social reformer**, or a **rebel**. Indeed, while Jesus clearly comes from a Pharisaic and an Essene background, he breaks dramatically with both of these traditions and sets out in his own, unique style. And who is his mentor? The biggest rebel of them all – John the Baptist, whose nonconformity is even more extreme than Jesus'. Indeed, it is Jesus' message of a new Kingdom based on love and compassion (vs. purity) which is so revolutionary, and that threatens the very cornerstone of contemporary 1st Century temple Judaism. We see this, never more clearly, than in the parable of the Good Samaritan, in which the priest and the Levite pass a "half dead" traveler because they do not wish to violate the purity laws (that forbid contact with the dead). Only the Samaritan, who is impure/unclean by birth, shows the compassion to stop and assist the injured traveler

It is as a social reformer that Jesus' **extraordinary curing abilities** are best understood. As told in the many "miracles" or acts of power he performed in which the blind were made to see, the deaf to hear, and the lame to walk, Jesus' patients were almost always from the disadvantaged (hence impure) classes. There were many wonder workers and exorcists in 1st Century Israel, but none whose clientele came from the weak and the wretched, as did Jesus' patients. As he sought to heal himself from the impurity of his birth, so now he healed others.

Nowhere was Jesus' basic nature and his rebelliousness better illustrated than in his attempt to **create a new society**. He preached the formation of a new basis for family, and a new system of table fellowship. He rejected wealth and stressed service. He stressed works, not blind adherence. He preached inclusion, not exclusion. Jesus' views are probably best summed up by his saying that "...the last shall be first, and the first last (Matthew 20:16)."

Summary

While the Gospels tell us very little about Jesus' personal life, apart from his vocation as a carpenter, we can infer a great deal. It's obvious that Jesus had a very good education, due to his extremely capable verbal skills, his ability to read and (possibly) write, and to speak Aramaic and Greek (although we don't know how well he spoke Greek). It's equally obvious he wasn't a carpenter, since carpenters did not have such a good education, and since none of the many experiences he relates in his parables come from the experiences of a carpenter. Our extensive analysis of his appearance suggests that, contrary to popular belief, he was small, not conventionally attractive, had short hair, and was beardless. He was, without doubt, a Jew, but our analysis suggests that he was an Essene rather than a Pharisee. He had conventional attitudes toward sex in general, leaning toward the conservative side. While we can't be certain, the bulk of the evidence suggests that he was married, most likely to Mary Magdalene, but there is no evidence that they had children.

Jesus Who?

With regard to his personality, we've noted that Jesus exhibited many leadership qualities: he was self-assured and had good organizational skills, although he could be highly controlling and manipulative and a harsh task master. He viewed himself as a teacher and a reformer, and drew support and friendship from a wide variety of people. Yet he was prone to depression, fueled by his eschatological fatalism and by the constant stigma associated with his birth circumstances. These demands on his psyche could lead to contradictory impulses and account for the long periods of self isolation that marked his career.

This mosaic is on the dome of the Ravenna Catacombs. It dates from about 500 A.D. and shows a short haired, beardless, Jesus being baptized by John the Baptist, surrounded by the disciples.

CHAPTER SEVEN

Ministry

When Did Jesus Preach?

"Now when all the people were baptized, it came to pass, that Jesus also being baptized, and praying, the heaven was opened, And the Holy Ghost descended in a bodily shape like a dove upon him, and a voice came from heaven, which said, Thou art my beloved Son; in thee I am well pleased. And Jesus himself began to be about thirty years of age..." (Luke 3:21-23)

It's not clear from the Gospels how long Jesus preached. Most experts and scholars believe that Jesus' ministry was a single year, while a significant minority believes that it was three years, using the *Gospel of John* as their reference and the mention of three Passovers. In fact, a little detective work allows us to put forward a more realistic estimate of the length of Jesus' ministry. Are you ready?

Let's start with the facts, as we know them. Jesus was born somewhere between 17 and 4 B.C., but our best bet is 6 B.C., given that he was born while Herod the Great still ruled, and given that he was about two years old when Herod died. According to the *Gospel of Luke*, he began his ministry when he was "about 30 years of age" (3:23)[137] and we know from the *Gospel of John* that he was preaching when he was less than 50 years of age (8:57). We also know that he started his ministry after being baptized by John the Baptist. Using these figures, we can see that he started his ministry sometime between 23 and 26 A.D. (e.g., If Jesus were born in 6 B.C. he would have been 30 years old in 24 A.D.). This time period corresponds to the time when John the Baptist was preaching[138]. So far, so good.

Jesus was preaching right up until his death, and we know his death occurred while Caiaphas was the High Priest in Jerusalem, while Pontius Pilate was the Prefect, but after John the Baptist was beheaded. All these dates are known. For example, John the Baptist was beheaded on the day that Herod Antipas celebrated his birthday, after his half brother, Philip, had died and after Herod had married his

---

[137] In the Talmud, age 30 is identified in the "Sayings of the Fathers" as the time when a man reaches his "full strength" (Avoth 5:24). In the Old Testament, King David began his reign at age 30 (2 Samuel v. 4). The Egyptian God Horus started his career at age 30 (Harpur, 2004). This may account for the use of age 30 by Luke in this regard, and given Luke's tendencies to be more of a novelist than a historian, 30 is not to be taken literally.

[138] Indeed, in the Slavonic version of Josephus, John the Baptist was said to have appeared before Archelaus, the Ethnarch of Judea, who was deposed in 6 A.D. This date is reinforced by Jesus' statement - "From the time of John the Baptist until now the Kingdom of Heaven is being stormed, and men of violence take it by force" (Mt., 11:12), referring to the War of Varus and the activities of Judas of Galilee which date from 6 A.D. In addition, Matthew's Gospel notes that after Jesus' family returned to Galilee, "In those days came John the Baptist, preaching in the wilderness of Judea" (3:1) and since the family moved to Galilee after Archelaus succeeded Herod the Great, this substantiates the fact that John the Baptist was already preaching near the turn of the millennium. Luke, however, dates John's preaching from the 15th year of the reign of Tiberius, which would be the year 28 or 29 A.D., or if we start the clock from the time Tiberius co-reigned, it could be as early as 24 or 25 A.D. Luke is clearly at odds with the rest of the evidence, although the earliest date (24 A.D.) possible under Luke is within our time period for the start of Jesus' ministry. But bear in mind from his dating of the birth of Jesus, that Luke is often at odds with the evidence.

half brother's wife, Herodias (although there is some evidence that is beyond the scope of this book that indicates that he was married to Herodias' daughter Salome, a theory which makes more sense). We know that Philip died in 34 A.D., in the 20th year of the reign of Tiberius. We know further that the defeat of Herod Antipas' army in 36 A.D. was attributed to celestial punishment for his killing of John the Baptist. Ipso factor, John the Baptist, then, died in 35 or 36 A.D., and most people mark the date as August 29, 35 A.D.

If Christ began his ministry between 23 and 26 A.D., and was still preaching in 35 or 36 A.D., it means that his ministry lasted at least 9 years, and possibly as many as 13 years at the time of John the Baptist's death.

How much longer after the death of John the Baptist did Jesus live? Most people believe it was within the year, and, in fact, that seems to be true. From Josephus and other sources we know that both Caiaphas and Pilate were deposed in 36 A.D., and since both were in power when Jesus was crucified, it makes sense to date the crucifixion in the Spring of 36[139].

Putting together Jesus' birth (6 B.C.) and his death (36 A.D.) leads us to the conclusion that Jesus was 42 years of age when he died. If he began preaching about 30 years of age, his ministry lasted more than a decade, not a single year or even three years.

We know intuitively that it makes more sense that Jesus' ministry lasted a long time. He traveled to many places, mostly on foot, and in those days, travel could be difficult, not merely because the roads were poor but also due to the number of brigands who frequented the main roads. Moreover he seemed to have attracted a large number of devoted followers, some wealthy supporters, and even had significant support within some of the opposition groups. Such accomplishments would have taken years, especially in those days. There was no "Larry King" in Jesus' time.

---

[139] Another argument in favor of Jesus' death around 36 A.D. is the fact that taxes were very much on everyone's mind, and the census year for tax purposes (held every 14 years) had been 34-35 A.D.

The idea that Jesus was in his 40s when he died is supported by comments attributed to the Temple priests in John (2:19-20). Jesus has said: "Destroy this temple and in three days I will raise it up" and the response came: "It has taken 46 years to build this temple, and will you raise it up in three days?" Many scholars have noted the subtext in many (most/all) of Jesus sayings, and it cannot but tempt our interest to suggest that they were talking about Jesus himself when they said it took 46 years for him to live, and when he dies, he will be raised in three days.

As well, the comment of the Judeans from John: "You are not 50 yet, and you have seen Abraham? (8:57)" suggests a Jesus in his mid 40s. Certainly it doesn't suggest a man in his early 30s.

Irenaeus, Bishop of Lyon, (130-202 A.D.) in his principal work *Against Heresies*, believed (on the basis of oral testimony from the disciples) that Jesus was nearly 50 when he died.

Isaac Asimov (1968) calculated that in 29 A.D. Jesus "must have been at least 33 years old, very likely 35, and just possibly even older (p. 802)." Knowing that he died in 36 A.D., by Asimov's calculations he would have been "very likely" 42 years old (35 + 7 (36 A.D.-29 A.D.)). Bloom (2005) put Jesus' age at 40, correctly giving his birth at 6 B.C. but mistakenly putting his crucifixion at 34 A.D.

To summarize, Jesus was actively preaching from the time he was about 30 years of age until he was in his early to mid 40s, a period of more than 10 years.

How Large Was His Following?

And he appointed twelve, whom he also named apostles, to be with him, and to be sent out to proclaim the message…" (Mark 3:14-15)

Jesus Who?

The Numbers

We all know about the 12 disciples (who really are 14 or more). Most people believe that the number 12 was chosen because it referred to the 12 tribes of Israel. In fact, both the 12 disciples and the 12 tribes of Israel came from a more ancient source, the 12 signs of the Zodiac. Indeed, many of the disciples' names can be traced to Zodiac signs (e.g., the Sons of Thunder[140] refer to Jupiter, the God of Thunder; Alpheus comes from the Babylonian word *alpu* which refers to the Bull or Zodiac sign Taurus; Thomas the Twin refers to Gemini, etc.).

In addition to the 12, there were the people closely related to Jesus: Mary Magdalene, Lazarus and his sisters Mary and Martha, his mother Mary and his brothers, especially James, his uncle Cleophas (aka Clopas) and cousin Simeon, Nicodemus, and Joseph of Arimathea. Schonfield (1974) estimates that Jesus' "traveling company" alone numbered 60 or 70 people. Moreover, Jesus had a support system that also included Simon the leper[141] (Mark 14: 3), the woman with the alabaster jar (Mark 14:3), the villagers who provided a donkey for his ride into Jerusalem (Mark 11:2), the supporters who spread their cloaks and leafy branches when he entered Jerusalem (Mark 11:8), the supporters who arranged for the last supper (Mark 14:13), "a certain young man was following him... (Mark 14:51)", the "many other women who had come up with him to Jerusalem (Mark 15:41)", "some women who had been cured of evil spirits and infirmities (Luke 8:1)", and "many others, who provided for him out of their resources (Luke 8:3)", etc.

Beyond this, there were various references to another 70 disciples[142] (Luke 10:1), the Gentile converts (John 12:20), 120 "believers" (Acts,

---

[140] The original "Sons of Thunder" were the Greek brothers Castor and Pollux, said to be the torchbearers for the Sun God Mithras.

[141] The word "tsaraat" in Hebrew and Aramaic meant an outbreak of the skin. It was translated as "lepra" in Greek, and later leprosy in English. But the original condition simply referred to a skin outbreak which was curable (Chilton, 2000).

[142] Schonfield (1965) claims that Luke's use of the number "70" is symbolic of Jesus sending his disciples to the Gentiles, who were said to inhabit 70 nations.

1:15), the Samaritan converts (John 4:40-41), and a group of 500 disciples (1 Cor. 15:6). Add to this, the 4000 and/or 5000 people whom he fed at the Sermons, and the unspecified numbers in the crowds who gathered about him and followed him or were baptized/initiated by him. Jesus influence even went beyond his immediate followers to the extent that others began using his name in their spells (Acts 19:13).

All told, we can estimate that Jesus' followers numbered between 5000 and 10,000[143] people, which for that time, was an enormous number. Josephus estimated that the total membership of the Essene community was 4000, and the Pharisees only 6000. Wilson (1992) claims that among the Essenes, Pharisees, and Sadducees, "None of these groups numbered more than a few thousand adherents... (p. 97)." So the Jesus cult, at 5000 to 10,000 followers, was a major force. No wonder the chief priests and the Pharisees feared Jesus' influence. No wonder the political undertones of the Gospels (e.g., John 6:15) are so tempting. Indeed, in several places, the Jewish authorities are frozen with fear, worried about the reactions of Jesus' followers (e.g., Acts 5 24-26; Luke 19:47-48; Matthew 21:46; 7:45-49). The *Gospel of John* records the Pharisees saying to one another: "Look, the whole world has gone after him (John 12:19)" and Klinghoffer (2005) observes – "...on the days leading up to Passover...his movement suddenly exploded in numbers and enthusiasm...(p. 74)." Johnson (1976) makes the point: "Jesus had succeeded in uniting an improbable, indeed unprecedented, coalition against him: the Roman authorities, the Sadducees, the Pharisees, even Herod Antipas (p. 29)."

The Nature

If you examine the stories associated with Jesus' followers, you see two recurrent themes: the women are steadfast and the men, particularly the disciples, are undependable. For example...

---

[143] The *Ascent of Jacob*, quoted in Schonfield (1974) chronicles an event shortly after Jesus' death, at the conclusion of which "...we went down to Jericho, to the number of 5000 men (p. 124)."

Jesus Who?

- The only witnesses at his crucifixion were women: Mary Magdalene, Mary the mother of James, Salome, and "many other women" who were his followers (Mark 15:40-41). All the male disciples fled.
- The first ones to visit his tomb were women (Mark 16:1).
- Jesus was anointed by a woman (Mark 14:3), who was then criticized by the men, and defended by Jesus, who claimed: "She had performed a good service for me (Mark 14:6)."
- Peter denied he knew Jesus three times (Mark 14: 30).
- Jesus asked Peter, James, and John to remain with him while he prayed in Gethsemane, but they all fell asleep (Mark 14:41).
- Jesus is betrayed by a man - Judas (Mark 14:10).
- Despite all his teachings, the disciples never seemed to understand what he was truly saying (Mark 4:13, 6:51, 8:21, 9:19; Matthew 15:16; Thomas 51).
- Everyone involved in his arrest, trial, punishment, and crucifixion was a male. The only person who believed Jesus was "innocent" was Pilate's wife (Matthew 27:19).
- Among his family members, it was the brothers who doubted him (John 7:5) and who believed he was out of his mind (Mark 3:21). His sisters were never mentioned from a negative perspective[144].
- Male followers typically had little faith, even among his disciples (e.g., Matthew 14:31; 16:8; 17:20), while female followers were said to have great faith (e.g., Matthew 15:28). Male followers wondered what's in it for them (e.g., Matthew 19:27; Mark 10:35), but women followers had no selfish interests (e.g., Matthew 26:10)

Craveri notes: "Jesus must often have had to suffer patiently under the ignorance and pettiness of his disciples (1967, p. 284)."

---

[144] Actually, Jesus' sisters aren't mentioned very much, positively or negatively. Given the context of Jewish society at that time, this is not surprising.

Whatever Happened To...?

Peter was crucified upside down in Rome around 64 A.D.

Matthew/Levi suffered martyrdom in Ethiopia, killed by a sword.

James, son of Zebedee was beheaded in Jerusalem around 44 A.D.

James the Just was thrown from the Temple and stoned to death in 62 A.D.

Andrew was crucified on an x-shaped cross in Patras, Greece.

Thomas was stabbed with a spear in India.

Phillip was crucified in Hieropolis where he was buried along with his virgin daughters.

Bartholomew was skinned alive, and then beheaded in Derbent on the Caspian Sea.

Jude was killed in Persia, along with **Simon**, who was hacked to death.

Judas either hanged himself or his insides exploded, shortly after Jesus was crucified.

John, son of Zebedee was the only Apostle to die a peaceful death, around 100 A.D. on the Isle of Patmos.

Of these accounts, we only have historical information about James The Just. The lives and deaths of the other disciples are the stuff of legend and myth.

Another interesting characteristic of Jesus' followers was their diversity. Most were fishermen[145] (which was appropriate considering that fishing was a major industry in Galilee), but others included a tax collector (Matthew), a zealot (Simon), and a member of the assassin cult (Judas Iscariot). His inclusion of so many women followers was revolutionary for its time, as was his inclusion of the poor. In summary, Jesus had a large and diverse following. They numbered in the thousands and rivaled the largest contemporary groups. In addition, Jesus' followers were marked by the inclusion and relatively high status of women and poor people.

Was Jesus a Miracle Worker?

"And he cured many who were sick with various diseases, and cast out many demons..." (Mark 1:34)

Jesus is remembered today, as much for his miracles as for his teachings[146], yet it must be noted that it wasn't until the 2nd Century that the Gospels writers first began to talk about the miracles. Nothing in the letters of Paul referred to any miracles, nor were they mentioned in the *Letter of the Hebrews*. In addition, being a miracle worker was not part of the expectations for a Messiah as laid out in the Old Testament. Indeed, in the eyes of his contemporary Jewish audience, being a "miracle worker" would detract from any claims he made to be a Messiah. It had the tinge of "magic" and "sorcery". The true Messiah was in the business of restoring Israel's greatness and smiting its foes. There was no time for miracle working, unless it was directly related to that great enterprise.

We live in an age when it's a miracle to get decent services from a handyman, so that the stories of Biblical miracles are foreign indeed. When was the last time you saw a miracle on your TV (news, that is, not the X-files!)? Or read about a miracle in the newspaper (The New York Times, not the National Enquirer!)? Yet miracles seemed to be

---

[145] The four fishermen who follow Jesus mirror the four fishermen who served the Egyptian God Horus.
[146] See Morton Smith's provocative book *Jesus the Magician* (1978).

happening all the time 2000 years ago. In fact, miracle workers were a dime a dozen in Israel at the start of the millennium.

The Nature of the Miracles

There are more than 200 miraculous references in the Gospels[147], 44 of which are described in much detail – 28 in Matthew, 22 in Mark, 22 in Luke, and 9 in John. Most of the miracles appear in more than one Gospel, although 18 appear in only one Gospel. The only miracle to appear in all four Gospels is the feeding of the 5000.

Most scholars make a distinction between the various types of miracles – the **healings** (e.g., restoring sight and hearing, curing leprosy), **exorcisms** (e.g., the "legions"), the **re-animations** (e.g., raising Lazarus, raising Jairus' daughter[148]) and the **natural miracles** (e.g., walking on water, feeding 5000, cursing the fig tree, turning wine into water, the coin in the fish's mouth).

While we come to speak of these acts as miracles, the Greek word *dynameis* means "acts of power", and *semeia* (used in John) means "signs", rather than *terata* that would translate better into miracles or amazing wonders. Thus, the New Testament regarded these acts of Jesus as acts of power or signs, not as miracles that were probably associated, in those days, with magic, sorcery and/or Satanism.

One of the characteristics of the acts or signs in the New Testament is that they become more miraculous with the telling. What starts out in the *Gospel of Mark* as healing one blind man and one possessed man, turns quickly into two blind men and two possessed men in Matthew. Jesus feeds 4000, which grows in the next telling to 5000, and leaves 12 baskets of leftovers instead of 7.

---

[147] It's interesting to note that the Jesus Seminar considers only eight of the miracle stories to be authentic.
[148] When he arrives at Jairus' house, Jesus proclaims that Jairus' daughter is not dead, but merely sleeping, and he proceeds to awaken her. As such, this is not technically a miracle nor is she raised from the dead, yet this remains in many Gospel discussions, another example of Jesus' miracles.

Jesus Who?

Not only do the miracles become more miraculous, Jesus himself changes. In the *Gospel of Mark* he is a healer who uses touch, lifting, spit, rubbing, and a whole black bag of tricks to effect his cures (1:31; 7:33; 8:23). In the *Gospel of Matthew* he specializes in touch (8:15; 9:27; 12:22; 20:34). In the *Gospel of Luke* all his tools are gone. Now Jesus cures by word alone (4:38; 11:14; 18:42).

Curiously enough, none of the miracle healings deal with sexual disorders (e.g., infertility, impotence, sexually transmitted diseases, etc.). Virtually every other major bodily group is represented, from the eyes and ears down to the hands and feet, and many groups are mentioned repeatedly, blindness being the clear ring winner. Another curious element in his miracle stories is that once he enters Jerusalem, the miracles stop. And, of course, his ability to perform miracles is seriously constricted when he is in his hometown and among the people who knew him before he started his ministry.

Scholars are not in complete agreement over the fundamental meaning of the miracles. Some believe that the miracles are a sign of Jesus' divinity (e.g., Acts 2:22). Others argue that they are signs of the coming Kingdom of God, where afflictions will disappear (e.g., Luke 11:20). Still others believe that Jesus' miracles represented a radical alternative to the Temple sacrifice institution, and as such, were an economic and political threat to the status quo (e.g., John Dominic Crosson). Some validation for this point of view can be seen in the *Gospel of Mark* - the first time that the Temple authorities decide to kill Jesus comes when they witness one of his healings (Mark 3:6).[149]

What Kind of a Miracle Worker Was Jesus?

One of the curious aspects of Jesus' miracles is that often he appears to be reluctant to perform them, and reluctant for the recipients and onlookers to tell others. Moreover, he never accepts payment for his services, which seems strange for an itinerant preacher with no visible means of support, and an entourage of more than a dozen people to

---

[149] "...he saith unto the man, Stretch forth thy hand. And he stretched it forth; and his hand was restored. And the Pharisees went out, and straightway with the Herodians took counsel against him, how they might destroy him (3:6-7)."

support. As well, many of the healing miracles are ascribed to the faith of the people involved (e.g., the Centurion's servant, the bleeding woman, the blind man near Jericho) rather than to any actions that Jesus took. Finally, almost no one ever thanks him for the miracle. They accept the cure and then go off on their merry way

Jesus used a number of techniques to accomplish his healing miracles. As noted above, he often relied on touch, spit, rubbing, and lifting. At other times, his healers were exorcisms in which demons were cast out of the afflicted person. Generally speaking, Jesus' exorcisms were not directed at people with specific physical complaints, as for example, when he confronts the unclean spirit in the synagogue (Mark 1:23), or the "legions" in the cemetery in Gerasenes (Mark 5:1), or the unclean spirit in the Syro-Phoenician woman's daughter (Mark 7:24) or even the seven demons in Mary Magdalene (Luke 8:2). The only exorcism directed at a specific physical complaint (epilepsy) is the exorcism that takes place immediately after the transfiguration (Mark 9:20). On the other hand, his healing miracles are almost always directed at people with specific physical problems – he takes hold of Peter's mother-in-law and her fever departs (Mark 1:30-31), he touches a leper and cleanses him (Mark 1:40-42), a bleeding woman touches his fringe and stops bleeding (Mark 5:25-34), he puts his finger in the deaf man's ear, spits and then touches the man's tongue and lo and behold the man now hears and speaks (Mark 7:32-35), etc. Thus, Jesus worked his healing miracles in a number of ways, using exorcisms for the possessed and various natural techniques for people with physical complaints. What does this tell us about Jesus?

There were several kinds of miracle workers or magicians in 1st Century Israel. The first kind was the *goetes*, who professed magical powers but were often charlatans. The second kind was the *magos* (from which we get the Magi), who originally were a priestly clan from Media in the 6th Century B.C. While the Magi were believed to have true powers, they also had a reputation for unsavory acts, including incest, polygamy, cannibalism, and human sacrifice[150]. The third kind of magician was the "divine man", believed to be a God or demon in

---

[150] Curiously enough, the early Christians were also criticized for these types of practices.

human form. While the magi needed rituals, spells, and objects to perform his magic, the divine man drew upon his inner spirit.

The Jesus described in the *Gospel of Mark* appears to be a Magi in that he employed various tools (e.g., spit, laying on of hands, special sayings) to achieve his cures. In this aspect he is well within the tradition of the Essenes who were well known for their healing abilities, and a branch of the Essenes were even known as the Therapeuts. As we move from Mark to Matthew and Luke, the nature of Jesus' abilities change from the Magi to the Divine Man. Jesus no longer needs his tools, and soon the mere mention of his name has healing properties.

While being a divine man seems better than being either a Magi or a goetes, the divine man had an accompanying disadvantage – insanity. Possession of a human body by a God or a demon often led to a state of insanity, as true in ancient Israel as it is today among the witchdoctors of Southern Africa with whom I worked in the 1970s.

Healers and Possession

I spent one year working in a "blacks-only" psychiatric hospital in Sterkfontain, South Africa during the time that Apartheid ruled in that country. There I supervised psychotherapy sessions by my black graduate students. Most of the sessions were in Zulu. We encountered many "witchdoctors" among the inmates, and their history was the same. At some point they felt "the calling" to become a witchdoctor, but resisted. As the calling became stronger, and they continued to resist, they suffered physical and mental problems until the point when they were no longer able to function – hence their involuntary incarceration. This same "calling" is reported in the backgrounds of witchdoctors who were successfully living and functioning in the community. The key difference was that the successful ones obeyed the calling while the patients with whom I worked had resisted it.

The account in the *Gospel of Mark* when Jesus was baptized and the spirit, in the form of a dove, appeared, is very much like the stories of "divine man" magicians. Note that Jesus' miracles began after this, indicating to contemporaneous readers that the dove imparted Jesus with the divine spirit[151]. It was the strength of this new spirit which aided Jesus in his miracles. It was also this new spirit whom the demons recognized (e.g., Luke 4:34) even while ordinary people took no note of it. In many respects, following the baptism, Jesus was a split personality – the ordinary man and the spirit man. As is common in such cases of dissociative states, both personalities existed side-by-side, with one being dominant at any one time.

Perhaps this split-personality explains why in his hometown he has no power, because the ordinary Jesus has lived there for so many years that it's the dominant voice there. Yet under the influence of the spirit, he ventures into new cities where his powers are greatly increased and he speaks with authority. Perhaps it also explains the apparent contradictions in Jesus' spoken words. He preaches "love your enemies (Luke 6:35)" yet claims that "Whoever come to me and does not hate his father, mother, wife and children, brothers and sisters...cannot be my disciple (Luke 14:26)." He extols "blessed are the peacemakers (Matthew 5:9)" but also says "I have not come to bring peace, but a sword (Matthew 10:34)." Much later, at his death, we will see many interpretations that correspond to the one raised here. They will claim that the humanly Jesus died on the cross while the spiritual Jesus arose to the heavens. Such beliefs were well within the theology surrounding the "divine man" theory.

Prior Accounts

One problem with the veracity of the miracle stories as they apply to Jesus is that many of his miracles had been associated with prior acts by so-called Pagan Gods, Old Testament prophecies, and acts of contemporaneous wonder workers. For example, turning water into wine was associated with Dionysus (Lietzmann, 1961; Shorto, 1997), raising the dead was a common feat for Asclepius who also cured the

---

[151] This transcending function of the dove is also part of the belief system among African witchdoctors.

Jesus Who?

sick (Hoffman, 1987)[152], Pythagoras calmed the waters and produced large catches of fish (predicting the exact number)[153], in addition to his healings (Guthrie, 1987), Eleusis exorcised demons by using pigs thrown into the sea (Burkert, 1985), etc.

In the Old Testament, Isaiah prophesizes that the "...dead shall live, their corpses shall rise... (26:19)" and "...the deaf shall hear...the eyes of the blind shall see... (29:18)" Sound familiar? In the 2nd *Book of Kings*, Elisha feeds the throngs with a mere 20 loaves of barley, and has some left over (4:42-22). Does that story ring a bell? We have seen before in our discussions (especially with regard to the *Gospel of Matthew*) that events in the Gospel appear to be created in order to fulfill Old Testament prophecy. Shorto (1997) goes so far as to say that "Reading Mark (the most miracle-packed gospel)...one can almost see the writer ticking off his list of mighty deeds (p. 126)." Having thus created the event (e.g., Jesus is born in Bethlehem), the event itself is given validity because it is said to fulfill the prophecy. Were these true miracles that Jesus caused to happen, or were they chosen from the list of miracles in the Old Testament?

Not only do we have a long list of miracles performed by Pagan Gods and prophesized in the Old Testament, Josephus relates many tales of miracle workers who were contemporaneous with Jesus. Honi the Circledrawer, also from Galilee, was renowned for his ability to bring rain through prayer/magic, and Eleazar performed an exorcism in front of General Vespasian. Simon Magus (meaning Simon the Magician) had a thriving practice in Samaria, and it's his identity that undoubtedly leads to the accusation that Jesus is "...a Samaritan, and have a

---

[152] Origen quotes Celsus as making a strong case that Asclepius was the true savior and that Jesus' so-called miracles were mere copies of the original.

[153] Indeed, the number of fish caught by Jesus (John 21:11) was 153, which was a sacred number to the Pythagoreans, known for their geometry, and was called "the measure of the fish" because the ratio of height to length of two intersecting circles which produced the sign of the fish was 153:265. In other words, the Christian symbol of the fish, which originally came from the "nasrani" or the name of the little fish in the Sea of Galilee (from whence the Nasorean name came), was produced by this equation (see Freke & Gandy, 1999, p. 40 for a complete explanation).

demon (John 8:48)." Hanina ben Dosa[154], also from Galilee, a so-called "man of deed", enacted miraculous cures for the sick through prayer. He was best known for achieving a "long distance" cure for the fever that threatened the son of a leading Pharisee (Gamaliel) in Jerusalem.[155] Apollonius of Tyana, a contemporary of Paul, was an itinerant preacher who had a devoted following, and among the miracles he performed were exorcisms, healings, prophecies, and raising the dead (Sound familiar!). He was said to be fathered by the Gods, went off into the wilderness in his youth where he encountered and overcame demons, and was opposed by the religious authorities who attempted to have him killed. Unlike Jesus, Apollonius magically escaped his captors, and upon his death in old age, he ascended to heaven and subsequently appeared to his followers.[156]

How do we explain the fact that miracles ascribed to Jesus are copies of miracles ascribed to past Gods and Old Testament prophecies, and in his own time, other miracle workers were producing miracles on a par with Jesus? Do we believe that everyone was capable of producing such miracles? If so, were these people also divinely inspired, as they claimed, and was their divinity more or less than Jesus'? If not, how do we dismiss their claims and accept the claim for Jesus alone? Did Jesus produce these exact miracles because others had been known to produce them? Unlikely, since there is no mention in the Gospels about any of these miracles having been produced by others either in the past, or by Jesus' contemporaries. Do we accept Jesus as the only true claimant to the title of miracle worker, and reject the others, because Jesus was the Son of God? Unlikely, since part of his claim to be the Son of God comes from his miracles, we can't then accept the miracles because of the claim, unless circular reasoning is dear to our hearts. The most likely scenario is that the writers of the Gospels chose these miracles because they were familiar with them, and ascribed them to Jesus.

---

[154] Sometimes called Chanina ben Dosa (e.g., Chilton, 2000).
[155] This story may have formed the nexus of the Gospel story of Jesus' own "long distance" cure in Luke 7:1-10 (Chilton 2000).
[156] *Life of Apollonius* by Flavius Philostratus, 217 A.D. Quoted in Smith (1977).

Jesus Who?

Alternate Explanations

Of course, many of the miracles in the Gospels can be explained today in non-miraculous ways. Most of the healing episodes (36 of the 44 detailed miracles) in which the blind are made to see, the deaf to hear, and the lame to walk are all theoretically possible and indeed, do appear to happen even today, though not frequently. Of course, the fact that these remediations can occur non-miraculously does not prove that Jesus' cures were not miraculous. They may have been. But given the non-miraculous possibilities, there is no reason to posit a miraculous cure when non-miraculous alternatives are available to us. This is especially so since the Gospels tell us that Jesus had difficulty working his miracles in his home town, wherein few people believed in his power; leading Jesus to say that "A prophet is not without honor, except in his own home town... (Matthew 13:57)." In other words, Jesus' power to heal came from the belief of his followers, thus tending to argue for the non-miraculous cause of the cures.

Many more (but still not all) of the so-called miracles ascribed to Jesus are not miracles at all, but are failures of the readers to understand the context in which the stories are being told, and the nature of the words being used. This is partly because we are 2000 years away from the customs of the day, and also because the words of the Bible come through dozens of translations from nearly half a dozen different languages. Even more to the point, many of the customs and word usages were peculiar to the religious sects of the time, and until the discovery of the Nag Hammadi, Qumran, and other documents, these customs and word usages were not known. For example...

- Jesus is credited with bringing many people from death to life. Seems like a miracle, doesn't it? Yet among the Essenes, the words "life" and "death" had specific meanings. The people of "The Way", those who were devout and followed the way of the Lord, were alive. People outside this sect were dead. Thus when Jesus says, "Let the dead bury the dead (Matthew 8:22)" what he means is that the non-believers should tend to themselves. It's not possible for dead people to bury dead people, so the comment makes no sense, unless you realize that his use of the word "dead" is very specific, and means non-believer. So when Jesus is said to bring the dead into the living, it means that Jesus is converting non-believers into believers. Hence, we can explain easily the fact that Peter and Paul, who are not the sons of God, also bring the dead back to life, because this is a metaphor for conversion, not miracle working.

- The miracle of the feeding of the 5000 is the only miracle mentioned in all four Gospels, yet it has some curious aspects. Once the miracle is accomplished (and this applies to the feeding of the 4000 too), no one appears to be taken aback. Mark says: "They all ate and were satisfied (6:42; 8:8)." Yet following most every other miracle, his disciples and the onlookers are "utterly astonished" (Mark 6:51), "overcome with amazement" (Mark 5:42), "filled with great awe" (Mark 4:35), "amazed" (Mark 1:27; 2:12), "astounded beyond measure" (Mark 7:37), etc. How is it that his most famous miracle, and one of his most powerful, produces no reaction from his easily impressed disciples and followers? Perhaps the answer lies in the nature of what it meant to "feed" the multitudes. If we realize that the sacrament of the bread was an induction ceremony, and that Jesus was inducting lots of people (the numbers 4000 and 5000 are not to be taken literally, but surely mean "a lot" of people) with a slice/crumb in much the same fashion as Catholics do today, then it's entirely possible that a multitude could be fed from five loaves. And what of the fishes? The "fishes" were undoubtedly "fishers", who in the language of the Essenes, were people capable of giving the sacrament. Thus, an alternate reading of the feeding of the 5000 would be: "With the help of two priests, and five loaves of bread, Jesus gave the sacraments to several hundred of his followers." Not so miraculous when you look at it this way?

- In the *Gospel of Mark* (6:48) it says that on the "fourth watch of the night he cometh unto them, walking on the sea..." Sounds miraculous, doesn't it? Yet the proper Hebrew translation is "<u>by</u> the sea" not "<u>on</u> the sea" (Schonfield, 1965, p. 272), which doesn't make it much of a miracle at all.

Jesus Who?

Thus, knowing the language and customs of the times helps translate what appears to the literalists to be miracles to be natural events (Shorton, 1997; Schillebeeckx, 1979).

In summary, there can be no question that Jesus performed "miracles" within the traditions of the "pious ones" or the "holy ones" of 1st Century Israel. Many of these so-called miracles can be explained today using less than miraculous theories, but notwithstanding these alternate theories, Jesus' ability to cure should not be doubted. However, the ability to work wonders, as praise worthy as it was, does not advance the concept of his divinity nor does it contribute to the belief that he was the Messiah.

Was Jesus an Exorcist?

"And he went throughout Galilee, proclaiming the message in their synagogues and casting out demons." (Mark 1:39)

Just as the Jewish Messiah wasn't expected to perform miracles, so too he wasn't expected to perform exorcisms. Yet the synoptic Gospels tell us about 12 exorcisms performed directly by Jesus, and others performed by his disciples (Mark 3:15; Matthew 10:1; Luke 9:1) and his followers (Luke 10:17)[157]. Jesus' most famous exorcism was when he cast out the "legions" from the man who lived in the cemetery (Mark 5:1-13), sending them into the bodies of pigs who then drown in the sea; and his most intriguing exorcism was casting out the seven demons from Mary Magdalene (Luke 8:2), which is not described in any detail, but referred to. Exorcisms were not uncommon during the 1st Century B.C., and they were referred to several times in the New Testament (Mark 9:38; Matthew 7:22). A contemporary of Jesus, Rabbi Hanina ben Dosa, also from Galilee, was a well-known exorcist.

What made Jesus different from the run-of-the-mill exorcist was his ability to cast out demons with a word, rather than incantations, spells,

---

[157] The *Gospel of John* does not contain any exorcisms, although it does refer to demon possession.

or other rituals. Indeed, Jesus, it was claimed, was so powerful as an exorcist that some demons didn't even wait for him to approach them: instead, they willingly identified themselves when he came near. As skilled as he may have been, there was nothing in this power of exorcism that indicates either divine origins or status as a Messiah. In the grand scope of things, competence as an exorcist, however great, was more of an elective than a requirement.

Was Jesus a Prophet?

> *"Who do men say that the Son of man is? And they said, Some say John the Baptist; some, Elijah; and others, Jeremiah, or one of the prophets."* (Matthew 16:13-14)

In Jesus' time, being a prophet was different than it is today. Today we think of prophets as people who can predict the future, but in Jesus' time a prophet was someone who had an intimate relation with God. Either they spoke directly with God or God used them as a vehicle for communicating with others. Yet even here, implicit in this definition was the belief that the message was about some future event. Speaking about prophets, Jesus said: "By their fruits ye shall know them (Matthew 7:16)." Thus, the true prophet was inspired by God and spoke the truth about future events. Deuteronomy says: "When a prophet speaketh in the name of the LORD, if the thing follow not, nor come to pass, that is the thing which the LORD hath not spoken; the prophet hath spoken it presumptuously... (18:22)."

Jesus is equally well-known today as a prophet, however, a careful reading of the Gospels reveals that he never refers to himself as a prophet, although others do in the Gospels of Matthew, Luke, and John. For example...

- "And when he was come into Jerusalem, all the city was stirred, saying, Who is this? And the multitudes said, This is the prophet, Jesus, from Nazareth of Galilee (Matthew, 21: 10-11)."
- "And when the chief priests and the Pharisees heard his parables, they perceived that he spake of them. And when they

sought to lay hold on him, they feared the multitudes, because they took him for a prophet (Matthew 21: 45-46)."
- "And he that was dead sat up, and began to speak. And he gave him to his mother. And fear took hold on all: and they glorified God, saying, A great prophet is arisen among us: and, God hath visited his people (Luke 7:15-16)."
- "So they gathered them up, and filled twelve baskets with broken pieces from the five barley loaves, which remained over unto them that had eaten. When therefore the people saw the sign which he did, they said, This is of a truth the prophet that cometh into the world (John 6:13-14)."

Of course, these references cited above do not provide us with examples of prophecy. For example, the fact that Jesus spoke in parables, or raised the dead, or fed the multitudes are all praiseworthy endeavors, but hardly the stuff of prophecy.

Though Jesus never directly refers to himself as a prophet, some scholars believe that Jesus is referring to himself when he says "A prophet is not without honor, save in his own country, and among his own kin, and in his own house (Mark 6:4)" or "Jerusalem, Jerusalem, that killeth the prophets, and stoneth them that are sent unto her (Luke 13;33)." Indeed, this seems to be the case.

There are many examples in the Gospels in which Jesus does prophesize[158], but most scholars believe that these references were added by the Gospel writers to refer to later events. For example, when Jesus warns about "false messiahs", or disciples being persecuted and flogged in synagogues, or people loosing their faith, these are warnings to later generations put into the mouth of Jesus. In reality, there are few contemporaneous instances in which Jesus makes a prophecy and that prophecy comes true within the time of Jesus.

---

[158] We're using the word "prophesize" here to refer to current predictions about future events. Some scholars (e.g., Porter, 2004) have a broader definition of prophecy to include being able to uncover past events, as when Jesus informs the Samaritan woman about her past.

On the other hand, there are several occasions in which Jesus' prophecies do not come true. For example, he says: "for as Jonah was three days and three nights in the belly of the whale; so shall the Son of man be three days and three nights in the heart of the earth (Matthew 12:40)", yet he is only in the "heart of the earth" for two nights, not three. Referring to the Temple, he says that - "There shall not be left here one stone upon another, that shall not be thrown down (Matthew 24:2)", yet there are still standing today stones from the Temple that were not thrown down.

All things considered, Jesus does not deserve his reputation as a prophet, at least not in the narrow definition of the term. While he clearly believes that he speaks the word of God, there are precious few examples in which he predicts future events that come true, while there are cases in which his predictions about major events do not come true.

Was Jesus a Zealot?

"The Dead Sea Scrolls provide a context for understanding the role of Jesus and the political machinations that would have featured behind his birth, marriage, and active role in this Zealot aspiration for victory."
(Baigent, 2006, p. 38)

As indicated earlier, Jesus' followers included a high percentage of Zealots, including Simon the Zealot and Judas the Daggerman (and possibly the Sons of Thunder). Moreover, Jesus' own philosophy and the philosophy of the Zealots were similar in many ways. They both stressed the importance of the law and both were dissatisfied with the sad state of affairs in which the Temple authorities were corrupt and the Romans ruled Israel with an iron fist, exacting taxes that impoverished the people. Of course, Jesus, on the whole, professed peace while the Zealots were committed to the violent overthrow of the Roman authorities. However, there were occasions in which Jesus also advocated armed resistance, as when he urged his disciples to gather up swords (Luke 22:36) or when he said: "Think not that I came to send peace on the earth: I came not to send peace, but a sword (Matthew 10:34)."

Michael Baigent's in *The Jesus Papers* (2006) theorizes that Jesus was, in fact, a Zealot, and he claims that the two "lestai" who were crucified with him were also Zealots, as was Barabbas. Baigent adds to his list of Zealots, Paul (Acts 21:38) as well as the Essenes, and he claims that: "The Dead Sea Scrolls...provide original documents from the Zealots (p. 36)." There is some justification for linking the Essenes and the Zealots (see Eisenman, 1997). Hippolytus, a disciple of Irenaeus, in his 2nd Century text *Origenis Philosophumena sive Omnium Hæresium Refutatio* wrote:

> "Some of these [Essenes] observe a still more rigid practice in not handling or looking at a coin bearing an image, saying that one should neither carry nor look at nor fashion any image; nor will they enter a city at the gate of which statues are erected, since they consider it unlawful to walk under an image. Others threaten to slay any uncircumcised Gentile who listens to a discourse on God and His laws, unless he undergoes the rite of circumcision; should he refuse to do so, they kill him instantly. From this practice they have received the name of 'Zealots' or 'Sicarii.' Others again call no one Lord except God, even though one should torture or kill them (Jewish Encyclopedia v. 228-230)."

Thus, according to Hippolytus, the Zealots emerged as the military wing of the Essenes, in much the same way that the Therapeuts emerged as the healing wing of the Essenes. And given Jesus' involvement with the Essenes, it would be surprising if he had not been exposed to the Zealot philosophy and felt comfortable in the presence of Zealots among his disciples. Perhaps the situation is best described in contemporary terms. The Republican Party in the 21st Century has under its broad umbrella individuals and groups that advocate bombing abortion clinics, invading foreign countries, deposing leaders of sovereign countries, editing school books, and building enormous fiscal deficits to fund massive government spending. In these aspects they can be distinguished from the Libertarian and the Democratic parties, as well as from the 20th Century Republican Party. Yet not all

Republicans advocate all these positions. In a similar way, Jesus as an Essene may have adopted the Therapeut orientation to healing as well as the Essene eschatology, while rejecting the extreme violence of the Zealots.

Was Jesus Anti-Gentile?

"..do not heap up empty phrases as the Gentiles do." (Matthew 6:7)

Jesus lived in Galilee of the Gentiles, surrounded by cities whose inhabitants were mostly Gentiles (e.g., Tiberias, Tyre, Sidon, Gaulanitis, Hippos, Gadara, the Decapolis), yet it's clear that Jesus intended his preaching for the Jews, not the Gentiles. Here are some illuminating quotes:

> "Jesus...commanded them, saying, Go not into the way of the Gentiles, and into any city of the Samaritans, enter ye not (Matthew 10:5)."

> "God sent forth his son, born of a woman, born under the law, *to redeem those who were under the law* [i.e., the Jews] (Galatians 4:4)."

> "...he [Jesus] answered and said, I am not sent but unto the lost sheep of the house of Israel... It is not meet to take the children's bread, and cast it to dogs (Matthew 15:24-26)."

The latter quote from Jesus, referring to the Gentiles as dogs, shows that not only did he not intend his preaching for the Gentiles, he had very low regard for them. Indeed, calling someone a dog in Jesus' day was a far worse insult than it would be today. In the minds of the Jews at that time, dogs were "unclean" (like swine/pigs[159]), scavengers (Exodus 22:31), who ate their own vomit (Proverbs 26:11), and were to be excluded from heaven (Revelations 22:15).

---

[159] Note the familiar Jewish expression of the times: "He who rears dogs is like one who rears swine."

Jesus Who?

Here are some more choice quips about Gentiles, from Jesus:

> "..do not heap up empty phrases as the Gentiles do; for they think they will be heard for their many words. Do not be like them... (Matthew 6:7-8)."
>
> "Do not be anxious, saying 'What will we eat? Or 'What shall we drink?' of 'What shall we wear?' For the Gentiles seek all these things...(Matthew 6:31-32)."
>
> "For if you love those who love you, what reward have you? Do not even the tax collectors do the same?... Do not even the Gentiles do the same? (Matthew 5:46-47)."

Despite the fact that Galilee was primarily Gentile, Jesus performed healings and miracles almost exclusively for the Jews. Which is not to say that, on rare occasions, he didn't minister to Gentiles (e.g., the Centurion, the Canaanite woman's daughter), but the main (almost exclusive) focus of his healings was the Jews, and his preaching was to the Jews. Jesus made it clear when he said: "Think not that I am come to destroy the law, or the prophets: I am not come to destroy, but to fulfill (Matthew 5:17)."

Indeed, Jesus' attitude toward Gentiles was so negative that one of the major debates following his death was whether or not Gentiles could be recruited into the new faith. Pro Gentile enthusiasts searched high and low to find examples where Jesus' kind words about the Gentiles could be used to convince the ardent opponents like James and Peter. The search was in vain. All they could discover were some vague references that might be interpreted to indicate that Jesus was prepared to open his gates to the Gentiles. For example, Matthew quotes him as saying: "I tell you, many will come from east and west and sit at the table with Abraham, Isaac and Jacob in the kingdom of heaven... (8:11-12)" which was often interpreted as being pro-Gentile; however, coming from the "east and west" was not exactly a definition of the Gentile, when in Galilee the Gentiles were located in the east, west, <u>and</u> the north (Sanders, p. 27).

The bottom line is that Jesus was anti-Gentile, but not in the same ardent way that we look at anti-Semitism. Jesus did not preach attacking or killing the Gentiles. Jesus believed that his business was with the Jews, and generally speaking he ignored the Gentiles, occasionally poking fun at their unclean and inhuman practices as viewed by a 1st Century devout Jew.

What was Jesus' Relationship With John the Baptist?

> "The one who is more powerful than I is coming after me; I am not worthy to stoop down and untie the thong of his sandals. I have baptized you with water; but he will baptize you with the Holy Spirit."
> (Mark 1:7-8)

There are many points of comparison between John the Baptist and Jesus. In some respects they are opposites (John is born to an aged woman, Jesus to a very young girl), yet in other respects their fates are similar (both are sentenced to death by a "reluctant" ruler). The table below lists some of the obvious comparison points.

	John the Baptist	**Jesus**
Miraculous birth	Infertile mother	Unfertilized mother
Mother	Mother was very old	Mother was very young
Born	Summer solstice	Winter solstice
Baptizes	With water	With "fire"
Death	Cruel (beheaded)	Cruel (crucified)
Judge	Reluctant King	Reluctant Prefect
Day of death	Celebrating birthday	Celebrating Passover
Alternative to Temple	Baptism	Communal meal

Jesus Who?

We know that Jesus began his ministry after being baptized by John the Baptist[160], and we're told that John the Baptist began his ministry in the 14th year of Tiberius' reign. To many people this dating suggests 29 A.D., since Augustus died in 14 A.D. However, other scholars note that Tiberius reigned as a co-regent from 11 or 12 A.D., placing the start of John's ministry (assuming that the *Gospel of Luke* is correct, which, as we have pointed out, is a large assumption) as early as 25 or 26 A.D.. In fact, the Jewish Encyclopedia identifies John as an "Essene saint and preacher; flourished between 20 and 30" A.D. Jesus, having been born in 6 B.C., would have been "about 30 years old" in 24 A.D., and thus could well have been baptized by John.

John (sometimes called the Baptizer[161]) was a curious fellow. Matthew described him as being dressed in a "raiment of camel hair's, and a leathern girdle about his loins, and his meat was locusts and wild honey[162] (3:4)." John was so well known that he was mentioned in Josephus' *Antiquities* (while Jesus was not). Josephus says that John was "a good man, and commanded the Jews to exercise virtue, both as to righteousness towards one another, and piety towards God (18:116-119)."

John derived his name from the Greek word "baptize" which meant to "dip in water". As far as we know, the rite of baptism originated in Sumeria, and celebrated the water God, *Ea*, whose name in Greek was *Oannes*, which was similar to the Greek word for John, *Ioannes*.[163] Of course, John's baptism was no ordinary baptism, nor was the place we first encounter him an ordinary place. John baptized at the River Jordan, at the place where, legend has it, the Jewish people crossed over in their exodus from Egypt. This was the place

---

[160] It is curious that Jesus would be baptized at all. If he were the Son of God, and sinless, what need would he have of baptism, which was for the remission of sins?

[161] Also called the Immerser or the Forerunner. The Muslims call him Yahya, and he is 1 of 25 prophets mentioned in the Qur'an.

[162] Compare this to the description of Elijah from Kings 1:8: "...He was an hairy man, and girt with a girdle of leather about his loins..."

[163] Showing Pagan origins, John the Baptist was the Water God, while Jesus was the Sun God.

where Joshua led his people to the Promised Land and not far from the Essene headquarters at Qumran.

We get some feeling for the power of John's personality and his message when we realize that "all of Judea" was making the long pilgrimage into this inhospitable desert. The journey from Jerusalem to John was a journey of more than 25 miles across hot desert dunes with nary a place for shade, and the threat of bandits everywhere. Yet they came. From Jerusalem, from Judea, and as the Gospels tell us, even from Galilee (Matthew 3:14) – which would have required more than a week – the faithful came to hear John's message of repentance and receive his baptism.

Baptism at the River

Among the Sub Saharan "witchdoctors" with whom I worked for three years while living in South Africa, each one had a story about their journey to becoming a witchdoctor. At some key point, many of them found themselves in the wilderness and compelled to enter a body of water, usually a river. Once they entered the river, it seems they stayed there for a long time. During their immersion it wasn't unusual for them to have an encounter with a totem animal, usually a snake or fish. When they surfaced, they found an experienced witchdoctor. He or she would say: "I see you. I have been waiting for you." This would start their initiation process, and they would become an apprentice.

Although we can't be sure, there are hints that John's baptism was a replacement for the traditional Temple centered rites for the remission of sins. In Jerusalem a million dollar enterprise surrounded the Temple culture, with tens of thousands of employees and hundreds of thousands of dollars (shekels) filling the Temple coffers. At the center was the animal sacrifice industry (*korbanot*), that involved thousands of sheep, bulls, calves, pigeons, and doves, all of whom had to be unblemished (Leviticus 22:20). People were required to make sacrifices for individual peccadilloes as well as at the thrice yearly festivals (Passover, Pentecost and Sukkoth). John's one-stop one-time baptism for the remission of sins was a clear threat to this multi-million dollar industry, and some scholars believe that it's this economic threat and not the questionable husbandry of Herod Antipas that was behind his untimely death (e.g., Shorto, 1997).

Luke asserts that John and Jesus were related and that they were only six months apart in age[164], however, this assertion does not stand up to the facts, which indicate Jesus being born around 6 B.C. and John may have been preaching as early as 6 A.D. (under the reign of Archelaus, Herod's son). None of the other Gospels claim any relationship between Jesus and John, and even in Luke the only mention of this is during the birth and infancy stories. It isn't mentioned later when they were adults. So we can assume they were not related.

If the account in Luke is wrong, when was John born? One account by the Egyptian Bishop Serapion who lived in the late 4th Century claimed that John's mother and Herod the Great died on the same day, and John was 7 ½ years old at the time (Gibson, 2004). Accepting 4 B.C. as the date of Herod's death would place John's birth in 11 B.C. In confirmation of this, the Slavonic copy of *The Jewish Wars* by Josephus contains a passage about John: "And there went after him all Judea, that lies in the region round Jerusalem…And when he had been brought to Archelaus and the doctors of the Law had assembled, they asked him who he is and where he has been until then (II, vii, 2, 6-8)." The idea that John was active in the reign of Archelaus can also be deduced from the *Gospel of Matthew* that talks about Archelaus in 2:24 and then immediately says: "And in those days cometh John the Baptist… (3:1)", implying that John was active during Archelaus' reign. Thus, if John had been born in 11 B.C., he would have been 17 at the time of his encounter with Archelaus (who reigned in Judea from 4 B.C. to 6 A.D.), which is certainly possible.

---

[164] Assuming that Jesus and John were born 6 months apart, and assuming that Jesus was born during the Winter solstice, and therefore John was born in the Summer solstice, then the statement of John the Baptist that "He must grow greater, I must become less (John 3:30)" makes perfect astronomical sense.

The earliest Gospel (Mark) indicates that John the Baptist did not know Jesus and that Jesus' revelation during the Baptism was observed by Jesus alone. Later, the *Gospel of John* asserts that John knew Jesus, knew that he was the Messiah, and was subservient to him. However, we must realize that the later Gospels were written when sects devoted to John the Baptist as the Messiah competed with Christian sects for membership (e.g., Acts, 18:24-25). Hence, the writers of the later Gospels saw fit to claim that John the Baptist himself knew he was subservient to Jesus as a way of negating the impact of the sects devoted to John as Messiah (Gibson, 2004). Indeed the *Gospel of John* has John the Baptist say: "He must grow greater, I must grow smaller (3:30)" and goes so far as to claim that Jesus and his disciples were out-baptizing John (4:1).

Was John an Essene?

There is some evidence that John had once been a member of the Essene Sect[165]. The *Gospel of John* says that John the Baptist "...grew up and his spirit matured. He lived out in the wilderness until the day he appeared openly in Israel (1:80)." The "wilderness" was another name for the Qumran village where the Essenes had their capital, and it was only a half-day's walk from where John baptized in the River Jordan (Gibson, 2004). Given the proclivity of the Bible to speak using words with double meanings, it's likely, therefore, that he had lived in Qumran. Otherwise the *Gospel of John* could have used other words (desert, plains, etc) rather than the one word that also described the Essene capital. Finegan (1969) speculates that the relatively advanced age of John's parents made it likely that they died while John was still a child, and the practice of the Essenes of adopting "other men's children while yet pliable and docile, and regard them as their kin and mould them in accordance with their own principles (Josephus War, II, viii, 2:120)" raises the serious possibility that John was raised by the Essenes.

John's philosophy and way of life was also strongly in the Essene camp. He was apocalyptic as were they. He used water for baptism,

---

[165] Spoto, 1998, p. 38; Finegan, 1969, p. 6; Craveri, 1967, p. 73; Shorto, 1997, p. 95.

which was their custom (only John used it publicly while they were private in their purification rituals). He awaited the imminent coming of the true Messiah, as did they, and both relied upon the same scripture from Isaiah (40:3). Both preached fire and brimstone and warned that non-believers would suffer terribly while the true believers would enjoy peace. Both believed that the world was engaged in a struggle between Good and Evil. Neither exempted the Jews from God's ultimate judgment just because they were Jewish. Both believed in sharing possessions and both lived an ascetic life. John was said to eat "locusts and wild honey" and the Essenes were well known for raising bees and also eating locusts (Shorto, 1997).

Not only do many experts believe that John had been a member of the Essenes (e.g., Craveri, 1967; Vanderkam and Flint, 2002; Finegan, 1969; Shorto, 1997; Betz, 1990) , but John's membership was supported by American wellness expert and "sleeping prophet" Edgar Cayce (1877-1945). Cayce died in 1945, before the Dead Sea Scrolls were discovered, but nonetheless had a vision in which he identified John with this group[166], which was virtually unknown at the time. Lest his prophecies be dismissed, Cayce made many "fantastic" prophecies which turned out to be true, including rightfully predicting that, shortly before the end of the 2nd millennium, a room would be discovered beneath the Sphinx, and indeed such a room was found (Kittler, 1970).

Jesus too shared many of the customs and beliefs of the Essenes, and he too, like John the Baptist, probably had been brought up at Qumran. John, though older than Jesus, may have met him there. Can we go so far as imagine that the young Jesus may have been inspired by stories of John's exploits at Qumran and his ultimate rebellion, going off to preach a new style of the old religion. In the same way that new recruits in schools and military academies want to follow in the footsteps of distinguished alumni, do we dare imagine that John was such an inspiration for Jesus, and that the young Jesus, emerging from his time at Qumran, seeks out as his first public act, the legendary John, to whom he goes for baptism. Pure speculation, but enticing nonetheless, and supported by some evidence.

---

[166] He also identified Jesus' parents, Mary and Joseph, as members of the Essenes.

Was Jesus a Disciple of John?

Was Jesus a disciple of John? There is no clear evidence in the Gospels; however, the Mandaeans believed this to be the case, and believed that Jesus betrayed John. In this same regard, some scholars of the *Dead Sea Scrolls* believe that Jesus is the "wicked priest" who betrays John, the "teacher of righteousness". C.H. Dodd's (1953) interpretation of John 1:27 *Ho opiso mou erchomenos* is not "...the one who is coming after me..." but rather he translates the phrase as "he that follows me", implying "my disciple." Craveri (1967) says: "Unquestionably, Jesus was a follower of John, rather than otherwise. In one way or another...Christianity was born as a splinter from the sect of John (p. 80)."

We see hints that Jesus was a disciple of John in the strange question that Jesus puts to the Pharisees who ask him by what authority he preaches. Jesus answers by asking them a question: "The baptism of John, was it from heaven, or from men? Answer me (Mark 11:30)." At face value, the question makes little sense. What difference does it make how the Pharisees view John the Baptist vis-à-vis the authority of Jesus to preach. Looked at, now, from the point of view of Jesus as a disciple of John, the question makes a lot of sense. The Pharisees dare not say that John's authority came from God, because this admission would imply that Jesus, John's disciple, took his authority from John, whose authority came from God.

John was so powerful a figure that he had his own following, and after his death, many remained faithful to his memory (Acts, 18:24). Luke (3:15) says: "...all men mused in their hearts of John, whether he were the Christ, or not." Indeed, John was so well regarded that when Jesus asked the chief priests to tell him whether or not John's baptism was of heavenly or earthly origin, they refused to answer, partly because they were "afraid of the crowd" (Matthew 21:26). He remains the leading prophet of a group called Mandaeans, who date back to the 4th Century B.C. (Acharya, 1999) and who exist today in Southern Iran and Iraq[167]. This group believes that Jesus was a false prophet, that

---

[167] According to Acharya (1999), the Mandaeans derived from a blend of Judaism and Zoroastrianism and were a prominent Sect prior to Jesus and

Jesus Who?

Jerusalem was a wicked city, and the destruction of the Temple was God's wrath.

An alternate view of John the Baptist (e.g., Knight & Lomas, 1996) is that John represented the priestly Messiah and that Jesus represented the kingly Messiah, both of whom were foretold by the prophets. Luke (1:5) claimed that John's father belonged to the Abijah section of the Temple priesthood, thus making John eligible for the role of priestly Messiah. This dual leadership may explain the constant confusion between the two camps as to who is the true Messiah – in truth, they were both Messiahs. For the Jews to realize their goals, both Messiahs needed to be present, and it's the death of John the Baptist that appears to accelerate Jesus' own mission.

There is an oft-overlooked aspect to the relationship between John the Baptist and Jesus, and that is their competition with each other. No sooner does Jesus go to John to be baptized, then Jesus starts baptizing people himself (John 3:22). Pretty soon "all are going over to him [Jesus]" and he "was making and baptizing more disciples than John (John 4:1)." Indeed, Jesus not only steals John's followers, he steals his disciples too (John 1:35), and he claims to "have a testimony greater than John's (John 5:36)." John's concern to know whether or not Jesus is the Messiah may reflect his concern that Jesus has stolen his thunder, which would be appropriate for the Messiah but not for a competing prophet. Jesus, on the other hand, is cagey, and refuses to give a direct answer to the question, again, possibly reflecting this rivalry for souls.

Regardless of whether or not Jesus was a disciple of John, or whether they were co-Messiahs destined to change the fate of Israel, there can be no doubt that it was while being baptized by John that Jesus underwent a classic religious awakening or conversion (James, 1901). From the Gospels we know virtually nothing about Jesus' life up until this point, when at approximately 30 years of age, he decided to leave

---

John the Baptist. During the Christian era, they became lumped in with other Gnostic groups and ultimately declared heretical and persecuted. St Augustine himself was a Mandaean, who later converted to orthodox Christianity.

Galilee and make the week-long arduous journey to the River Jordan. In any event, it's clear that once having started on a similar path with John the Baptist (and the Essenes), Jesus soon found his own way. Rather than emphasize external purification, Jesus focused on the internal - "...the things which come out of a man are what defile him (Mark 7:19)." Rather than wait in one spot for followers to appear, Jesus actively sought them out. Rather than focus on the coming End Times, Jesus held that the End Times had begun, and his focus was on how people acted today. Jesus substituted a God of love and mercy for the God of fire and vengeance that John preached.

What Did Jesus Actually Say?

"These are the secret words which Jesus the Living spoke..."
(Gospel of Thomas v. 1)

Nearly 2000 years after he died, it's impossible to discover, with accuracy, the actual sayings of Jesus. There are several problems here. The first is that, as far as we know, Jesus never wrote anything down, so we are forced to rely upon "biographers" or scribes. As already noted in the first chapter, problems in translations, writer bias, political and theological considerations, confound our ability to discover what Jesus said. For example, we know that many of the sayings attributed to him in the canonical Gospels were not really sayings of Jesus, but rather were sayings that the authors of those Gospels wanted Jesus to have said because they reinforced issues that were relevant to their times. This practice is commonly called "false attribution". For example, in the canonical Gospels, Jesus is always warning his followers to beware of false prophets who came in his name. In Jesus' time there were no such people, so these warnings make no sense. But 50 to 100 years later there were many such false prophets, so the writers of the Gospels put these words into Jesus' mouth as a warning to the people of their times. In a similar vein, the constant harping on the faithlessness of his followers makes no sense when we realize the Jesus Cult was a major success and rivaled even the largest of the existing religious groups. But it does make sense when you realize that in the 2nd Century the struggling Christian

Jesus Who?

religion was having great problems with faithlessness, so the authors of the Gospels put these words in Jesus' mouth.

A second problem as we search for the true sayings of Jesus is that there is very little framework upon which to base our speculations. Jesus did not offer a complete theology, since his original impetus was to make the Jews more righteous. That is, he accepted the Law of Moses and sought not to replace the law, but to get people to conform to its requirements. Yet within his own teachings he allowed for deviations from the law, as when he preached that it was acceptable to heal on the Sabbath. Lacking a new structure, and allowing for deviations from the old structure, makes it almost impossible to decide whether or not a given saying could be attributed to Jesus. As such, we have a large number of discrepant sayings all of which are attributed to Jesus. Perhaps more than any other historical figure, Jesus' sayings contradict each other.

A third problem we encounter looking at Jesus' sayings is that the nature of the oral tradition used by the Jews at that time tended to alter the speaker's exact words so that they were easier to recall and recite (Garitte, 1957; Grant and Freedman, 1993). For example, in the *Gospel of Thomas*, Sayings 59 to 62 are all linked by the words "life", "living", and "dying" while Sayings 25 to 27 are linked by references to "eye". These linkings made it easier for the sayings to be remembered. In all probability, the oral tradition continued for nearly 100 years before the Gospels were first codified, and in all that time, who knows how many oral adaptations were made to the original sayings.

With these caveats in mind, let's begin our search for the real sayings of Jesus. Are you ready?

It was long known that there was a collection of sayings of Jesus that preceded the canonical Gospels. This long lost document was referred to by Bishop Papias and others, and ultimately given the name of the Q document by German scholars. After much research and debate, the Jesus Seminar (1993) concluded: "Eighty-two percent of the words ascribed to Jesus in the gospels were not actually spoken by him (p. 5)." What did he say? The Table on the following page contains the 10 sayings that the Jesus Seminar determined were most likely said by

Jesus, listed in rank order. Before you read the list, think for a minute about those sayings of Jesus that you remember best. Jot them down on a piece of paper. Now go ahead and see how many of these appear in the Table. A score of 2 would be average. Four right would be exceptional, and if you got more than five correct, you should be writing your own book.

Cayce in his book *What Did Jesus Really Say* (2005) provides very little about what Jesus really said, but instead focuses on the meaning of what Jesus spoke. He identifies four essential points:

1. "Love God with all your heart, soul, and mind
2. Do to others only what you would have them do to you
3. Do not judge others or you'll risk judgment upon yourself
4. Love your neighbor as yourself (p 58)."

The Jesus Seminar dealt not only with what they believed Jesus actually said, but also the manner in which he said things. Some of the common attributes they noted include:

- "cut against the social and religious grain (p. 31)."
- "surprise and shock...characteristically call for a reversal of roles or frustrate ordinary everyday expectations (p. 31)."
- "often characterized by exaggeration, humor, and paradox (p. 31)."
- "images are concrete and vivid, his sayings and parables customarily metaphorical and without explicit application (p. 32)."
- "rarely makes pronouncements or speaks about himself in the first person (p. 32)."
- "refuses[s] to give straightforward answers (p. 32)."
- "does not initiate debates or controversies. He is passive until a question is put to him, or until he or his disciples are criticized (p. 33)."

The Most Likely Sayings of Jesus

1. "Don't react violently against the one who is evil: when someone slaps you on the right cheek, turn the other as well." (Matthew 5:39)
2. "When someone wants to sue you for your shirt, let the person have your coat along with it." (Matthew 5:40)
3. "Congratulations to the poor, for to you belongs Heaven's domain." (Thomas 54)
4. "Further, when anyone conscripts you for one miles, go an extra mile." (Matthew 5:41)
5. "...love your enemies..." (Matthew 5:44)
6. "Heaven's imperial rule is like leaven which a woman took and concealed in fifty pounds of flour until it was all leavened." (Matthew 13:33)
7. "Give the emperor what belongs to the emperor, give God what belongs to God..." (Thomas 100)
8. "Give to the one who begs from you..." (Matthew 5:42)
9. "There was a man going from Jerusalem down to Jericho when he fell into the hands of robbers. They stripped him, beat him up, and went off, leaving him half dead. Now by coincidence a priest was going down that road; when he caught sight of him, he went out of his way to avoid him. In the same way, when a Levite came to the place, he took one look at him and crossed the road to avoid him. But this Samaritan who was traveling that way came to where he was and was moved to pity at the sight of him. He went up to him and bandaged his wounds, pouring olive oil and wine on them..." (Luke 10: 30-35)
10. "Congratulations you hungry! You will have a feast." (Luke 6:21)

Funk & Hoover, 1993, p. 549

Of course, the Jesus Seminar is not the "final word" on Jesus' actual sayings, and there have been many scholars who seriously question the validity of their methods as well as the accuracy of their conclusions (e.g., Witherington, 1997).

Another way to look for the actual sayings of Jesus is to go to the *Gospel of Thomas*. Discovered in 1945 at Nag Hammadi, the document is said to date from 340 A.D., based on an original text that was written between 50 and 90 A.D., making it one of the oldest documents ever discovered (Meyer, 2005). The advantage that the *Gospel of Thomas* has for studying the historical Jesus is that Thomas did not undergo the numerous changes that the canonical Gospels did, and therefore is more "original" and less "biased" than the canonical Gospels. Some authors go so far as to suggest that the *Gospel of Thomas* is the original Q document, and the *Gospel of Thomas* was used by the Jesus Seminar as part of their quest for the historical Jesus.

A great many of Jesus' sayings in the *Gospel of Thomas* can be found in a similar, if not identical, form in the Gospels of Matthew (62 of 114) and Luke (52 of 114). Between the two Gospels there are 72 similar sayings. The *Gospel of John* has only 16 similar sayings, although 9 of them are not found in either Matthew or Luke. In other words, 71% (81 of 114) of the sayings in the *Gospel of Thomas* can be found in Matthew, Luke, or John. Adding the Apocryphal Gospels (Egyptians and Hebrews) raises the number to 75% (85 of 114). Since so much of what is in Thomas can be found elsewhere, it's interesting to note what is <u>only</u> in Thomas. There's a selection on the next page.

While these sayings do not appear in the other Gospels, they are not completely without foundation. For example, referents for verse 24 can be found in Ecclesiastes (7:28) and verse 26 in Leviticus (19:17-18). Moreover, similar sayings appear later in the works of Paul (v. 30, 43, 54), Origen (v. 74, 82), Clement of Alexandria (v. 28), and in the *Pistis Sophia* (v. 24), suggesting that these secret sayings that are not taken up by the Gospels were, nonetheless, sufficiently well known to survive centuries later.

Secret Sayings of Jesus in the Gospel of Thomas

6. "Blessed is the lion which man will eat, that the lion may become a man; and cursed is the man whom the lion will eat, that the lion will become a man."
24. "I will choose you, one from a thousand and two from ten thousand, and they will stand because they are a single one."
26. "Love your brother as your soul; keep him like the apple of your eye."
28. "If you do not fast to the world, you will not find the kingdom; if you do not truly keep the Sabbath, you will not see the Father."
30. "If the flesh came into existence for the sake of the spirit, [it is] a wonder; but if the spirit [came into existence] for the sake of the body, it is a wonder of [wonders]; but I wonder at how [this] great wealth has dwelt in this poverty."
43. "Come into being as you pass away."
53. "You have abandoned the one who lives before your eyes, and you have spoken concerning the dead."
54. "If it [circumcision] were profitable, their father would have begotten them circumcised from their mother. But the true circumcision in the Spirit has found complete usefulness."
71. "When you beget in yourselves him whom you have, he will save you. If you do not have him within yourselves, he whom you do not have within yourselves will kill you."
74. "O Lord, there are many about the well, but there are none in the well."
80. "He who has known the world has found the body, but he who has found the body, of him the world is not worthy."
82. "He who is near me is near the fire, ad he who is far from me is far from the kingdom."
83. "The images appear to man, and the light which is within them is hidden in the image of the light of the Father. He will be revealed, and his image is hidden through his light."
87. "Wretched is the body which hangs upon a body, and wretched is the soul which hangs upon them both."

Grant and Freedman, 1993, pp.125-183

Yet despite its credentials, the *Gospel of Thomas* shares with the traditional texts the same problem of trying to discern what Jesus really said. In the end, I am inclined to agree with the great German Jesus scholar Rudolf Bultmann (1925) who said "…none of his words can be regarded as purely authentic (p. 33)."

Summary

Most scholars believe that Jesus' ministry was brief, from one to three years, that his following was extremely small, and predominately male. Our research, however, concludes that it was more than 10 years in length when we date the start of his ministry from his baptism by John in the mid 20s to his death in 36 A.D. Moreover, we uncovered evidence that Jesus had thousands of followers and at its peak his group was larger than the Pharisees, Sadducees, or the Essenes, which explains the reluctance of the Jewish authorities to openly oppose him. In addition, our research indicates that women played a much more substantial role in Jesus' ministry, and in fact, the women were far better and more devoted to Jesus than were the men. Indeed, a careful reading of the Gospels shows the male disciples to be relatively dumb and faithless.

With respect to Jesus' miracles and exorcisms, we can recognize their existence, however, they add nothing to the claims of some supporters that he was the Messiah or that his origins were divine. Most of his miracles can be explained by non-supernatural means, often as a result of understanding the nature of the language and customs of his time and his particular sub-culture. In any event, his achievements were not extraordinary when compared to many of his contemporaries, such as Honi the Circledrawer and Simon Magus, to name a few. That he had skills in these areas, however, should not be denied, but it may indicate that he believed he was possessed by a spirit, which was the popular way in Jesus' time to conceive of the special gifts of healing and prophecy that Jesus displayed.

For all intents and purposes, Jesus appears to have been a disciple of John the Baptist. Just as John rebelled against the teachings of the Essenes and established his own practice and philosophy, Jesus too, in his own time, rebelled against John's teaching and brought the

Jesus Who?

Essene concerns to the masses. Judging from our best estimates as to the true sayings of Jesus, he appears to have been concerned with issues of brotherly love and obedience to the Mosaic Law, tempered by a concern with the broadest spectrum of humanity.

This is one of the earliest depictions of a crucifixion, from the 2nd Century, in a piece of wall graffiti near the Palatine Hill in Rome. It shows the victim on a T shaped cross.

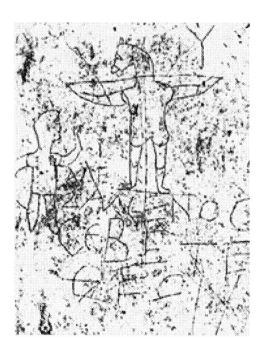

CHAPTER EIGHT

Death

The story of Jesus' death occupies the largest single part of the Gospels. In the *Gospel of Mark*, the Passion week (from Latin *patior* meaning "to suffer") occupies half of the Gospel. Some scholars believe that what occupied a single week in the Gospels actually took place over several months (Chilton, 2000; Cohn 1963). Others argue that most of the Passion account and language were lifted from the Old Testament, and they question whether it happened at all (Brown, 1994; Shorto, 1997). Indeed, the lack of any mention in the epistles of Paul also raises the issue of the validity of the Passion events. Moreover, the lack of agreement between the four Gospels on significant events during the week (e.g., when the Last Supper occurred, Jesus' last words, whether or not Jesus saw Aninas or Herod, etc) raises our suspicions that the Passion Week was not an historical event.

Having raised the issue of the veracity of the Passion Week, let's examine what we do have. Are you ready?

What Was Jesus Accused of?

> "And the chief priests accused him of many things." Mark 15:3

During his long career, Jesus was accused of many things. Here's a list of the major complaints by category:

Magic/Demon Possession

- magician (Mark 27:63)
- Egyptian magician (Celsus)
- "doer of evil" (Babylonian Talmud)
- possessed of a demon (John 7:20)
- possessed of Beelzebub, prince of demons (Mark 3:22; Luke 11:14-15)
- possessed of Satan (Mark 3:23)
- possessing the spirit of John the Baptist (Mark 6:16)
- possessing the spirit of Elijah (Mark 6:15)
- Samaritan (i.e., a magician like Simon Magus) (John 8:48)
- unclean spirit (Mark 3:30)

Anti-Social Acts

- beggar (Celsus)
- fugitive (Celsus)
- bandit (Celsus)
- eating human flesh (Typhos)
- nocturnal orgies (Typhos)
- invented the virgin birth story (Celsus)
- insane (Mark 3:21; John 10:20)
- sedition (i.e., claiming to be a King) (John 18:37)
- prohibiting the payment of tribute to the emperor (Luke 23:2)
- stirs up the people (Luke 23:2)
- deceiving the crowd (John 7:12)
- criminal (John 18:30)

Blasphemous Practices

- godless and lawless and unholy things (Trypho)
- sinner (John 9:24)
- blasphemy (John 10:33)

Jesus Who?

- eating with sinners and tax collectors (Mark 2:16)
- neglect of fasts (Mark 7:5)
- working on the Sabbath (Mark 3:2; Luke 6:1; John 5:9)
- neglect of purity rules (Mark 7:5)
- doer of evil (John 18:30)
- claiming he came down from heaven (John 6:42)
- made himself a son of a God (John 19:7)
- making himself God (Mark 2:7; John 10:33)
- making himself "equal to God" (John 5:18)
- perverting the nation (Luke 23:2)
- saying that he himself is the Messiah, a king (Luke 23:2)
- claiming that he could "destroy the temple" (Matthew 26:61)
- "performed magic, enticed, and led astray Israel." (Sanhedrin 43a)

From this long list of complaints, only four surfaced in the final hours. Before the Jewish authorities he was accused of blasphemy by claiming to be the Son of God (Luke 22:71), and before Pilate he was accused of "...perverting our nation, and forbidding to give tribute to Caesar, and saying that he himself is Christ a king (Luke 23:3)."

Why Was Jesus Arrested?

"'You have heard his blasphemy. What is your decision?' All of them condemned him as deserving death." (Mark 14:64)

Jesus was arrested in Jerusalem while attending the Passover season. Passover is the celebration of the Jews flight out of Egypt, and specifically refers to God's advice to the Jews to smear the blood of a lamb on their front door so that he would "pass over" their homes while he sought out the first born of the Egyptians to slay them in the night. Passover was one of the three pilgrim festivals, the others being Shavuot (Pentecost or Weeks; early summer) and Sukkoth (Tabernacles or Booths; autumn) requiring all male Jews to travel to Jerusalem and participate in the festivities (and pay dues to the Temple). In some senses, Passover was the equivalent of the 4th of

July or Bastille Day, and so came Jesus into Jerusalem along with his entourage that included at least two Zealots (Judas and Simon). Festivals in Jerusalem could be problematic. Josephus recounts more than 400 riots and disruptions in the 150 years preceding Jesus' birth, meaning, on average, there was one major riot per festival per year. Because of this, the Romans "beefed" up their garrison there in anticipation of any trouble. 36 A.D. was a particularly raucous year and tensions were high. The recent crop failure had added to the woes of the citizenry, and civil unrest intensified the mood. Only one year earlier, John the Baptist had been slain, and the smell of rebellion was in the air. Klinghoffer (2005) describes the situation as "a powder keg with everyone milling around armed to the teeth (p.74)."

For whatever his reasons were, Jesus took a provocative stand. Not only was he accompanied by his Zealots, he stage-managed the event to fulfill the prophecy of Zechariah (9:9) that said: "Shout aloud, O daughter of Jerusalem! Lo your king comes to you; triumphant and victorious is he, humble and riding on an ass..." To add emphasis to the prophecy, he has his Galileans gather palm branches, which was the traditional Jewish symbol of victory over the enemy (1 Maccabeas 13:49-51; Revelations 7:9). As he entered, the crowd yelled, "Blessed is the King..."

The *Gospel of John* explains the motivation for having Jesus arrested. Following the incident with Lazarus, "...the chief priests and the Pharisees called a meeting of the council, and said, "What are we to do? This man is performing many signs [miracles]. If we let him go like this, everyone will believe in him, and the Romans will come and destroy both our holy place [temple] and our nation." The High Priest Caiaphas suggests: "...it is better for you to have one man die for the people than to have the whole nation destroyed (47-50)."

The quote from Caiaphas is reinforced from our own research that indicates Jesus' followers numbered in the thousands and rivaled/exceeded the other religious sects. Any coordinated movement by so large a force would undoubtedly bring down the wrath of the Romans. Indeed, some 30 years later, the acts of a much smaller group of rebels provoked the Romans to destroy the Temple in Jerusalem.

Jesus Who?

If we know the motivation for why Jesus was arrested, the next question is – What were the charges? Basically, there were two sets of charges; one before the Sanhedrin (blasphemy) and three before Pilate (perverting the Jewish nation, refusing tribute to Caesar, and claiming to be a King).

The *Gospel of John* states that Jesus was brought before Pilate because the High Priest Caiaphas claimed: "It is not lawful for us to put any man to death (81:32)." This is incorrect. Jewish law provided for the death penalty and in fact it was used on many occasions (Cohn, 1963). In any event, once before Pilate, the religious charges of blasphemy were laid aside as were the other two charges, and what remained was the claim that Jesus was the King of Jews. Within the framework of Roman law, such a claim was "tantamount to insurrection and high treason" and was subject to capital punishment as *crimen laesae maistatis*, i.e., causing injury to the emperor (Cohn, 1963, p. 171).

Was Jesus Beaten?

"Some began to spit on him, to blindfold him, and to strike him, saying to him 'Prophesy!' The guards also took him over and beat him."
(Mark 14:65)

Mel Gibson notwithstanding, there is very little evidence that Jesus suffered much before crucifixion. For example, Luke says that: "now the men who were holding Jesus began to mock him and beat him (22:63)." Matthew says that: "and after flogging Jesus, he handed him over to be crucified (27:26)." John notes that Jesus was "flogged" (19:1) and that the guards were "striking him on the face (19:3)." Mark's description is the harshest – "some began to spit on him, to blindfold him, and to strike him, saying to him, 'Prophesy'. The guards also took him over and beat him (14:65)." Later, he notes: "So Pilate, wishing to satisfy the crowd, released Barabbas for them; and after flogging Jesus, he handed him over to be crucified (15:15)."

Needless to say, being struck in the face, beaten, and flogged is not very gentle treatment. In those days there were two types of instruments used to flog hapless victims – the *flagella* which was an ordinary leather strap, and the *flagra*, which was an iron chain with spikes made of iron or bone. The more severe instrument, the flagra, was not in general use and was reserved for slaves who committed heinous crimes. Most likely Jesus would have been punished with the *flagella* (or strap) since there is no indication that the punishment in this case was life threatening or even that he was seriously injured as a result[168]. Indeed, the *Gospel of John* indicates that Jesus was "carrying the cross by himself (19:17)" which clearly implies that he was not injured, and none of the other Gospel writers who claim that Simon of Cyrene carried the cross (Luke 23:26; Mark 15:21; Matthew: 27:32), indicate that he carried the cross because Jesus was unable to do so. Moreover, while on the cross, Jesus was conscious and sufficiently self-possessed to carry on conversations with the other two victims, address his mother and inquire about her future treatment, etc. Obviously his physical punishment had not incapacitated him.

In an extensive analysis of the laws and customs surrounding the trial and death of Jesus, Israeli Supreme Court Justice Haim Cohn concluded: "if Jesus suffered, it was from the taunts rather than from the blows, from the assault rather on his dignity than on his body (p. 202)." He continues: "no dependable tradition or information exists that there were any aftereffects, wounds, or other external injury...(p. 202)."

Had Jesus' punishment been great, the New Testament writers would surely have noted it. For example, compare those descriptions of Jesus' treatment with the treatment of Polycarp: "...their skin was ripped to shreds by whips, revealing the very anatomy of their flesh, down to the inner veins and arteries...(2:2)." Clearly, Jesus' punishment did not rise to these standards. Cohn affirms this position.

---

[168] There are cases reported in Josephus in which a victim of flogging died during the process, although these cases were rare. As a prelude to crucifixion, flogging was designed to make the victim less likely to resist, and the extent of the flogging was left to the Roman Lictors to decide. Given Jesus' demeanor, it undoubtedly did not call for extensive flogging to get Jesus to be subservient.

He notes: "...if the evangelists did not describe the pitiable condition of a scourged Jesus, it was because there was none, and that he was in fact unscathed, his outward appearance unchanged (p. 202)."

While there is no evidence that Jesus was harshly treated, there is some evidence to the contrary, that his treatment was stellar. The *Gospel of Nicodemus,* dated to the 4th Century[169], claims that Pilate instructed his soldiers: "Let Jesus be brought with gentleness (I, 1-2)." Most scholars dismiss the validity of this document, as shall we, however, it is worth noting. But Cohn (1963), in his exhaustive examination of the trial of Jesus, noted: "not only were Jesus' hands not bound to the beams of the cross, but he had not even to bear it himself[170] (p. 201)." In addition, he noted: "not only was he not divested in nakedness, but he was given his own garments when led to the place of crucifixion...[and]...the usual beatings on the way were not his portion either (p. 207)." He concluded: "the soldiers must have taken pity on him (p. 201)."

Was Jesus Crucified?

"So Pilate, wishing to satisfy the crowd, released Barabbas for them: and after flogging Jesus, he handed him over to be crucified."
(Mark 15:15)

Crucifixion in Jesus' Time

Crucifixion was a fairly common form of execution, dating as far back as the 6th Century B.C., and used by Greeks, Persians, Egyptians, Carthaginians, and, of course, Romans. The methods varied from culture to culture, and from time to time. Most scholars believe it

---

[169] Mention of the *Acts of Pilate*, that constitute the bulk of the *Gospel of Nicodemus*, was referred to centuries earlier by Justin Martyr, Tertullian, and Eusebius; however, the earliest copy of the document is traditionally ascribed to 425 A.D.

[170] The normal procedure would have been to bind the hands to the cross and whip the victim while he carried the cross.

evolved from the Persian practice of impalement. As practiced by the Romans at the time of Jesus, Gardner (2001) says:

> "Crucifixion was both punishment and execution: death by torturous ordeal extended over a number of days. First the victim's outstretched arms were strapped by the wrists to a beam which was then hoisted into place horizontally across an upright post. Sometimes the hands were transfixed by nails as well, but nails alone would have been useless. Suspended with all his weight on his arms, a man's lungs would be compressed and he would die fairly quickly through suffocation. To prolong the agony, chest pressure was relieved by fixing the victim's feet to the upright post. Supported in this manner a man could live for many days, possibly even a week or more (p. 65)."

Prior to crucifixion, the Romans would "soften up" the victims by scourging. This made the victims more compliant. Following death, it was the custom to leave the victims hanging there, to be consumed by vultures and other animals. For Jews this was especially humiliating, since their religion prescribed immediate burial.

While this is how crucifixion was carried out, it's noteworthy to consider whether Jesus was crucified at all. Although most accounts of Jesus' death involve crucifixion, there are a few that do not, and some that claim that while he was crucified, he didn't die on the cross. We will explore all these theories.

Was it Jesus on the Cross?

Among the claims that it wasn't Jesus on the cross, the Qur'an says: "...they killed him not, nor crucified him, but so it was made to appear to them.[171] (Sura 4:157)." The Mandaeans, an ancient sect who worshipped John the Baptist as their Messiah, claimed that it was Jesus' brother, Judas Thomas, who was crucified, and Jesus spent the rest of his life impersonating his dead brother (Roberts, 1995). Indeed, Gnostic beliefs spoke about the twin aspects of our *eidolon* or ego as

---

[171] The Qur'an claims that it was Simon of Cyrene who was actually crucified, while Jesus watched from a hiding place.

the "real" self and the "false" self, and it was believed that the "false" self (aka the "evil" twin) had to die so that the real self could achieve gnosis or knowledge. Thus, among the Canaanites, the evil brother Mot dies[172], just as among the Egyptians it is the evil brother Set who dies. The stories about Jesus being replaced by his twin brother follow this line of reasoning.

The Samaritans believed that it was Simon Magus who died on the cross (Acharya, 1999), as does the Australian scholar Barbara Thiering (1992) who ascribed the subsequent appearances of the "resurrected" Jesus to real-life encounters. Bloom (2005) conjectured:

> "I suspect that, as lore has it, he had the wisdom to escape execution, and then made his way to Hellenistic northern India...where some traditions place his grave (p. 18)."

The 2nd Century historian Basilides of Alexandria also believed that Simon was a substitute, and a 2nd Century Coptic tractate (part of the Nag Hammadi findings) entitled *The Second Treatise of the Great Seth* that professed to be the word of Jesus also indicated that Simon was Jesus' substitute (Gardner, 2001). Here is a section from that text:

> "They hatched a plot against me, to counter the destruction of their error and foolishness, but I did not give in to them as they had planned. I was not hurt at all. Though they punished me, I did not die in actuality but only in appearance...They nailed their man to their death. Their thoughts did not perceive me since they were deaf and blind....As for me, they saw me and punished me, but someone else, their father, drank the gall and the vinegar, it was not I. They were striking me with a scourge, but someone else, Simon, bore the cross on his shoulder. Someone else wore the crown of thorns...I was laughing at their ignorance (v. 55 – 57)."

Thus, there is a considerable body of opinion that it was not Jesus on the cross and that someone else took his place. Dismissing the stories

---

[172] Mot's last words to his Father are: "My God, My God, why have you forsaken me?" Quoted in Freke & Gandy, 2001, p. 122.

about Simon, the only likely candidate for this would have been his "twin" brother, but there is very little evidence that Jesus had a twin.

If you are not a lover of conspiracy stories, there is another explanation for the accounts that claim someone else took Jesus' place on the cross. We see it most clearly in the *Book of Baruch*, a 2nd Century Gnostic text best known from the refutation by Hippolytus in the 3rd Century (Meyer, 2005):

> "Naas also wanted to deceive Jesus, but he was unable to do so, because Jesus remained faithful to Baruch. Naas was furious that he could not lead him astray; and he had him crucified. But Jesus left the body of Eden on the cross and ascended to the Good. Jesus said to Eden 'Woman, here is your son' – the psychical and earthly person – and he yielded the spirit into the hands of the father and ascended to the Good (v. 31-32)."

A careful reading of this passage indicates that by leaving his body and ascending to heaven, Jesus was no longer on the cross, only his physical body. In this way, they did not crucify Jesus, only his body. We see this same theme in the *Gospel of Philip* – "He spoke these words on the cross, for he had left that place (v. 68)." It's easy to see how such subtleties can result in a new story in which it is not Jesus at all who goes up on the cross. Now re-read the passage from *The Second Treatise of the Great Seth* quoted above and see if a similar meaning is not inherent therein.

For all intents and purposes, then, it's likely that the person who was punished was Jesus. He may have attained gnosis in accepting his fate, in which case, it would have been his "false" self that died. Or his spirit may have left his body and so it was only his corporeal self that died. But in either case, it was probably Jesus in the flesh who suffered.

History of the Latin Cross

The traditional or Latin Cross has a history far older than the crucifixion of Jesus. It was the symbol of the God Tammuz in ancient Chaldea, and it can be found on ancient carvings on the breasts of Egyptian mummies and in the hands of deceased pharaohs, indicating their coming rebirth. In slightly altered form, as an ankh, with the top center piece of the cross enlarged into a circle, it symbolized eternal life. The ankh was a symbol adopted by the early Christians and was in use through the Middle Ages. The Latin Cross was rarely used, and only achieved prominence after the 3rd century. It was only in 692 A.D. that the church declared, through the Trullan Council, that the figure of Jesus on the Latin Cross was the official symbol of Christianity.

Among the ancient Hebrews, the Latin Cross was equivalent to the letter Taw, the last letter of the alphabet, and also carried the name that meant "mark" or "sign". It was used for thousands of years and even appears in Qumran documents. On occasions it's tilted to resemble the Greek letter Chi or the Roman letter X. In the Old Testament, the Taw appears two times (Job 31:35; Ezk. 9:4-6), most notably in Ezekiel where it was the symbol used by the Jews to denote the righteous in Jerusalem who were to be protected. The Qumran documents refer to this passage in talking about the return of the Messiah and the last judgment, when the Taw again would be used to mark the righteous for salvation.

OK – What Kind of a Cross?

If we assume for a moment that Jesus was crucified on a cross, can we at least agree upon what type of a cross it was, had he, in fact, been crucified. Most scholars agree that if Jesus was crucified, it would have been on a **T** shaped cross (called a *Tau or* Saint Anthony's Cross or *crux commissa*) rather than the traditional cross (called the Latin Cross or *crux immissa*). The reasons for this are obvious to anyone who has ever tried to build a cross: it is time-consuming and requires a reasonable amount of skill. To construct a cross heavy enough to bear the weight of a person, you have to carve the two wooden shapes so that where they intersect, each supports the other. Simply nailing the two pieces together will not sustain the weight of a person. And if one of the shapes is carved too deeply, the entire shaft will break. On the other hand, the Tau is simple. You place the vertical pole *(stripes)* in the ground, place the horizontal pole *(patibulum)* centered on top, nail them into place, and gravity does the rest. Simple mechanics dictates that the Tau was used instead of the Latin Cross. Indeed, the earliest depiction of a crucifixion comes from the 2nd Century in a piece of wall graffiti near the Palantine Hill in Rome (See page 182). Similarly, all early Christian and Coptic images of the crucifixion (e.g., Sardonyx in Munich, Cornelian in the British Museum) show the Tau.

There is little doubt that if Jesus was crucified, it was not on a Latin Cross. It may have been a T-shaped cross, since this was what was commonly used by the Romans, or he may simply have been staked out on a single pole. Or he may not have been crucified on a cross at all, and the folklore and customs of associating the *Taw* with the salvation of the righteous may have been transformed into a story about crucifixion on a cross.

When was Jesus Crucified?

> *"It was nine o'clock in the morning when they crucified him."*
> (Mark 15:25)

Jesus was said to have been crucified at 9 am on Friday, March 30, in the year 36 A.D. There is a long and complicated method for measuring the date of Jesus' death, involving the mixture of solar and lunar timetables used by the Jews in association with their holidays.[173] The dates most commonly used are April 7, 30 and April 3, 33 because these date correspond to a Friday that matches the 14/15 month of Nisan date suggested by the Gospels. However, the other date that matches this same conjuncture is March 30, 36, and since

---

[173] See Meier (2001) for a complete discussion.

Jesus Who?

Jesus died after John the Baptist, whose death can be dated after 34 A.D., the date – March 30, 36 is our date.

According to Mark "It was nine o'clock in the morning when they crucified him…(Mark 15:25-27)." John claims it was noon (19:14). At 3 pm he was taken down. It was the beginning of Passover, according to Mark. The *Gospel of John* claims that it happened on Passover eve.

But let's back up, for a moment, and consider what is said to have happened in these critical 12 hours, between the last supper and his crucifixion. Here is a summary of the sequence of events, using Mark's chronology as a basis, and adding, as appropriate, the other Gospels.

1. In the evening, Jesus and the disciples had their "last supper". Among other things,

    - they shared in the bread and wine,
    - discussed Jesus' imminent betrayal ,
    - had a lengthy discussion about love (John 13:12 to 17:25),
    - sang a hymn, and
    - Jesus took time to wash each disciples' feet (John 13:5).

2. They journey to the Mount of Olives, which is about ½ mile high, and ½ mile East of Jerusalem. They pray. Jesus forecasts that they will desert him, including Peter, who will deny him (Jesus) three times before "the cock crows twice."

3. Jesus takes Peter, James, and John, and they journey to Gethsemane to pray. The Garden of Gethsemane stood just outside the walls of Jerusalem, near Herod's Temple, at the bottom of the Mount of Olives. The disciples fall asleep.

    - While still at Gethsemane, Judas and "a crowd with swords and clubs" arrive. They question Jesus. He is arrested. There is a scuffle and they cut off the ear of "the slave of the high priest". Jesus heals the ear with a touch (Luke 22:51). A "certain young man" who was following Jesus is grabbed by the authorities, but he escapes, wearing nothing.

4. Jesus is taken to Annas, father-in-law of Caiaphas. Annas interrogates him, then sends him to Caiaphas. (John 18:13-24)

5. Jesus is taken from Gethsemane to the house of the High Priest, Caiaphas, where "the chief priests and the whole council" are assembled. The House of Caiaphas is in the Upper City, near Herod's Palace, more than a mile from Gethsemane.

    - Many people give testimony, but there are large disagreements.
    - The High Priest interrogates Jesus.
    - Jesus is blindfolded, spat upon, and beaten.
    - Observing this, Peter denies he knows Jesus, as the cock crows.

6. In the morning, the chief priests consult with the elders, Scribes, and the council.

    - Jesus is bound, led away, and turned over to Pilate. Pilate's house is near the Pool of Bethesda, at the Eastern end of the second North wall, about one mile from Caiaphas' House.

7. Pilate, at the governor's headquarters/palace, interrogates Jesus. Discovering that he is a Galilean, he sends him to Herod (Luke 23:7). Herod's Palace is on the West side, beyond the Gennath Gate, about one mile from Pilate's House.

8. Herod interrogates Jesus and sends him back to Pilate (Luke 23:8-11).

9. Pilate talks with the priests and council members (Luke 23:13-16).

- Pilate asks the crowd if he should release Jesus or Barabbas. They vote for Barabbas.
- Pilate releases Barabbas
- Jesus is flogged.
- Jesus is taken into the courtyard, stripped, mocked, and a crown of thorns is placed on his head.

10. Jesus is taken from Pilate's House to Golgotha[174] to be crucified. No one is sure where Golgotha was. Asimov (1968) speculates that it was "just outside Jerusalem" (p. 893) and Perkins (1988) places it along the Via Dolorosa, just past the Ephraim Gates (See Heb. 13:12), about ½ mile from Pilate's House.

- Along the way, Simon of Cyrene is compelled to carry his cross.
- Two "criminals" are "led away to be put to death with" Jesus (Luke 23:32).

11. At Golgotha

- Jesus is offered wine mixed with myrrh. He declines.
- He is stripped and the guards cast lots for his clothes.
- He is crucified.

If you begin to set a timeline for all these activities, you'll see that it's impossible to accomplish all of this, and still have Jesus on the cross at 9 am. Even if the evening's activities could have taken place in the time allotted, certainly the daytime activities could not. At that time of the year, in Jerusalem, the sun would rise about 6 am. That leaves three hours for:

- the council to discuss their actions among themselves (at least 30 minutes),

---

[174] Golgotha comes from the Hebrew *Gol-Goath* which means "the hill of Goath". It was said to refer to "the place of the skull." In Latin, the word for skull is *calva*, and Golgotha was called *Calvariae locus*, which in English became Calvary.

- sent from Caiaphas House to Pilate's Headquarters – one mile (60 minutes),
- interrogated by Pilate (15 minutes),
- sent to Herod's Palace from Pilate's HQ – one mile (60 minutes),
- interrogated by Herod (5 minutes),
- sent back to Pilate's HQ from Herod's Palace – one mile (60 minutes),
- Pilate and the council debate Jesus' fate (15 minutes),
- Pilate arranges for Barabbas to be brought before the crowd, he explains the holiday exemption, and the crowd chooses Barabbas (30 minutes),
- Jesus is flogged, stripped, redressed, crowned, etc. while the two criminals are gathered to accompany him (30 minutes),
- Jesus leaves Pilate's HQ and carries the cross to Golgotha, and is helped along the way by Simon (60 minutes), and
- At Golgotha, Jesus is offered drink that he declines, he is stripped, and nailed to the cross. The cross is placed upright (30 minutes).

Using these minimal estimates, the total time required would exceed six hours. These minimal estimates assume that Pilate is awake and dressed and prepared to receive guests at 6:45 am, and Herod is similarly in governing mode at 7:15 am. Unlikely in both cases; but possible. It assumes also that the prison officials can easily find and extricate Barabbas and the two criminals. Also unlikely, but possible. Finally, it assumes that the discussions within the council, and between the council and Pilate, and the council and Herod, took place in a very short period of time. Again, unlikely, but possible. In other words, under the best of circumstances, it's impossible for these activities to take place within three hours.

The point of this exercise is to show that while the Gospels say that Jesus was crucified at 9 am, it's unlikely that this was the actual time. In fact, it's unlikely that all these events happened in the framework proposed by the Gospel writers. Chilton (2000) notes: "The Gospel's technique of compacting episodes tightly together is never stronger than when they relate the events leading up to Jesus' capture, and what awaited him at Pilate's hands (p. 248)." Indeed, Chilton estimates that these events occurred over months, rather than in a single day. In a similar vein, Cohn (1963) maintains that a proper Jewish trial would have taken at least a month for the gathering of witnesses and testimony.

Was There a Last Supper?

And he said unto them, With desire I have desired to eat this passover with you before I suffer." Luke 22:15

Mark (14:22-25) and John (13:17) both indicate that prior to his arrest, Jesus had a last supper with his disciples, thus giving Leonardo an opportunity to work his magic. However, the last supper is not mentioned in the other Gospels nor in the *Gospel of Thomas* nor in the *Didache*. It is mentioned in the *Gospel of the Hebrews*, which claims that Jesus' brother, James, was also present.

The idea of a Last Supper is only one of the many threads in the Gospels that center on food. Here's a list of some of the major roles that food plays in the Gospels...

- Jesus' most well known miracle involves feeding thousands of people (Mark 6:35-44).
- The Lord's Prayer asks, first and foremost, to "give us this day our daily bread... (Matthew 6:9)."
- The *Gospel of John* begins with Jesus turning water into wine (John 2:9).
- Jesus is criticized for eating and drinking with sinners and tax collectors (Matthew 11:19).
- Jesus is anointed, in preparation for his death, during a meal (Luke 7:37).
- The risen Jesus eats a meal with his disciples (Luke 24:42).
- According to Jesus, the first criteria used by God to accept people into his kingdom is "...for I was hungry, and you gave me food...(Matthew 25:31)."

Did the Last Supper exist? Of course. Everyone has a Last Supper. The trick is in knowing when. In that sense, Jesus' eschatology is very apt. He urged his followers that the End Times were near and they needed to be prepared at any moment for the Kingdom of God. For Jesus, every supper was a last supper.

How Old Was Jesus When He Died?

There are claims that Jesus escaped his execution and lived to the ripe old ages of 106 and even 120. Putting these aside for the moment, if we accept the common theory that Jesus died as a result of his crucifixion or hanging, there are several ways to date his death. It can be dated with respect to the central players (i.e., Pilate, the High Priest Caiaphas, and John the Baptist) for whom there is a reasonable amount of historical information. Or it can be dated with respect to the Gospel text, or even with respect to other canonical publications. Hopefully, all three ways coincide.

Historical Data

The best way to date the death of Jesus is to look for the key players in his death drama, about whom there is considerable information, and to establish the context surrounding Jesus' death. We begin by acknowledging that Jesus' death followed the death of John the Baptist, and occurred while Caiaphas was High Priest and while Pilate was Prefect. We know that John the Baptist met his gruesome death in 35 A.D.,[175] Caiaphas was deposed by Lucius Vitellius, the legate of Syria, in 36 A.D. and Pilate was recalled to Rome at the end of 36 A.D[176]. Ipso facto, Jesus must have been crucified in the year 36 A.D. Having been born in 6 B.C. and having died in 36 A.D. means that Jesus was in his 40s when he died, probably 42 years old.

The Gospel Record

---

[175] Schonfield, 1974, p. 51.
[176] Josephus, *Antiquities*, XVIII, 90, vol. ix. p. 65.

Jesus Who?

Further proof that Jesus was in his 40s when he died comes directly from the *Gospel of John*. Jesus is discussing the destruction of the temple and he says: "Destroy this temple, and in three days I will raise it up." The Jews then said, "This temple has been under construction for 46 years, and you will raise it up in days?' But he was speaking of the temple of his body (John 2:20-21)." John points out that later, when he was crucified, Jesus' disciples remembered his prophecy of the three days; however, no one seemed to recall the 46 years. Taken at his word, Jesus was clearly saying that he was 46 years old, and that when he died, he would resurrect in three days.

We find further proof that Jesus is in his 40s from the *Gospel of John*. Jesus is in a Temple, close to the Mount of Olives, talking to the Scribes and Pharisees. The subject turns to Abraham, and the "Jews" ask Jesus: "You are not yet 50 years old, and have you seen Abraham? (8:57)."Jesus answers: "...before Abraham was, I am", but the important thing to observe here is that the questioners described Jesus as not yet being 50. Were he in his 20s or 30s, they would have chosen a different year, but by saying that he was not yet 50, they clearly identified him as being in his forties.

Other Christian Sources

The noted Christian Irenaeus (130-202 A.D.), Bishop of Lyon, who was a disciple of Polycarp (who claimed to be a disciple of John the Evangelist), wrote in his classic work *Against Heresies* that Jesus was nearly 50 years old when he died (2:22:6).

All this evidence shows a significant divergence from the commonly accepted idea that Jesus was in his 30s when he died. All three methods used to date the year of Jesus' death suggest 36 A.D., and given his birth in 6 B.C., we come up with an age of 42. It also suggests that Jesus' ministry was significantly longer than the one to three years that are traditionally attributed to it, because if he began his ministry when he was about 30, and he died at 42, his ministry was 12 years, not one or three.

How Was Jesus Crucified?

According to Cicero (106-43 B.C.), crucifixion was "the worst and cruelest" form of torture (*Contra Verres*, II, 5-14). The victim was attached to two pieces of wood (shaped in a T, called a Tau or Saint Anthony's cross), by ropes[177], and left to hang. Death was by suffocation, which could be delayed by pressing one's feet against the titled ledge (*sedula* in Latin, *pegma* in Greek) midway down the post. If the victim survived too long, his legs were broken, preventing him from pressing his feet for support, and rushing on the eventual suffocation. Typically, victims were left on the cross as food for wild beasts and birds of prey (Hengel, 1977), and typically "the agony of the crucified never ended in less than two days (Craveri, 1967, p. 418)."

We have only one corpse from this era who shows the effects of crucifixion. He was 1 of 35 individuals discovered in 1968 at Giv'at ha Mivtar, in northeastern Jerusalem. The adult male had been 5'5" tall. His arms had been hung to the cross, not nailed, and his feet had been nailed to a small olive wood plaque set behind his heel. His legs had not been broken.

The earliest artifacts show people being hung from the cross, not nailed. A brown jasper gem, dated from 200 A.D., shows the victim hung by his wrists. Neither his hands nor his feet are nailed. An equally ancient artifact, scribbled on the walls of the Imperial Palace in Palatine Hill in Rome between 193 and 235 A.D., shows a crucified figure also hung, not nailed (Morton, 1977). A ring seal amulet dating from the 3rd Century depicting Dionysus crucified also omits any signs of being nailed (Freke & Gandy, 1999).

Tradition says that Jesus was crucified by driving nails into his hands and feet. Jesus' legs weren't broken, as were the legs of his unfortunate companions[178], probably because of the long-standing belief that resurrection was only possible for someone whose bones

---

[177] Cohn (1963) – "it was normal Roman practice to bind the convict to the cross by ropes, not to nail him to it (p. 219)."

[178] Called "robbers" by Mark and Matthew, "criminals" by Luke, and "others" by John. At least they all agreed there were two.

had not been broken. Jesus was not left on the cross, but taken down after a few hours.

Neither Mark nor Matthew mentions anything about Jesus being nailed to the cross. Nor does Luke, however, he has a passage where the risen Jesus says to his disciples: "Look at my hands and my feet; see that it is I myself. Touch me and see; for a ghost does not have flesh and bones as you see that I have (24:39)." Nothing here refers to wounds. John's description of the crucifixion also omits any reference to being nailed, but again, as in Luke, the risen Jesus "...showed them his hands and his side (20:20)." It is only when Thomas says: "Unless I see the mark of the nails in his hands, and put my finger in the mark of the nails and my hand in his side, I will not believe (20:25)." What can we infer from this? The earliest Gospels omit and references whatsoever about being nailed, and it's only mentioned specifically in John, and only then for Jesus' hands. The fact is, however, that John's version is suspect, because he introduces the wound in the side along with the wound in the hands. Only eye witnesses to the crucifixion would have known that Jesus' side was pierced, and according to John, Thomas was not among them (19:25) nor was he in attendance when Jesus first appeared to them (20:24). Hence, he should have had no knowledge of the wound in the side.

In any event, while it was not uncommon for someone to be nailed to the cross, nailing through the hands was rarely done because the composition of the hands was not sufficient to support a person's body weight. Thus, nailing through the hands would result in a person's hands splitting and the person would fall to the ground. If nailed, a person was nailed between the bones of the forearm (being sure not to sever an artery which would quicken the death). In other words, had Jesus been nailed through the hands, his hands would have split apart and there would be no need to look for "wounds". Thus, Thomas' demand to see the "mark of the nails in his hands" cannot be accurate.

Did Jesus Die on the Cross?

"Then Jesus gave a loud cry and breathed his last." (Mark 15:37)

There are many theories that while Jesus was crucified, he did not die on the cross (Harpur, 2004; Kaiser, 1977; Schonfield, 1965; Thiering, 1992) and this has also been the subject of some fictional books (e.g., George Moore's *The Brook Kerith* and D.H. Lawrence's *The Man Who Died*). Indeed, the blind poet John Milton's *Paradise Lost* simple says" "so he dies/But soon revives". These theories rely on the fact that Jesus was on the cross for only three to six hours, which was not sufficiently long enough to produce death. The *Gospel of Peter*, for example, says that he was crucified at noon (v. 15) and "they pulled the nails from the Lord's hands and placed him on the ground. All the ground shook and everyone was terrified. Then the sun shone and it was found to be three in the afternoon (v. 20-22)."[179]. Three hours on the cross, as harrowing as that might be, was normally not sufficient to kill a person. Indeed some people lingered for days under these conditions.

In cases where the person had not died and (for whatever reason) the crucifixion was finished, their legs were broken so that their lungs collapsed and death followed shortly thereafter. The two men who accompanied Jesus had their legs broken, but he did not.[180] Kaiser (1977) makes the point that if the two thieves hadn't died, there was no reason for Jesus to have died either. Indeed, when Joseph of Arimathea begs the body of Jesus from Pilate, Pilate is astonished that Jesus died so quickly (Mark 15:44). The evidence that Jesus is truly dead comes from a Legionnaire's account that Jesus bled when pierced with a spear (John 19:24), but, in reality, the fact that Jesus bled was just as likely to be an indication that he was still alive (Gardner, 2001; Kaiser, 1977). Even Joseph's own words, asking for the *soma* (body) of Jesus instead of his *ptoma* (corpse) implies that Jesus was still alive.

---

[179] Mark also says that Jesus died at 3 o'clock in the afternoon, but he contends that he was placed on the cross at 9 am (15: 25-34).

[180] Indeed, Josephus tells the story of three acquaintances of his who were crucified, and when he learned of this, he requested Titus to release them. After they were taken down, two subsequently died, however, one lived Kaiser (1977).

Jesus Who?

In addition to these theories, there are numerous suggestions in the Old Testament that the Messiah would survive his ordeal.

> "Though I walk in the midst of trouble, thou wilt revive me...The bands of the grave compassed me about...In my distress I called upon the Lord...He delivered me from my strong enemy. God shall redeem my soul from the grasp of the grave. My flesh also shall rest in hope...(I Cor., XV, 51-3)."

> "He professes to have knowledge of God, and calls himself a child of the Lord...Let us see if his words are true, And let us test what will happen at the end of his life; For if the righteous man is God's son, he will help him, And deliver him from the hand of his adversaries...Let us condemn him to a shameful death, For, according to what he says, he will be protected (*Wisdom of Solomon*, ii, 12-20)."

These Old Testament prophecies receive some validation from Qumran documents. For example...

> "The Wicked watches out for the Righteous and seeks to slay him. The Lord will not abandon him into his hand or let him be condemned when he is tried... (Schonfield, 1965, p. 215)."

The *Gospel of Philip* indicates that: "Those who say that the lord died first and then rose up are in error, for he rose up first and then died (56: 15-20)." The *Gospel of Peter* actually seems to indicate that Jesus did not die at all, and was resuscitated (not resurrected). Verse 39 says: "...they [the guards] see three men coming out of the tomb, and the two supporting the one..." It's hard to imagine that a resurrected Jesus needed to be supported between two men. In addition, we are told that the "exceeding large" stone was moved, implying that Jesus was alive since he had to exit through an open door. Had he been dead, and later risen as a spirit, there would be no need to move the stone.

Later, when the Gospels claim he rose and visited his disciplines, Jesus appears to have a healthy appetite (John 21:13). He partakes of a meal of bread and fish. Why would a dead man eat?

Thus, there is considerable evidence that Jesus did not die on the cross. All things considered, however, the theories of the "fake" death of Jesus on the cross seem far too complicated. They would have relied on Joseph of Arimathea's ability to plead Jesus' body, which certainly wasn't a foregone conclusion given Pilate's reputation. Moreover, it would have required Jesus to be crucified on Joseph's estate, again a vital piece of the puzzle that could not be assured. Next it would rely on Jesus being able to feign death, whether aided by a drug or not, and not being subjected to intense scrutiny by the guards. If this were accomplished through the aid of drugs, Jesus lapse into unconsciousness would have brought about the same death that breaking the legs brought.

If there was no conspiracy to "fake" death, it does not rule out that Jesus, for whatever reason, did not die on the cross (or from being hung from a tree). One of the earliest Christian leaders, Irenaeus (c 130-202 A.D.) believed that Jesus lived to be an old man (*Against Heresies*, Book 2, 22:5), a theory he shared with Bishop Papias (c 60-135 A.D.) who supposedly learned this from the Apostle John.

Was Jesus Hung From a Tree?

> *"On the eve of Passover they hanged Yeshu. And an announcer went out, in front of him, for forty days (saying): 'He is going to be stoned, because he practiced sorcery and enticed and led Israel astray. Anyone who knows anything in his favor, let him come and plead in his behalf.' But, not having found anything in his favor, they hanged him on the eve of Passover." (Sanhedrin 43a)*

As shocking as it may be, there is a wealth of evidence that Jesus was hung from a tree, rather than crucified. For example...

- In *The Acts of the Apostles*, Paul says: "The God of our ancestors raised up Jesus whom you had killed by hanging[181]

---

[181] In some versions of the Bible this passage is changed to indicate crucifixion instead of hanging, but the original and most translations refer to hanging.

[*kremannumi*] him on a tree (5:30)[182]." He repeats this account two more times (10:39, 13:29). The word used for "tree" is "xulon" which refers to a living tree, rather than a post or stake.
- Galatians says: "Christ redeemed us from the curse of the law by becoming a curse for us - for it is written, 'Cursed is everyone who hangs on a tree' (3:13)."
- *1 Peter* (2:24) says: "He himself carried up our sins in his body to the tree..."
- *The Letter of Polycarp to the Philippians* says: "Jesus Christ, who bore our sins in his own body on the tree...(v. 8)."
- The *Sefer Toledot Yeshu* (Book of Life of Jesus), a medieval retelling of the Gospels from the point of view of the Jews, dates from 800 A.D. but is based on earlier oral traditions. They maintain that Jesus was first hung on a tree, but when it broke, they finished the job on a cabbage stalk.
- Jesus himself seems to be saying much the same thing in the *Acts of John* when he says: "One hanged was I, and yet not hanged (101)."
- Both the noun (stauros) and the verb (stauroo) signify "to fasten to a stake or pale," without any indication that a cross is involved. Even today, Jehovah Witnesses deny that Jesus was crucified on a cross.

Putting aside, for a moment, the cabbage stalk story, many Christian scholars argue that the use of the terms "hanged from a tree" should be translated as "crucified" since the crucifixion involved someone being fastened to a piece of wood which formerly had been a tree. The word *kremannumi* is usually translated as hanged, but also can be translated as "suspended". The more familiar analogy in everyday life is hanging a picture. We hang a picture in a very different way from the way we hang a person. There is another word for hanging which more specifically applies to hanging a person, and that is *talah* in Hebrew. In Galatians and elsewhere, the wording involves kremannumi, and not talah, implying being suspended from a tree and not being hung. But, the Christian myth is that Jesus was "nailed" to the cross, in which case he wasn't hung at all, but rather he was fastened. There was an alternate form of crucifixion in which the person was hung/suspended

---

[182] Some translations indicate: "...whom you slew and hanged on a tree..."

by ropes, instead of being nailed, but this was not the case in the traditional view of Jesus. Moreover, the reference to Deuteronomy (21:22-23) in Galatians is to a case of someone being hanged to death on a tree, not suspended/crucified on a wooden structure/pole: "If a man has committed a capital offense, and is put to death, thou shalt hang him on a tree: his body shall not remain all night upon the tree, but thou shalt in any wise bury him that day, for he that is hanged, is accursed of God..."

The bottom line is - to hang from a tree is not the same as to be crucified.

In terms of recruiting new followers, the story of a man hanged from a tree has far less appeal than a man crucified, especially since the Gentiles were more familiar with crucifixion.

The Romans used crucifixion as a penalty for treason by non-Romans. The most infamous example of crucifixion of Jews by Romans occurred shortly after Jesus was born, in 4 B.C., when 2000 Jews in a messianic revolt in Judea, were crucified by Publius Quinctilius Varus (c 46 B.C. – 9 A.D.). The charges against Jesus were "subverting the nation, forbidding payment of tribute to Caesar, and claiming to be the Messiah, a king (Luke, 23:2)." According to the *Gospel of John*, the specific charges written (in Hebrew, Latin, and Greek) on the *titulus* of the cross were: *Iesus Nazarenus Rex Iudaeorum: INRI* (Jesus the Nazarene, King of the Jews). But these are not the types of charges that generally warranted crucifixion by the Romans, although lesser punishments could be handed out. In any event, there are no similar cases of people charged with similar offenses being crucified. These charges are, however, the types of charges that would warrant stoning and/or hanging, yet these were the punishments that the Jewish authorities were charged with enforcing.

One final indication that Jesus may have been hung instead of crucified comes from Deuteronomy in which punishment for a capital offense is specified: "If a man has committed a capital offense, and is put to death, thou shalt hang him on a tree; his body shall not remain all night upon the tree, but thou shalt in any wise bury him that day...(21:22)." In the Gospels, Jesus is specifically taken down before the end of the day, in compliance with the law not to let a hanged man remain all night. This implies that he was hung, not crucified. Of course, it can be argued that being crucified was like being hung, and therefore the law applied to crucifixion as well. While that may be the case, that point of law was never argued, and had it been the case, one might have expected it to be raised. Moreover, the Roman law and custom was that the victims of crucifixion "were left on the cross until beats and birds of prey devoured them (Cohn, 1963, p. 238)."

Faced with two documented traditions, hanging from a tree vs. crucifixion, we have to weigh the merits of each case. The crucifixion is the better-known scenario, however, this comes mainly from the Gospels, while the hanging scenario comes pre-Gospel (Acts, 1 Peter, Galatians) and post-Gospel (Babylonian Talmud), and from both Christian and Jewish sources. The evidence seems to favor the hanging scenario. On the other hand, if Jesus were killed by the Romans, as a violation of the dignity of their Emperor by claiming to be a King, then it was more likely he was crucified. Trying to reconcile these two strong traditions, the most likely case is that the historical Jesus was killed by the Jewish authorities by stoning, and was then hung from a tree. We know this was the case with the previous Jesus (ben Stada) and we know that the apostle Stephen was also stoned to death (Acts 7:59). One hundred years later, when the Gospels were being written, sensitivities about such an ignoble death undoubtedly prompted the writers to change the scenario from death by stoning/hanging to crucifixion. But trying to account for the crucifixion scenario was difficult indeed, and hence the many anomalies and impossibilities that crept into the account (e.g., Pilate and Herod Antipas becoming friends, the Sanhedrin meeting at night, Pilate as a wishy-washy meek prefect, etc.), which remain to this day.

Summary

The death of Jesus has been a contentious issue for nearly 2000 years. Our research indicates that the Jewish authorities feared the strength of Jesus' movement, especially since it involved so many highly placed Zealots. To prevent further escalation and possibly revolt, followed by Roman retaliation, the Jewish authorities accused Jesus of blasphemy by claiming to be the Son of God, perverting the Jewish nation, forbidding tribute to Caesar, and saying that he was a king. The common tradition is that Jesus was flogged and sentenced to death, most likely on a Cross. However, it seems more likely that he was stoned to death and then hung from a tree. In either event, he died and was subsequently laid in a common grave, but his body was stolen by his disciples (probably to give him an honorable burial), hence giving birth to the legend that he was resurrected. Over time, his story was merged with the stories of Pagan Gods and other revolutionaries, until eventually it came down to us in the form it is today. These many transmutations of his story accounted for the many discrepancies between the Gospel accounts, none of which reflected true historical events, and most of which stretched the laws of physiology and physics to attain their goals. In the end, Jesus died in 36 A.D., at the age of 42.

CHAPTER NINE

Lasting Questions

We've explored everything about Jesus' lifetime, but there are still a few issues that remain because they go beyond his life as a person and refer instead to the Jesus of faith. Was he the Son of God? the Messiah? the suffering servant? Was he resurrected? Is he coming again? While these issues are not as grounded in history as the issues of his birth, ministry, and death, we can explore them with the same dedication and resolve that we applied to these other issues. Are you ready?

Is The 2nd Coming, Coming? Or Has It Gone?

"It was not long afterwards that He rose into the sky and disappeared into a cloud, leaving them staring after Him. As they were straining their eyes for another glimpse, suddenly two white-robed men were standing there among them, and said, 'Men of Galilee, why are you standing here staring at the sky? Jesus has gone away to heaven, and some day, just as He went, He will return!'" (Acts 1:10-11)

The Second Coming had a twofold objective. First, it served to qualify Jesus as the true Messiah, in that upon his Second Coming he would perform the duties which were expected of a Messiah, duties he did not fulfill in his First Coming (e.g., bringing peace, triumphing over his enemies, etc.). Second, the Second Coming would inaugurate judgment day, an event that would allow all of the converts to Christianity to ascend to Heaven with him.

Throughout the New Testament, the Gospels spoke of a Second Coming. Here are some examples...

> "Truly, I say to you, there are some standing here who will not taste death before they see the Son of Man coming in his kingdom (Matthew 16:28)."
>
> "There will be signs in the sun, the moon, and the stars, and on the earth distress among nations confused by the roaring of the seas and the waves. People will faint from fear and foreboding of what is coming upon the world, for the powers of the heavens will be shaken. Then they will see the Son of Man coming in a cloud, with power and great glory (Luke 21:25-27)."
>
> "I go to prepare a place for you. And...I will come again, and receive you unto myself (John 14:2-3)."

Clearly, the Second Coming was expected within the lifetime of Jesus' apostles, and apparently there were many false predictions about the Second Coming, prompting warnings about false prophets (e.g., 2 Thessalonians 2:1-2; Matthew 24:4). Yet still they waited. As they began to die off, more and more questions were asked. Indeed, the Gospels themselves were written more than 50 years after his death, and still no appearance. Bloom (2005) suggests that the radically different tone of the *Gospel of John* compared to the synoptic Gospels is due to the fact that John is the last one written, long after the Second Coming was to have occurred, so that the apocalyptic hopes had "ebbed away" and all that was left was the "anxiety of frustrated expectations (p. 79)."

These frustrated expectations are illustrated in *2 Peter*, that says: "First of all, you must understand that in the last days scoffers will come, scoffing and following their own evil desires. They will say, 'Where is this 'coming' he promised? Ever since our fathers died, everything goes on as it has since the beginning of creation.' (3:3-4)" The Gospel goes on to say: "But don't forget this, dear friends, that a day or a thousand years from now is like tomorrow to the Lord. He isn't really being slow about His promised return, even though it sometimes seems that way. But He is waiting, for the good reason that He is not willing that any should perish, and He is giving more time for sinners to repent (3:8-9)."

Most Christians are still waiting for the Second Coming. Funk and Hoover (1993) call it the "Christian wrinkle". Some, however, believe it has already come (e.g., 7th Day Adventists), and some scholars (Ellegard, 1999) believe that his so-called return is actually his coming. Huh?? That's right! Swedish scholar Alvar Ellegard (1999) argues that the proper translation of the word *parousia* is "arrival" or "presence", and that references to the Second Coming are merely references to Jesus' First Coming to Earth. In other words, Ellegard observes that almost all 1st Century accounts of Jesus are "spiritual" or "visionary" sightings in which a heavenly Jesus imparts wisdom to his apostles (This is certainly the case with Paul). Because there was no Earthly Jesus - an idea Ellegard shared with the Gnostics and the Docetists discussed earlier – his coming was to be palpable proof of his existence, which prior to that event could be doubted.

In summary, the Second Coming may still be coming, or it may have already come and gone. Are you waiting?

Was Jesus Resurrected?

"...and he said to them, 'Thus it is written, that the Messiah is to suffer and to rise from the dead on the third day...'" (Luke 24: 46)

Resurrection Defined

What does it mean to be resurrected (in Greek *anastasis* or 'awakening')? What does this mean to us today? to the early Christians who composed the New Testament? to the Jews who heard the stories? to Jesus himself? Unless we understand what is meant by the resurrection, we can't begin to discuss whether or not Jesus was resurrected. Returning to the first question, what does it mean to be resurrected? we can note several features from the Old Testament and the Gospel stories[183]:

- To be resurrected, someone must die first.
- A person must be resurrected within three days after he dies (Hosea 6:2; Job 14:20-22).[184]
- Once resurrected, a person can't die again (Luke 20:36).
- In some manner, resurrection affects the body as well as the soul. In other words, unlike a ghost (Luke 24:39), who can float about even while the body remains behind, a resurrected person's body also experiences the resurrection, and doesn't stay behind.
- A resurrected person appears in a different (altered) form, in which they are not recognizable, even to their closest associates (Luke 24:16; John 20:14).
- Resurrected people do not obey the normal laws of physics. They can appear (Luke 24:36; John 20:26) and disappear in a flash (Luke 24:31).
- Resurrected people engage in normal activities. They can speak (Matthew 28:10) and eat (Luke 24:43; John 21:15).
- Resurrected people have a corporeal reality. You can hold their feet (Matthew 28:9) and touch their hands (Luke 24:39), but sometimes they don't want to be touched (John 20:17).
- People who are resurrected are not yet ascended (Mark 16:19; Luke 24:51; John 20:17). The earth is their home.

Assume for a moment that it was Jesus on the cross and that he did actually die there. That's the accepted Christian view. The next obvious question is: "Was he resurrected?" To some extent, this question goes beyond the scope of history and enters into the realm of

---

[183] The Gospel stories accept a Literalist interpretation of resurrection. The Gnostic interpretation is very different, and a thorough discussion can be found in Freke & Gandy (2001).

[184] See Carrier, 2005, p. 158, for the Jewish origins of this belief, which are undoubtedly the "scriptures" to which Paul refers in 1 Cor. 15:4. But deeper than this, the Egyptians equated the number 3 with resurrection because it took three days for the old moon to die and the new moon cycle to begin (Harpur, 2004).

theology. Historically speaking, there are no documented instances of people being resurrected, although there are many cases of people being resuscitated. The distinction is a fine one. In other words, suppose Jesus had "died" on the cross (or from being hung on a tree) and was promptly taken to the crypt where devoted followers worked on him and revived him. This is certainly possible, since he wasn't on the cross/tree long enough to suffer any fatal damage. Yet those who argue that he was resurrected do not have this scenario in mind. Rather, they believe that with no help at all, apart from heavenly intervention, Jesus who died, later came to life. While we don't know exactly how long he was "dead", it appears to be about 39 hours, from just before sunset on Friday to Sunday morning (hence, 9 hours on Friday + 24 hours on Saturday + 6 hours on Sunday). Contrary to Jesus' own words, that he would "be in the heart of the earth for three days and three nights" (Matthew 12:40), apparently it was only two nights.

The Background

The concept of resurrection existed before the time of Jesus. Examples of resurrected deities included Adonis (from Greek legends via Syria), Dionysus (Greece), Attis (Asia Minor), Tammuz (Babylon), Bacchus (Italy), Mithra (Persia), and Osiris (Egyptian God of Death and the Underworld)[185], all of whose resurrections were tied to agricultural renewal. Note this description of the resurrection of Attis: "...the tomb was opened; the god had risen from the dead...The resurrection of the god was hailed by his disciples as a promise that they too would issue triumphantly from the corruption of the grave... (Frazer, 1922, p. 350)."

While the Jews had no tradition of resurrection, the concept was an established part of the 13 principles set down by Maimonides - "I believe with complete (perfect) faith, that there will be *techiat hameitim* - revival of the dead, whenever it will be God's, blessed be He, will (desire) to arise and do so. May (God's) Name be blessed, and may His remembrance arise, forever and ever". In *2nd Maccabees*, the

---

[185] See Freke & Gandy's 1999 excellent book, *The Jesus Mysteries*, for a full discussion.

second brother tells his torturers – "You accursed wretch, you dismiss us from this present life, but the King of the universe will raise us up to an everlasting renewal of life because we have died for his laws (7:9)." Despite this literary tradition, there were no examples of people who were resurrected in the Old Testament. The best they could do was Elijah's ascension, in which a living person ascended into Heaven without having to stop and die first. But this was not the resurrection.

The Evidence for the Resurrection

The original version of Mark ended at Chapter 16, verse 8, with the women running away from the empty tomb. There was no mention of a resurrection[186]. Nor was there any mention of Jesus being resurrected in many of the Gnostic Gospels (e.g., Philip, Thomas, Judas) that date from that period. Nor was the resurrection discussed in James, or Jude, or the epistles of John. Nor, of course, was it mentioned in any of the non-religious books of the time. Indeed, the only discussion of the resurrection came from Paul's letters (e.g., 1 Cor. 15:3-5) and the Gospels of Matthew, Luke, and John, and almost every element of the story varied considerably from one to the other. For example, the *Gospel of John* reports two angels, Luke reports two men, Matthew reports only one angel, and Mark has no angels at all. John says Mary Magdalene alone went to the tomb; the others say three women went there (Mary, Jesus' mother Mary, and another). The resurrection stories in Luke (explicitly) and John (implicitly) occur in Jerusalem, indoors, while Matthew's story occurs in Galilee, outdoors.

So, our information is scant, and not exactly reliable. But this shouldn't prevent us from looking at what we have.

Is Mark's Gospel Historic or Literary?

While Paul's mention of the resurrection is the first historical reference, he doesn't offer many details; rather, his focus is on the theological importance of the event. It is Mark's record of the resurrection that

---

[186] Years later Mark was edited to put a resurrection scene into the Gospel, but it was not a part of the original, and undoubtedly was adapted from the resurrection stories in Luke and John (Carrier, 2005).

offers our first glimpse at what might have actually happened, and the stories in the other Gospels derive from Mark's account. Since Mark's "empty tomb" is the linchpin around which the other three Gospels' stories revolve, we need to turn our attention there. Carrier (2005) offers an extensive analysis of the "empty tomb" concept in the *Gospel of Mark*, noting some of the possible historical, religious, and literary antecedents, which include…

- the myth of Osiris, who was persecuted by 72 conspirators (the Sanhedrin had 71 members + Judas = 72), whose dead body was sealed in a casket (cave), and who arose during the full moon (Passover) after three days.
- passages in Psalms, especially Jesus' cry on the cross (Mk. 15:34; Ps. 22:1), the taunts of onlookers (Mk. 15:29, Ps 22:7), casting lots for the garments (Mk. 15:24, Ps 22:18), piercing the body (Ps. 22:16), and the third day resurrection (Ps. 24).
- Orphic theology, dating back as far as 400 B.C., that speaks of "white cypress on the right hand side" of the tomb (Mk. 16:5), the guardians in the tomb (Mk. 16:6) who advise that the searchers must seek elsewhere (Mk. 16:7), and the admonition to drink of the sacred waters (Mk. 14:24).

It's likely that the writers of Mark were familiar with these myths and legends, and this may account for the close similarities. Indeed, it brings into question whether or not Mark's account is truly historical or merely derivative, a retelling of the myths and legends already identified. And without Mark's account as a firm basis, any further retelling by Matthew, Luke, and John is without empirical merit.

Would Jesus Have Been Buried At All?

Not only is the idea of the empty tomb suspect due to the many literary precursors, the idea does not square with the practices at the time (Hengel, 1977; McCane, 2003). To the Romans, crucifixion was both a punishment and a deterrent, so they tended to deny burial to people who were crucified. Typically victims were left to hang for days, their corpses rotting in the sun, picked clean by the birds, the pathetic remains savaged by dogs. [187] Would an exception have been made for Jesus? One has to ask: "Why?" After all, according to the Gospels, he was found guilty of blasphemy by the Sanhedrin and guilty of treason by the Romans. At the time of his death, contrary to the popular opinion that his followers were a small group of rag-tag fishermen, Jesus had gathered a large following and a wide support system. To show mercy or favoritism to him would only encourage his followers and add some substance to his claims, an act the Romans would not likely take.

Moreover, according to Jewish law, having been found guilty of blasphemy, Jesus would not have been entitled to an honorable burial. As an executed criminal, he would have been buried in a public graveyard and denied such niceties as anointing, wrappings in linen, placement in a tomb, etc. (Lowder, 2005; Schonfield, 1965). Given their influence with the Roman authorities, the Sanhedrin surely would have insisted on a dishonorable burial, something that the Romans would have been inclined to anyway. Indeed, there is evidence of such a dishonorable burial in the *Secret Book of James*, written about the same time as the Gospels of Luke and John (i.e., early 1st Century), which indicates that Jesus was buried "in the sand[188] (v. 5)."

Another factor that brings Jesus' tomb burial into question is the fact that there was no tradition prior to the 4th Century of veneration of his tomb or grave sight. Surely the man who inspired thousands of people during his lifetime, and hundreds of thousands thereafter, would have also inspired people to visit his tomb, if it existed! This is true especially since the tomb served two important spiritual functions – his death served as atonement for the sins of humanity, and his resurrection served as a sign of his divinity. This omission is made more poignant when we realize that the tombs of lesser men were well

---

[187] This practice accounts for why only one crucified corpse has ever been uncovered.

[188] Some authors translate this as "shamefully", but Kirby (2005) notes that it's translated as "shamefully" because the original meaning of being buried in the sand was shameful. In any event, Jesus' burial as described by Mark (anointed, wrapped in linens, in a tomb, etc.) would not qualify as a shameful burial.

known at the time of their deaths. For example, John the Baptist's tomb was said to be in Samaria-Sebaste[189]. Herod Agrippa I was buried at Caesarea, James the Just was buried near Jerusalem, Lazarus' tomb was in Bethany, etc. (Finegan, 1969).

What Does The Empty Tomb Really Mean?

Suppose, for a moment, we ignore these literary precursors and the unlikely chances of an honorable burial, and assume that the empty tomb, as told by Mark, was historical. Does that lead us any closer to a historical resurrection? No! First of all, it should be noted that no one reports seeing Jesus arise from the dead. Most agree that he died and was put in the tomb; then, a few days later, he wasn't in the tomb, and shortly after that, his disciples reporting seeing someone who identified himself as Jesus (but who didn't resemble him), and even later, a convert (Paul) reports hearing his voice. In other words, no one sees him arise. No one sees the resurrection, in the same way that Peter, James and John see the transfiguration, or in the way that thousands see the miracles. It is all speculation based on the empty tomb. But what does an empty tomb tell us? Not much! He could have revived himself, or been resuscitated by his colleagues, or his body could have been stolen or simply moved by a gardener anxious to avoid the crowds trampling his vegetables[190]. An empty tomb, if it is true, signifies nothing.

Looked at closely, the empty tomb story as described by all the Gospels actually speaks against a supernatural explanation of Jesus' disappearance. All four Gospels note that the "exceedingly great" stone door had been moved (Mark 16:3; John 20:1). Why would a spirit need to move a door? Later Jesus is described as moving through walls (John 20:26). Why didn't he move through the cave walls, or through the stone door? In fact, the idea that the stone had

---

[189] A church was built over the gravesite in the 4th Century. Nearly a thousand years later, Crusaders built a cathedral there, some portions of which remain extant today.

[190] The vegetable theory was put forward by Tertullian and exists in a modified version in the *Book of the Resurrection*, a Coptic manuscript in the British museum attributed to the apostle Bartholomew.

been moved indicates that Jesus was not dead and he had to go out through the doorway just like anyone else.

If Believers Believe, Should We?

The first reports of Jesus' resurrection are taken with a grain of salt. The revised ending of Mark has Mary Magdalene reporting his appearance to his followers, "But when they heard that he was alive and had been seen by her, they would not believe it (16:9)." Then he appears "in another form" to two more, who recount their experience, "...but they did not believe them (16:13)." Luke confirms this. He says of the reaction of the 11 disciples to Mary Magdalene's report: "...they did not believe them (24:11)." Later, Matthew reports that even among the 11 remaining disciples, "some doubted (28:17)." Only John has a more trusting group. In his recounting of the resurrection, only Thomas doubts.

It's important to note that Jesus only appears to people who believed in him. From an historical point of view, a careful researcher would like to have an account of a non-believer to support the accounts of the believers. In other words, if the disciples of the infamous false prophet James Jones said they saw him risen from the dead, the average person would doubt the veracity of this claim, attributing it to self-serving hallucinations, or even to deliberate fraud. So too, the risen Jesus who only appears to those who believe in him, is a relatively weak proof of his resurrection.

What is the Evidence?

So far we have considered various problems with the theory of the resurrection, including (a) the fact that Jesus' resurrection is a one-of-a-kind event despite Paul's "first fruits" prophecy, (b) Mark's Gospel appears to have many literary precursors that suggest his account is literary rather than historical, (c) the fact that the empty tomb, per se, has very little meaning, (d) the account of the stone door being moved suggests a human rather than a spiritual exit, and (e) the fact that the only accounts of a risen Jesus are from his true believers. All of these issues suggest that the resurrection did not happen. Yet they would be mute testimony if there were some empirical evidence substantiating the claim. For example if a resurrected Jesus wrote a document that could be dated from 60 A.D., this would go a long way toward substantiating his return. If we recovered an ossuary[191] containing his bones, which could be carbon dated to 50 A.D., we could say that indeed there must have been a resurrection. Yet in nearly 2000 years no empirical evidence has been produced to substantiate any life after death.

Is the "Sky Falling" on Mark?

As if all these problems were not sufficient to question the historicity of the empty tomb, we have the additional problem of Mark's other unsupportable claims surrounding the death of Jesus. For example, Mark records: "When it was noon, darkness came over the whole land, until three in the afternoon (15:33)", and later he notes: "Then Jesus gave a loud cry and breathed his last. And the curtain of the temple was torn in two, from top to bottom (15:37-38)." Neither one of these events are mentioned in any non-Gospel sources, yet given their magnitude, one would expect some reference to them, especially in the works of Josephus or Pliny. This lack of reference leads many authors to conclude that Mark was simply using symbolism here, yet if he uses symbolism in these two cases, why isn't the empty tomb another case of symbolism. Indeed, Carrier (2005) makes exactly this case – the empty tomb is symbolic, not historical.

Does the Resurrection Nullify the Sacrifice?

The concept of resurrection, even if true, is a curious one. On the one hand, it is said to be essential to the Christian faith. Two thousand years ago Paul in a letter to the Corinthians said, "If Christ has not been raised, then our preaching is in vain and your faith is in vain... If Christ has not been raised, your faith is futile (1 Cor. 15:14-17)." The resurrection is a key concept in the Apostles Creed ("...the 3rd day he rose again from the dead") and the Nicene Creed ("...the 3rd day he rose again according to Scriptures."). Yet much is made in the Gospels that Jesus' <u>death</u> was the key to salvation, that "he died for our sins".

---

[191] An ossuary with the inscription "James, Son of Joseph, Brother of Jesus" was unearthed in 2002 (Shanks & Witherington, 2003).

Indeed, a death with a resurrection is not much of a death at all. Had Jesus died, once and for all, for our sins and remained dead, then his sacrifice would have been great. If he died and then, after 39 hours, lived forever, it wasn't much of a sacrifice, was it? In fact, his life after death is so much greater than his life before death, one wonders why he didn't choose to die sooner. Thus, in many ways, the idea of a resurrection belittles the idea of a sacrifice, yet we're told that the sacrifice is the key.

To summarize the evidence about the resurrection, it's clear that the resurrection story is symbolic. There was no empirical evidence for the resurrection, no one actually saw Jesus arise, and the only people who claimed to see him afterwards were firm believers, and there were precious few of them, and even they claim that the person they saw didn't look like Jesus. Moreover, the main literary evidence for a resurrection came from the *Gospel of Mark*, and it's clear that most of the features of his story were taken from prior accounts drawn from myths and legends going back hundreds of years. Even more telling, there are so many inconsistencies and improbabilities involved in the story of the empty tomb (e.g., neither the Romans nor the Jews would have allowed an honorable burial, there is no tradition of tomb veneration, there are alternate stories of being buried in the sand, etc.), that it must be dismissed as metaphor or symbolism.

Having examined and rejected both the story of the empty tomb and the idea of the resurrection, does this mean that Jesus was not the Son of God? Not necessarily. It certainly argues strongly that the reasoning of the Paulists that Jesus' divinity was defined by his resurrection is deeply flawed. But it does not preclude other grounds on which to claim that Jesus was the Messiah and that he was the Son of God. These are considered next.

Was Jesus the Old Testament Messiah?

"Who do people say I am? And they answered him, 'John the Baptist; and others, Elijah; and still others, one of the prophets.' He asked them, 'But who do you say I am?' Peter answered him, 'You are the Messiah.'" (Mark 8: 27-29)

Jesus Who?

Who Was The Messiah?

In the Old Testament, the word "messiah" (*moschiach or mashiach*) appears 39 times. It signified "anointed", and generally referred to people who were "anointed" for a specific task (e.g., King Cyrus of Persia who returned the Jews from their exile in Babylon). The Messiah associated with King David assumed a more general meaning, and this meaning came to be associated with the return of the exiles of Israel, and the bringing of peace (Micah 5:1-4). Many people, including experts (e.g., Morton, 1978, p. 3) confuse the issue of Messiahship with divinity. The two are separate issues. In the Jewish tradition, the Messiah *was* to restore the greatness of Israel. He was expected to be a wise and understanding man who would bring peace and justice to Israel, and usher in an age of world peace. As an extra bonus, he would do terrible things to Israel's enemies in the process. Most of the requirements for the Messiah were spelled out in the Old Testament in the Books of Isaiah and Ezekiel.

Looking at the formula, the messiah would: (1) spring from David's loins[192], (2) exiles would return to Israel (especially the lost tribes)[193], (3) under his reign Israel would defeat its enemies[194], (4) disease and death would be conquered[195], (5) a new Temple would arise[196], and (6) world peace would be initiated[197]. In addition, it was believed that the Messiah would not know his powers until Elijah anointed him[198].

At the time of Jesus, many Jews expected two Messiahs[199], not one –

---

[192] Isaiah 11:1
[193] Isaiah 11:12
[194] Isaiah 11:4
[195] Isaiah 25:8;
[196] Ezekiel 40
[197] Isaiah 52:7
[198] "...he [the Messiah] does not even know himself, nor has he any power until Elijah comes, anoints him, and reveals him to all (*Dialogue with Trypho*, 8)."
[199] The tradition of two Messiahs can be traced back to Pythagoras and Gnostic beliefs in the God and Goddess (Freke & Gandy, 2001) as well as to Persian concepts of the end of times (Renan, 1927).

"For the Lord shall raise up from Levi as it were a High Priest, and from Judah as it were a King: he shall save all the race of Israel."[200]

For the Essenes, the Priestly Messiah was the superior of the two, whereas for the Pharisees the Kingly Messiah was the chosen one, who would be preceded by the Priestly Messiah (as the returned prophet Elijah). But under no circumstances was the messiah associated with King David believed to be divine. He was to "issue from [David's] loins…and have the "afflictions of human beings…(2 Samuel 7:12-16)."

The Coming of the Messiah

Times were indeed difficult. Previous messianic claims by the Maccabees, and by John Hyrcanus I (died 104 B.C.) had failed to come to pass. Now Israel seemed to be at its lowest point. In power was Herod the Great (37-4 B.C.) who engaged in wholesale slaughter, including in his victim list the remaining Hasmoneans and his own family. Recent years had seen earthquakes, droughts and pestilence, made worse by the tax collection policies of the Romans. People fled the cities and moved into the wilderness, giving strength and numbers to the communities like those around Qumran by the Dead Sea. The call for a Messiah grew.

John the Baptist gave many hints about how the coming Messiah would behave. For example, he said that he "will baptize you with the Holy Spirit and fire (Matthew 3:11)," and "he will clear his threshing floor and will gather his wheat into the granary; but the chaff he will burn with unquenchable fire (Matthew 3:12)." But Jesus did not fit John's picture, so John sent his disciples to question Jesus: "Are you the one who is to come, or have we got to wait for someone else? (Matthew 11:1-15)."

Of course there were many Messiahs before Jesus, and many after him. During Jesus' own lifetime, the rebellion of 6 A.D. featured Judas

---

[200] *Testaments of the XII Patriarchs*, Test Simeon, vii, 1-2. Quoted in Schonfield, 1965, p. 29. See also Jer., xxxiii, 15-26.

Jesus Who?

the Galilean, and prior to him there was Theudas – both of them mentioned by Gamaliel in the Acts of the Apostles (5:36-37). Shortly after Jesus' death and the destruction of the Temple in 70 A.D., Simon Bar Kochba emerged around 130 A.D. to add his name to the long list of Messiahs for Israel.

Was Jesus the Messiah?

Now, let's look at Jesus' career, in light of these expectations...

Expectation	Jesus' Life
Spring from David's Loins	No according to Mark & John/ Yes according to Luke and Matthew
Unaware until anointed	Yes in Mark/ No according to Matthew, Luke and John
Exiles return to Israel	No
Defeat Israel's enemies	No. In fact, within 35 years, the Romans would nearly destroy the Jews.
Defeat disease and death	No (although Jesus does cure many people)
Build a New Temple	No. In fact, within a few years, the 2nd Temple would be destroyed and it would never be rebuilt.
Initiate World Peace	Hardly!

In other words, based on the Jewish expectations of who the Messiah was and what he would accomplish, Jesus didn't stack up very well. This was exactly why most Jews refused to accept Jesus as the Messiah. He simply didn't fit the profile. Indeed, Jesus himself was very cagey about his credentials as Messiah and never claimed it for himself. For example, in the *Gospel of Luke* - "All of them asked, 'Are you then the Son of God?' He said to them, 'You say that I am... (Luke 22:70)." Or from the *Gospel of Mark* - "'...who do you say I am?' Simon Peter answered, 'You are the Messiah, the Son of the living God.' And Jesus answered him, 'Blessed are you, Simon son of Jonah[201] For

---

[201] Craveri (1967, p. 91) claims that Simon bar Jona ordinarily means "Simon, son of Jonah", but as used in Israel at the time, it meant "Simon, the terrorist".

flesh and blood has not revealed this to you, but my Father in heaven (Mark 16:15-17).'" In both cases, Jesus himself made no claims but allowed others to make the claim.

Not only didn't Jesus fit the Jewish expectations of the Messiah, those characteristics he did manifest were not commonly associated with the Messiah. His miracles and exorcisms were not feats expected of the Messiah, as laudable as they may have been. More importantly, the Messiah was not expected to die. Perkins (1988) says: "...none of the 'anointed' figures that were expected to serve as God's agent were expected to die even a martyr's death (p. 102)." Nor was being resurrected, if indeed this happened, an expectation of the Messiah (Klinghoffer, 2005). The Messiah was not expected to die, so there was no expectation of his resurrection. Indeed, the idea that the Messiah died was anathema to the Jews. Craveri (1967) says: "A dead Messiah who could no longer act for the welfare of the people of Israel was an absurdity (p. 323)." When the Apostle Paul offered the description of the dead/resurrected Messiah to the Jews of Thessalonica, they "...gathered a crowd, set the city in an uproar, and attacked the house... (Acts 17:5)."

Was Jesus the "Suffering Servant?

If Jesus was not the expected Messiah of the Jews, was he, at least, the so-called "suffering servant" whom Christianity identified as a secondary vision of the Messiah, to replace the Kingly version. The basis of the suffering servant prophecies is Isaiah, particularly verse 53. Let's examine some relevant sections...

> "He was despised and isolated from men, a man of pains and accustomed to illness...But in truth, it was our ills that he bore, and our pains that he carried – though we had regarded him diseased, stricken by God, and afflicted. He was pained because of our rebellious sins and oppressed through our iniquities: the chastisement upon him was for our benefit, and through his wounds we were healed....He was persecuted and afflicted, but he did not open his mouth; like a sheep being led to the slaughter or a ewe that is silent before her shearers, he

Jesus Who?

did not open his mouth. He was taken from prison and from judgment...for the transgression of my people was he stricken. And he made his grave with the wicked, and with the rich in his death... (53: 3-9)"

Does this sound like Jesus? Let's examine the similarities...

- He was hardly despised and isolated. In fact, he had thousands of adherents.
- As far as we know, he never had any illnesses or pains.
- He certainly wasn't regarded as "diseased", or stricken, or afflicted.
- The only wounds he had occurred after his trial.
- He wasn't persecuted. He was arrested, but that hardly qualifies as persecuted.
- And he certainly wasn't silent.
- He was never in prison, although he was arrested.
- He wasn't imprisoned/arrested for the transgression of the Jews, but rather for his claim to be the King of the Jews.
- His grave/tomb certainly wasn't with the wicked, but rather with the rich, since he was buried in the tomb of Joseph of Arimathea
- His death wasn't with the rich, but rather with the wicked, since he was crucified between two thieves.

In other words, Jesus hardly fits the profile of the suffering servant from Isaiah.[202]

There is another Old Testament reference that is often used to align Jesus with the suffering servant. In the *Gospel of Luke*, Jesus says: "Thus it is written, that the Christ should suffer and on the third day rise from the dead...(24:46)." But if we examine the full quote, from Hosea, we find this:

---

[202] Although Paul does fit this profile, which may be one of the reasons for Paul's own messianic beliefs. That issue, however, is another book. Stay tuned. Are you ready?

> "Come, let us return to the Lord, for He has mangled [us] and He will heal us; He has smitten and He will bandage us. He will heal us after two days; and on the third day He will raise us up and we will live before Him... (6: 1-2)."

The original quote from Hosea says nothing about being dead, or even rising from the dead, and the Jewish meaning to "raise up" bears no relationship to the idea of resurrection.

In summary, Jesus fits neither the profile of the Kingly Messiah nor the suffering servant. Hence, for most Jews, he was not accepted as the fulfillment of prophecy.

Was Jesus the Son of God?

> *"For God so loved the world that he gave his only Son, so that everyone who believes in him may not perish but may have eternal life."* (John 3:16)

Who is the Son of God?

It's difficult to address the question of Jesus being the "son of God" from an historical perspective. The divinity of Jesus has been a hot issue in the Christian literature since the 2nd Century. Despite numerous councils and decrees, the most contentious of which was the Arian Heresy that was defeated at the Nicaean Council in 325 A.D., it remains a paradox even today. Is Jesus the Son of God? yet equal to God? or shares his Goddom with God and the Holy Ghost? Was he God in human form? And did God remain in Godly form while Jesus became God in human form? The questions are endless, and there are no easy answers.

The term "Son of God" had many meanings to the Jews. In some cases it referred to "...an ancient title for everyone who was claiming kingship (Asimov, p. 489; Knight & Lomas, p. 49)." For example, *Psalm 2* celebrates the coronation of a new king thusly: "...the Lord hath said unto me, Thou art my Son; this day have I begotten thee (2:7)." In other cases, the title "Son of God" had a more general meaning, referring to all holders of the true faith (Mackey, 1979), as in *Exodus* – "Israel is my first-born son (4:22)." *Romans* (8:14) says: "All who are led by the spirit of God are sons of God." Two of Jesus' fellow Galilean wonder workers, Honi the Circledrawer and Hanina ben Dosa, were both referred to as Sons of God[203] (Wilson, 1992, p. 100). In no case, however, was there a tradition that implied that someone (anyone) was actually the biological Son of God (Harvey, 1971; Mackey, 1979; Perkins, 1988). It was only among the Pagans (including the Greeks) that Gods and humans had such a relationship.

Thus, when Matthew tells us that Jesus, after being baptized, heard God say to him; "…This is my beloved Son, in whom I am well pleased (3:17)" the implication is not necessarily that he is the biological son of God, but equally could mean that as a descendant of David, a "crown prince" if you will, his future status as a King is being realized. Being the King, Mel Brooks said, is a good thing. Maybe not as good as being the Son of God, but pretty good nonetheless.

Interestingly enough, in Hebrew, the words "Son of God" can be translated as "Barabbas" where "bar" stands for son of and "abba" stands for father. Abba, as noted earlier, was Jesus' name for "God, the father". Of even greater interest is the fact that Barabbas is the name of the "rebel" who was given his freedom in place of Jesus. In other words, the Son of God went free while the Son of God was crucified.

Reasons Why Jesus May Not Be The Literal Son of God

In looking at reasons why Jesus may not be the biological Son of God, the most obvious reason is that in the synoptic Gospels "the unequivocal phrase 'Son of God' was never used by Jesus when he was speaking of himself (Craveri, 1967, p. 106)."[204] In addition, when the term was used, it was often mistranslated, as in the temptation of

---

[203] More specifically, Honi was a "son of God's household" and Hanina was called "God's son".
[204] It does appear several times in the *Gospel of John*, however.

Jesus (Matthew 4:3-11; Luke 4:3) when the words "*hyos Theou*" are translated as "Son of God" when, in fact, they mean "protected by God". Had the writers meant to say "Son of God" they would have used the words "*ho hyos Theou*" instead of "*hyos Theou*".

According to Luke, eight days after he was born Jesus was circumcised. Circumcision was conducted as a renewal of the covenant between God and Abraham, one of four such covenants the Jews believed in. But if Jesus were the Son of God, or indeed God the Son, what would be the purpose of renewing a covenant with oneself? In other words, the act of circumcising Jesus implies that he was not the Son of God.

Another indication that Jesus was not the Son of God came at his baptism, a prominent feature in the synoptic Gospels, even if the details were quite varied from one gospel to another. If Jesus was the Son of God, what need did he have of baptism for the remission of sin? Matthew's Gospel attempted to deal with this thorny issue raised in the *Gospel of Mark*, by having Jesus and John agree that the baptism is "just for show" (the biblical translation is "to complete all righteousness"), but the explanation here is weak. Certainly for Mark, Jesus was not the Son of God, nor was he even the Son of David.

Another sign that Jesus may not have been the literal Son of God was the fact that following his baptism, he was taken by the Devil and then tempted. The idea that the Devil had influence over the Son of God must be questioned. While it's gratifying that Jesus overcame the Devil's temptations, were he truly the Son of God, these temptations would have been meaningless, and there would be no triumph overcoming them. For example, what was the temptation in offering Jesus "all the kingdoms of the world", when as the Son of God he already had dominion over them. Indeed, this temptation only works if Jesus was not the Son of God, but the Son of Man, to whom such a prospect might be tempting.

There is a curious tale from Luke (12:13-14) in which Jesus was asked to intervene in a family dispute. Jesus replied: "Man, who appointed me judge or arbitrator over [the two of] you?" If Jesus was the Son of God and he was going to sit at the head of the table when all peoples were judged for all eternity, it seems questionable that he would ask such a question. Hadn't Jesus been telling everyone that God appointed him? Yet now that he was being asked to judge, he rebuked the idea.

In a similar vein, Jesus appeared to deny his divinity when he was addressed as "good teacher" and he replied: "Why do you call me good? No one is good except God alone (Mark 10:17-18)." Ipso facto, if only God was good and Jesus questions why he should be called good, the implication is clear that Jesus was not God.

Another apparent contraindication that Jesus is the Son of God is the astonishment that people continue to express when he performs his various deeds of power. His mother and his brothers do not believe him (John 7:5), yet according to the stories in Luke and Matthew, his mother knows, more than anyone else, that Jesus is the Son of God, and therefore his deeds of power should have been expected.

From an historical perspective, Jesus is not the biological Son of God. The expression was used at the time to denote an honorary position, but never implied any biological connection. Moreover, Jesus' life provides many clues that he is a normal human being (e.g., circumcision, baptism, temptation) and without divine origins.

Summary

The story of Jesus Christ has purpose and meaning for millions of people today. For them he is the Messiah, the Son of God and his resurrection is the keystone of their salvation. But the story of Joshua ben Joseph is a different story. He was not the long expected Messiah of the Jews. That person was expected to spring from David's loins, return the exiles to Israel, defeat Israel's enemies, conquer disease and death, raise a new Temple, and bring world peace. Joshua ben Joseph accomplished none of these feats, although some apologists maintain that he will do all these things upon his Second Coming, for which we have been waiting nearly 2000 years. Was he the Son of God? Yes. Joshua ben Joseph was the Son of God, but he was the Son of God in the same way that Honi the Circledrawer and Hanina ben Dosa were Sons of God; in the same way that the Kings of Israel were Sons of God; in the same way that we are all Sons and Daughters of God.

CHAPTER TEN

Final Thoughts

On the journey to the historical Jesus, we found few signposts, only signs. Littered among the handful of certainties, we find mostly probabilities. Hints. Suggestions. Clues.

Our journey is nearly at an end. We went in search of the historical Jesus, and the man we found is not the man we thought we were looking for. Almost everything we thought we knew about Jesus, the man, is either clearly untrue or probably wrong:

> he wasn't born in the year 0
> or born in Bethlehem,
> or born on December 25th,
> three kings didn't attend his birth,
> his family didn't flee to Egypt,
> he didn't live in Nazareth,
> his mother wasn't a virgin,
> his father wasn't a carpenter,
> he wasn't a carpenter,
> he wasn't an only child,
> he wasn't estranged from his family,
> his family weren't poor peasants,

> his ministry wasn't a single year, or even three years,
> his followers weren't a small band of ragamuffins,
> he didn't die at age 30,
> in 30 A.D., and
> his story wasn't written by his disciples

Beyond this, we are in a cloud. We see shapes and we try to make sense of them. They represent our best guesses, but we attach no great certainty. And yet they are clearly more potent than the stories that precede them; more reality than myth.

> his parents were members of the Essenes,
> he was born in June/July,
> his birth was not orthodox,
> he was greatly troubled by his status as a "mamzer",
> he was raised in Qumran along with John the Baptist,
> he left Qumran to follow in the footsteps of John,
> to whom he became a Disciple,
> his ministry lasted a dozen years,
> his followers numbered in the thousands,
> and included his family,
> he died in his 40s,
> in 36 A.D., and
> his story was written down 100 years later.

Our findings may be unsettling, largely because they do not fit the archetypical remembrances we had of who Jesus was. But these remembrances were based on myth, not fact, and for whatever the reasons, over the centuries, Jesus became shrouded in the myths despite the fact that the evidence remained in clear sight for anyone to see. Jesus must be smiling. If we listen closely we can even hear his words - *If any man hath ears to hear, let him hear*. Going back to the basics, and reading them appropriately through the lenses of the times, we can see more clearly now who he really was.

Unsettling? Yes. Heretical? Maybe. Sacrilegious? No. Nothing we've encountered in our journey implies that the Jesus of faith is less worthy of devotion as a result of our new discoveries. He is still the same person who preached love and fidelity, who taught us to "turn the other cheek", and who offered his faith to women, sinners, and the whole host of humanity at a time when religion was for the wealthy and privileged. If he seems less supernatural under our microscope, he must then also appear more exceptional. If his strength did not come from divine origins, we must be all the more amazed that his strength came from his inner self. And a Jesus who was so strong and so good must be a model for us all. Not the divine God placed on earth for us to worship; instead the divine spark that is in all of us, and when ignited, can so light the world.

A Roman guard places the crown of thorns on Jesus' head. This detail is from a mid 4th Century sarcophagus from the Catacomb of Domitilla. Note that Jesus is clean shaven and has short hair.

Appendix 1
Dateline

1812 BC	Abraham born.
1300 BC	Jews flee Egypt (the Exodus).
1000 BC	King David reigns from approximately 1010 to 970 B.C., followed by King Solomon and the building for the First Temple.
922 BC	The Jewish kingdom splits into North (Israel) and South (Judah).
753 BC	The founding of Rome.
721 BC	Northern kingdom conquered by Assyria.
597 BC	Southern kingdom conquered by Babylon; First Temple destroyed.
539 BC	Cyrus the Great allows Jews to return; they build the Second Temple about 520 B.C.
332 BC	Alexander the Great conquers Israel.
323 BC	Death of Alexander. Control of Israel falls to Ptolemy, one of his generals.
200 BC	Translation of Jewish Bible (Septuagint) completed in Egypt.
175 BC	Antiochus IV Epiphanes of Syria invades Jerusalem. Outlaws Judaism. He installs a new High Priest, Jason, breaking the Zadok line. Jason builds a gymnasium and renames the city Antioch-at-Jerusalem, a Greek city. Essenes founded as a protest.
169 BC	Antiochus enters the Holy of Holies and erects a statue of Zeus. Pigs are sacrificed in the Temple.
168 BC	Maccabean uprising.
165 BC	Book of Daniel appears, introducing the concept of an afterlife.
	Maccabeans capture Jerusalem (cause of the celebration of Hanukkah).

161 BC	Romans and Maccabees forge a strategic alliance against the Carthaginians that recognizes the Jewish religion.
152 BC	Jonathan Maccabeus appoints himself High Priest of the Temple. In protest, Essenes leave Jerusalem and establish their headquarters in the desert (Some scholars date the exodus to 130 B.C.)
128 BC	Samaritan temple at Mount Gerizim destroyed by John Hycranus.
125 BC	Maccabeans under John Hycranus conquer Idumea and convert the inhabitants to Judaism.
78 BC	Herod Antipater II appointed Governor of Idumea following the death of his father.
63 BC	The Romans under General Pompey are asked to arbitrate in a civil war between the last two sons of the Maccadean dynasty (Hycranus II and Aristobulus). Hycranus II is installed as High Priest (and ultimately Ethnarch) and Aristobulus is exiled.
49 BC	The start of the "End Times". 49 BC was 70 weeks of years beyond 538 B.C., the time identified in the Book of Daniel as the start of the "End Times". Civil war between Pompey and Julius Caesar.
48 BC	Pompey is killed invading Egypt.
47 BC	Herod (the Great), age 25, appointed Governor of Galilee by his father, Herod Antipater II, who is now Procurator of Judea.
44 BC	Julius Caesar assassinated.
43 BC	Herod Antipater assassinated.
40 BC	Herod appointed King of Judea by Mark Anthony. Confirmed in 30 B.C. by Octavian.
31 BC	Large earthquake devastates Judea, killing 30,000 people, and reinforcing the "End Times" concept. The Essenes temporarily abandon Qumran.
25 BC	Drought, disease and famine ravage Israel. Further signs of the "End Times".
18 BC	Reconstruction of the Temple in Jerusalem begins. It will take 46 years to finish the first phase, which is completed around 28 A.D., and final completion will be 63 A.D.

Jesus Who?

11 B.C.	Probable birth of John the Baptist.
7 BC	Revolt against Herod by his two sons Alexander and Aristobulus. He has them strangled.
6 BC	Most likely date for the birth of Jesus.
4 BC	Herod the Great dies. Kingdom is split between Herod's sons: Herod Antipas (Galilee and Peraea), Philip (East and Northeast of The Sea of Galilee), and Archelaus (Judea).
	After suppressing a Jewish revolt, Publius Quinctilus Varus, Governor of Syria, crucifies 2000 rebels led by Judas of Galilee.
	Qumran re-occupied.
4 AD	Tiberius named to be Emperor Augustus' successor.
6 AD	Archelaus removed as Governor of Judea, Samaria, and Idumaea. Rule transfers to the Governor of Syria who appoints a series of Roman procurators, the first of whom is Coponius.
	Annas, son of Seth, appointed High Priest by Publius Sulpicius Quirinius, Governor of Syria
6-7 AD	First census in Israel. Luke mistakes this date for the birth of Jesus.
	Zealots rebel, under Judas of Galilee, saying "No Ruler but God".
10 AD	Tiberius reigns as co-regent.
13 AD	City of Tiberius founded by Herod Antipas. Built over an ancient Jewish cemetery.
14 AD	Tiberius' reign starts.
15 AD	Anna is deposed as High Priest.
18 AD	Caiaphas appointed High Priest by Valerius Gratius, Procurator of Judea.
19 AD	Jews ordered out of Rome.
24 AD	Jesus, age 30, is baptized.
26 AD	Pontius Pilate becomes the 5th Procurator of Judea (following Archelaus' removal).
30 AD	Pilate orders the slaughter of protestors in Jerusalem.
34 AD	King Philip (half brother to Herod Antipas) dies.
34 AD	Concurrence of Roman census year with Jewish land sabbatical year.

35 AD	Herod Antipas marries Herodias (wife of King Philip, his half brother, who died).
35 AD	John the Baptist killed.
36 AD	Pilate puts down a religious uprising in Samaria at Mt Gerizim.
36 AD	Jesus crucified, age 42.
36 AD	Pontius Pilate removed and leaves for Rome.
36 AD	Vitellius, Legate of Syria, removes Caiaphas.
37 AD	Death of Emperor Tiberius (March 16).
37 AD	The Mandaeans (followers of John the Baptist) flee from Judea and seek asylum in Hauran.
38 AD	Jewish pogrom in Alexandria.
38 AD	James the Just assumes control of the Jesus Cult.
45 AD	Theudas claims to be a Messiah. He leads a revolt at the River Jordan and he is beheaded and 400 of his followers are killed. The word "Christian" used for the first time (in Antioch). Jews expelled from Rome for causing "continuous disturbances at the instigation of Chrestus", according to Roman historian Suetonius.
48 AD	First letter of Paul.
49 AD	Jewish council allows Gentiles to join Jesus Cult without circumcision and without observing other Jewish rituals Jews ordered out of Rome
54 AD	Death of Claudius; ascension of Nero.
56 AD	Paul's final visit to Jerusalem.
57 AD	"The Egyptian" messiah appears, garnering 30,000 followers. They surround Jerusalem, are killed or dispersed, but the Egyptian escapes.
61 AD	Paul reaches Rome.
62 AD	Murder of James the Just. Simeon (aka Symeon), son of Clopas (Jesus' cousin) heads the Jesus Cult.
64 AD	Nero burns Rome, blames it on the Christians.
64 AD	Death of Peter in Rome (also possibly in 67 AD).
66 AD	Jewish revolt in Jerusalem begins.
70 AD	Temple in Jerusalem destroyed.
74-78 AD	Josephus publishes *The Jewish War*.
80 AD	Special malediction placed in the central Jewish prayer, the *Shermoneb Esrei*, cursing the Nazarenes and other

Jesus Who?

	Christian groups, cementing the schism between Christians and Jews (Note: Some scholars date this at 90 A.D.).
96 AD	Two grandsons of Jesus' brother Jude brought before Emperor Domitian for suspicion of sedition, however, they were released.
100 AD	Josephus publishes his two-part book *Against Apion*, many parts of which appear in slightly altered form in the *Gospel of Luke*.
107 AD	Simeon suffers martyrdom at the age of 120. Justus succeeds him.
110 AD	The *Didache* (aka *Teaching of the Apostles*) appears
110 AD	Ignatius of Antioch martyred. He wrote several letters en route to Rome.
110-115 AD	The *Gospel of the Egyptians* appears.
113-116 AD	Jewish revolt in Cyrenaica.
115 AD	First non-Christian mention of "Christus" by Roman Tacitus in *Annals*.
115-117 AD	Jewish revolts in Jerusalem, Cyrene, Libya, and Alexandria.
115-125 AD	The *Gospel of the Hebrews* appears.
130 AD	Earliest allusion to existence of Gospels appears in the works of Bishop Papias.
131 AD	Second Jewish rebellion, led by (Messiah) Simon Bar Kochba, begins.
136 AD	Jewish rebellion crushed. Emperor Hadrian institutes oppressive measures. Jerusalem renamed Aelia and Pagan statues placed where Jewish shrines had been. Jews forbidden to enter the city.
140 AD	First mention of Gospels in work of Aristedes of Athens
144 AD	Marcion excommunicated for rejecting the Old Testament.
150 AD	Justin Martyr specifically mentions the Gospels of Luke, Matthew, and Mark. The *Protoevangelium of James* appears. Hegesippus composes *Memoranda*.
161 AD	Council of Alexandria condemns Docetism as a heresy.
180 AD	Irenaeus certifies the existence of the four Gospels.
200 AD	First attempt to write down the Jewish Mishnah.

248 AD	Origen publishes *Against Celsus*.
257 AD	Pope Stephen I asserts the preeminence of the Bishop of Rome.
258 AD	Emperor Valerian orders the execution of all Christian clergy.
274 AD	Emperor Aurelian makes Pagan Cult Sol Invictus the official religion of Rome.
300 AD	Eusebius publishes *Ecclesiastical History*.
303 AD	Emperor Diocletian orders Christian books burned.
311 AD	Emperor Galerius grants Christians freedom of worship.
313 AD	Edit of Milan following Emperor Constantine's victory at the Milvian Bridge.
325 AD	Council of Nicea produces the Nicene Creed.
327 AD	Church built over a cave where Jesus was supposedly born. Supervised by Emperor Constantine's mother, Helena.
331 AD	Constantine requests Eusebius to create 50 bibles.
337 AD	Death of Constantine.
345 AD	Pope Julius sets Jesus' birth date as December 25th.
367 AD	First known listing of the 27 books of the NT by Bishop Athanasius of Alexandria.
381 AD	Christianity becomes State religion of the Roman Empire under Emperor Theodosius. The 1st Council of Constantinople defines the idea of the "trinity".
382-3 AD	St Jerome publishes the Latin Vulgate (official Bible of Catholic church).
386 AD	Priscillian, Bishop of Avila, becomes the first church sanctioned execution for heresy.
391 AD	Emperor Theodosius abolishes all non-Christian churches, launching widespread looting and destruction, including the library at Alexandria.
393 AD	Church council at Hippo affirms 27 canonical books. Emperor Theodosius abolishes the Olympics as a Pagan celebration.
400 AD	Palestinian Talmud written down.
416 AD	Christians successfully lobby for a law that bars Pagans from public employment.

Jesus Who?

431 AD	Council of Ephesus elevates Mary to "Mother of God" from "Mother of Christ".
451 AD	Council of Chalcedon, under Emperor Marcian and Pope Leo, accepts full humanity and full divinity of Jesus, resulting in the schism of the Egyptian Coptic Church.
494 AD	Pope Gelasius informs Emperor Anastasius I that the Pope is supreme over the King.
500 AD	Babylonian Talmud written down.
589 AD	Toledo Council of Bishops holds that Father, Son, and Holy Ghost are three substances of the same divine nature.
591 AD	Pope Gregory the Great claims that Mary Magdalene was a prostitute.
610 AD	Muhammad receives his first revelation.
649 AD	Lateran Council endorses the concept of Mary's "perpetual virginity", confirmed in 675 at Tolentino.
692 AD	At the Trullan Council, the Latin Cross is accepted as the official symbol of Christianity.
800 AD	Roman Pope crowns Charlemagne.
1054 AD	Eastern Orthodox Church breaks with Rome.
1099 AD	Crusades begin.
1139 AD	Catholic priests forbidden to have sex or be married.
1208 AD	Pope Innocent III offers indulgences and eternal salvation to recruit crusaders against the Cathars, who are eventually destroyed on March 16, 1244.
1215 AD	Fourth Lateran Council makes confession a requirement.
1216 AD	Order of the Dominicans formed under Spanish monk Dominic de Guzman, launching the Inquisition.
1307 AD	The Templars destroyed in France on Friday the 13th.
1456 AD	First printing of Latin (Vulgate) Bible following the invention of the printing press two years earlier.
1515 AD	First printing of Erasmus' edition of Greek New Testament.
1546 AD	Council of Trent declares Mary free of all sin.
1551 AD	4th edition of Greek New Testament divides text into verses for first time.

1611 AD	King James version of the Bible produced (based on Latin Vulgate).
1689 AD	Richard Simon, a French Catholic, publishes *Critical History of the Text of the New Testament*, identifying significant textual variations between the different versions.
1707 AD	John Mill, an English Protestant, published a version of Greek New Testament containing notes that identified more than 30,000 variations between previous versions.
1769 AD	Posthumous publication of Herman Reimarus' *The Aims of Jesus and of His Disciples*, which is the first systematic criticism of the story of Jesus.
1774 AD	German scholar Johann Griesbach coins the word "synoptic" for the Gospels of Mark, Matthew, and Luke.
1835 AD	Publication of two volume *Life of Jesus Critically Examined* by German scholar David Friedrich Strauss.
1844 AD	Discovery of *Codex Sinaiticus* at St. Catherine's monastery by Constantin Tischendorf. March 22, 1844 was the date of the 2nd Coming predicted by William Miller, the founder of the 7th Day Adventists.
1854 AD	Pope Pius IX makes "immaculate conception" a requirement of Catholic faith and adds that Mary herself was free from original sin. Four years later Mary appears to Bernadette at Lourdes.
1859 AD	Gravesite of Roman soldier Pandera discovered.
1869 AD	Pope Pius IX declares papal infallibility during First Vatican Council. Council of Bishops confirms on July 18, 1870.
1870 AD	Roman Catholic Church hegemony reduced to Vatican City by Italian troops on September 21.
1872 AD	Jehovah's Witnesses founded in U.S. by Charles Russell.
1873 AD	Discovery of the *Didache* in Constantinople.
1886 AD	Discovery of 8th Century fragments at Akhmin in Upper Egypt.
1896/7 AD	Discovery of Essene documents in Cairo synagogue storeroom.

Jesus Who?

1902 AD	Pope Leo XII creates Pontifical Biblical Commission to oversee all theological scholarship.
1907 AD	Pope Pius X issues formal ban against "Modernist" movement.
1945 AD	Discovery of Nag Hammadi library.
1947 AD	Discovery of Dead Sea Scrolls at Qumran.
1950 AD	Pope Pius XII declares that Mary ascended into heaven directly.
1961 AD	Discovery of inscription referring to Pontius Pilate as "praefectus" or Prefect.
1965 AD	The 2nd Vatican Council declares that the death of Jesus is not the fault of all Jews.
1969 AD	The Catholic Church officially denies that Mary Magdalene was a prostitute.
2002 AD	Ossuary of James the Just found.

This 3rd Century mosaic shows Jesus as the Sun God. Early Christianity competed with various Sun God cults and many of the traditions of the cults were adopted by the Christians in order to win converts. This mosaic is in the Vatican Grottoes under St. Peter's Basilica in Rome.

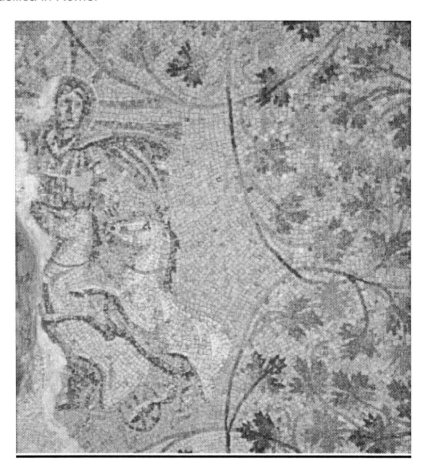

Appendix 2
Jesus – Myth vs. Reality

Jesus Christ was born in the year 0 in a manger in the town of Bethlehem.	Joshua ben Joseph was born around the year 6 B.C., either in a small village on the outskirts of Jerusalem, called Qumran, or in Galilee.
His mother, Mary, was a virgin and his father, Joseph, was a carpenter.	His mother, Miriam, was a nun and his father, Joseph, was a devoutly religious member of an orthodox Jewish sect called the Essenes. Joseph made a living as a general contractor, traveling from village to village in Galilee, and gave most of his money to the Essenes.
Mary became pregnant by the Holy Spirit while engaged to Joseph. An angel appeared to Joseph and dissuaded him from abandoning Mary and he went ahead and married her.	Mary became pregnant following the first marriage ceremony of the Essenes, but prior to the traditional December time period, thus violating one of the Essene rules. As unorthodox as this was, they received the blessings of the Essene leadership and proceeded to the 2nd marriage ceremony.
Jesus was born on December 25th.	Joshua was born in June/July, while shepherds tended their sheep in the fields. This was two

	months earlier than demanded by Essene principles which dictated that Davidic heirs be born in the Jewish month of Atonement (September)
At his birth, three kings came from the East to worship him, drawn there by a bright star. Shortly after his birth, the family returned to Nazareth where they lived, having come to Bethlehem to participate in the census.	
Jesus was the only child of Mary and Joseph.	Joshua was the oldest son, and had 4 brothers and 2 sisters, all of whom were raised to be devoutly religious within the context of the orthodox Essene sect.
The only thing we know about Jesus' early life is that he attended synagogue when he was 12 years old.	Joshua spent his formative years being raised in the Qumran community, as the "crown prince" who would someday assume the mantel of the Davidic Kings of Israel, from which his father, Joseph, was descended. Though raised within the sect, Joshua had problems reconciling their strict religious precepts with the reality of the Galilee he saw while touring with his father, from their home base in Capernaum.
Approximately 30 years later, following his baptism by John the Baptist, his cousin, Jesus	At the age of 30, inspired, perhaps, by the rebellion of another Essene devotee who left

commenced his ministry,	the fold and started his own sect (John the Baptist), Joshua left Qumran and became a disciple of John. After John died, Joshua established his own following throughout Galilee.
Jesus' ministry took place over a period of one to three years,	His ministry lasted more than a decade, from the mid 20s to 36 A.D.
Jesus had 12 disciples.	Joshua developed thousands of devout followers and an extensive network.
	As was common amongst Jews at that time, and especially among heirs to the Davidic line, Joshua married, to a woman named Mary Magdalene, who was one of his followers and supporters.
In 30 A.D. at the age of 30 by order of the Roman authorities, he was nailed on the cross, died, placed in a tomb, and was resurrected three days later.	In 36 A.D., at the age of 42, by order of the Jewish authorities, he was stoned to death and hung from a tree, placed in a common grave, however, his body was never found and a legend developed that he had been raised from the dead.
Peter, one of his disciples, assumed the leadership of the new religion.	His oldest brother, James, assumed the leadership of his following, and upon James'

	death, his brother Jude took over. The Christ Cult was eventually wiped out by the Romans in 130 A.D., although his teachings inspired a number of offshoots.

References

Acharya, S. *The Christ conspiracy.* 1999. Kempton, IL: Adventures Unlimited Press

Asimov, Isaac. *Asimov's guide to the Bible.* 1968. New York: Random House.

Bagnall, Roger & Frier, Bruce. *The demography of Roman Egypt.* 1994. Cambridge Press.

Baigent, M. *The Jesus papers.* 2006. San Francisco: HarperCollins.

Baigent, M & Leigh, R. *The Dead Sea Scrolls deception.* 1991. London: Jonathan Cape.

Baigent, M, Leigh, R., & Lincoln, H. *Holy blood, holy grail.* 1983. New York: Dell

Besdine, Matthew. *The Jocasta Complex, Mothering and Genius.* 1968. Psychoanalytic Review, 55, 259-277.

Betz, Otto. "Was John the Baptist an Essene?" *Biblical Review*, December 1990.

Bloom, Harold. *Jesus and Yahweh.* 2005. New York: Riverhead Books.

Borg, Marcus. *Meeting Jesus again for the first time.* 1994. New York: HarperCollins

Bridge, Steven. *Getting the Gospels.* 2004. Peabody, Mass: Hendrickson Publishers.

Brown, Raymond. *The death of the Messiah.* 1994. New York: Doubleday.

Bultmann, R. *Die Ersforschung der synoptischen Evangelien.* 1925. Goettingen.

Burkert, W. *Greek religion: Archaic and classical.* 1985. Oxford: Blackwell Publishers.

Butz, Jeffrey. *The brother of Jesus and the lost teachings of Christianity.* 2005. Rochester, Vermont: Inner Traditions.

Campbell, Joseph. *The hero with a thousand faces.* 1949. Boulder, Colorado: Paladin.

Carney, Thomas. *The shape of the past: Models and Antiquity.* 1975. Lawrence: Coronado Press.

Carrier, Richard. "The spiritual body of Christ and the legend of the empty tomb." In R. Price & J. Lowder (Eds.) *The empty tomb.* Pp. 105-231. 2005. New York: Prometheus Books.

Chilton, Bruce. *Rabbi Jesus.* 2000. New York: Doubleday

Chilton, Bruce. *Mary Magdalene.* 2005. New York: Doubleday.

Chilton, Bruce & Evans, Craig. *Studying the historical Jesus.* 1997. Boston: Brill Academic Publishers

Cohn, Haim. *The trial and death of Jesus.* 1963. New York: HarperCollins.

Craveri, Marcello. *The life of Jesus.* 1967. New York: Grove Press.

Crosson, John Dominic. "Mark and the relatives of Jesus". *Novum Testamentum*, 15, 1973

Crosson, John Dominic. *The historical Jesus. The life of a Mediterranean Jewish peasant.* 1991. San Francisco: Harper.

Crosson, John Dominic. *Jesus. A revolutionary biography*. 1994. San Francisco: Harper.

Crosson, John Dominic & Reed, Jonathan. *Excavating Jesus*. 2001. San Francisco: Harper.

Doane, Thomas. *Bible myths and their parallels in other religions*. 1985. Whitefish, MT: Kessinger Publishing

Dodd, C.H. *The interpretation of the fourth Gospel*. 1953. Cambridge University Press.

Downing, Gerald. *Cynics and Christian origins*. 1992. Edinburgh: T&T Clark.

Duquesne, Jacques. *Jesus: An unconventional biography*. 1994. Liquori, Missouri: Triumph Books

Edinger, Edward. *Ego and archetype*. 1972. New York: Putnam

Ehrman, Bart. *Misquoting Jesus: The story behind who changed the Bible and why*. 2005. New York: HarperCollins.

Eisenman, Robert. *James the Brother of Jesus: The Key to Unlocking the Secrets of Early Christianity and the Dead Sea Scrolls*. 1997. New York: Viking Penguin.

Eisenstadt, J. Marvin. *Parental loss and genius*. 1978. *American Psychologist*, 33, 211-222.

Eisler, R. *Orpheus the Fisher*. 1920. Whitefish, MT: Kessinger Publishing

Eisler, R. *The Messiah Jesus and John the Baptist*. 1931. London: Methuen.

Ellegard, Alvar. *Jesus: One hundred years before Christ*. 1999. New York: Overlook Press.

Fidler, D. *Jesus Christ, Son of God.* 1993. Wheaton, IL: Quest Books.

Finegan, Jack. *The archeology of the New Testament.* 1969. Princeton, New Jersey: Princeton University Press.

Fox, Robin. *Pagans and Christians.* 1989. New York: Alfred A Knopf.

Funk, Robert W. & Hoover, Roy W. *The five gospels: The search for the authentic words of Jesus.* 1993. New York: Polebridge Press.

Frazer, J. *The golden bough.* 1922. London: Wordsworth Reference Books.

Freke, Timothy, & Gandy, Peter. *The Jesus mysteries. Was the original Jesus a Pagan God?* 1999. New York: Harmony.

Freke, Timothy, & Gandy, Peter. *Jesus and the lost goddess. The secret teachings of the original Christians.* 2001. New York: Harmony.

Galambush, Julie. *The reluctant parting: How the New Testament's Jewish writers created a Christian book.* 2005. New York: HarperCollins.

Gardner, L. *The illustrated bloodline of the Holy Grail.* 2001. New York: Barnes and Noble.

Grant, Robert. *Jesus after the Gospels.* 1990. Louisville: John Knox Press.

Graves, Kersey. *The world's 16 crucified saviors: Christianity before Christ.* Kila, MT: Kessinger

Guthrie, K. *The Pythagorean sourcebook.* 1987. York Beach, ME: Phanes Press.

Harpur, Tom. *The Pagan Christ.* 2004. Toronto: Walker Publishing.

Harvey, A.E. *Companion to the New Testament.* 1970. Oxford: Oxford University Press.

Haskins, S. *Mary Magdalene: Myth and metaphor.* 1991. New York: HarperCollins.

Hengel, Martin. *Crucifixion in the ancient world and the folly of the message of the cross.* 1977. Philadelphia: Fortress Press.

Higgins, Godfrey. *Anacalypsis.* 1992. West Midlands, U.K.: A&B Books

Hoffman, R. *Celsus on the true doctrine.* 1987. Oxford: Oxford University Press.

Jackson, John G. *Christianity before Christ.* 1985. Parsippany, NJ: American Atheists Press

James, William. *The varieties of religious experiences.* 1901. New York: Modern Library.

Johnson, Paul. *A history of Christianity.* 1976. New York: Touchstone.

Kaiser, A. Faber. *Jesus died in Kashmir.* 1977. London: Gordon Cremonesi.

Keeler, Bronson. *A short history of the Bible.* 1965. London: Lightning Source

Kelly, Joseph F. *The origins of Christmas.* 2005. Collegeville, Minn: Liturgical Press.

Kidger, Mark. *The star of Bethlehem: An astronomer's view.* 1999. Princeton: Princeton University Press

Kittler, Glenn D. *Edgar Cayce on the Dead Sea Scrolls.* 1970. New York: Warner Books.

Klinghoffer, David. *Why the Jews rejected Jesus.* 2005 New York: Doubleday

Koester, Helmut. *Introduction to the New Testament.* 1980. New York: Gruyter.

Knight, Christopher & Lomas, Robert. *The Hiram key.* 1996. New York: Barnes & Noble.

Lazare, Daniel. "False Testament." *Harpers Magazine,* March 2002.

Lietzmann, H. *The history of the early church.* 1961. Cambridge: Lutterworth Press.

Loffreda, Stanislao. *Recovering Capharaum.* 1985. Jerusalem: Edizioni Custodia Terra Santa.

Lowder, Jeffrey "Historical evidence and the empty tomb story." In R. Price & J. Lowder (Eds.) *The empty tomb.* Pp. 261-306. 2005. New York: Prometheus Books.

MacDonald, Dennis. *The Homeric epic and the Gospel of Mark.* 2000. New Haven: Yale University Press.

Mack, Burton. *A myth of innocence: Mark and Christian origins.* 1988. Philadelphia: Fortress.

Mackey, James. *Jesus, the man and the myth.* 1979. London: SCM.

Malina, Bruce. *The New Testament world.* 2001. Louisville: Westminster John Knox Press.

Mason, Steve. *Josephus and the New Testament.* 2003. Peabody, MA: Hendrickson

Massey, Gerald. *Gnostic and historic Christianity.* 1985. Kila, MT: Kessinger

Massey, Gerald. *The historical Jesus and the mythical Christ.* 2002. Kila, MT: Kessinger

McCane, Bryon. *Roll back the stone: Death and burial in the world of Jesus.* 2003. Harrisburg: Trinity Press.

McClymond, Michael. *Familiar stranger: An introduction to Jesus of Nazareth.* 2004. Grand Rapids: Eerdmans.

Meier, John. *A marginal Jew. Rethinking the historical Jesus.* 2001. New York: Doubleday.

Meyer, Marvin. *The Gospel of Thomas: Hidden sayings of Jesus.* 1992. New York: HarperCollins.

Meyer, Marvin. *The Gnostic discoveries.* 2005. New York: HarperCollins.

Mitchell, Stephen. *Jesus: What he really said and did.* 2002. New York: HarperCollins.

Miller, John. *Jesus at thirty. A psychological and historical portrait.* 1997. Minneapolis: Fortress Press.

Notovitch, Nicolas. *The unknown life of Jesus.* 1894. San Francisco: Dragon Press

Painter, John. *Just James: The brother of Jesus in history and tradition.* 1999. Minneapolis: Fortress Press

Patzia, Arthur. *The making of the New Testament.* 1995. Downers Grove, Illinois: InterVarsity Press.

Perkins, Pheme. *Reading the New Testament.* 1988. New York: Paulist Press.

Porter, J. *Jesus Christ. The Jesus of history, the Christ of faith.* 2004. New York: Barnes & Noble.

Price, R. *Deconstructing Jesus.* 2000. New York: Prometheus Books.

Ratzinger, Joseph. *Introduction to Christianity.* 1969. San Francisco: Communio Books.

Renan, Ernest. *The life of Jesus.* 1927. New York: Prometheus Books.

Roberts, Paul William. *Journey of the Magi.* 1995. London: Tauris Parke

Robertson, John. *Christianity and mythology.* 1900. London: Watts.

Sanders. E.P. *The historical figure of Jesus.* 1993. New York: Penguin Books.

Schillebeeckx, Edward. *Jesus: An experiment in Christology.* 1979. New York: Seabury.

Schonfield. Hugh. *The Passover plot.* 1965. New York: Random House

Schonfield. Hugh. *The Jesus party.* 1974. New York : Macmillan

Schoeps, Hans. *Theologie und Geschichte des Judenchristentums.* 1948. Mohr: Tubingen

Shanks, Hershel & Witherington, Ben. *The Brother of Jesus.* 2003. San Francisco: Harper.

Shorto, Russell. *Gospel truth.* 1997. New York: Riverhead Books.

Sinclair, Upton. *A personal Jesus.* 1952. New York: Evans Publishing

Spoto, Donald. *The hidden Jesus.* 1998. New York: St. Martin's Press.

Stanton, G. *Gospel truth.* 1995. New York: Harper Collins.

Starbird, Margaret. *Mary Magdalene: Bride in exile.* 2005. Solon, Maine: Bear & Co.

Sullivan, Clayton. *Rescuing Jesus from the Christians.* 2002. Harrisburg: Trinity Press.

Taylor, Robert. The Diegesis. Quoted in Acharya, S. *The Christ conspiracy.* 1999.

Thiering, Barbara. *Jesus and the riddle of the Dead Sea Scrolls.* 1992. Sydney: Doubleday.

VanderKam, James & Flint, Peter. *The meaning of the Dead Sea Scrolls.* 2002. San Francisco: Harpers

Van Voorst, Robert. *Jesus outside the New Testament.* 2000. Grand Rapids: Eerdmans.

Vermes, Geza. *Jesus the Jew.* 1973. Minneapolis: Fortress Press.

Waite, Charles. *History of the Christian religion to the Year 200.* 1992. Chicago: C. V. Waite & Co.

Wells, G. *The historical evidence for Jesus.* 1988. New York: Prometheus.

Wheless, Joseph. *Forgery in Christianity.* 1990 Whitefish, MT: Kessinger Publishing

Wilson, A.N. *Jesus: A life.* 1992. New York: Norton & Co.

Witherington, Ben. *The Jesus quest.* 1997. Downers Grove, Illinois: InterVarsity Press.

"Yeshu." *Wikipedia, The Free Encyclopedia.* 7 Feb 2006, 19:29

Index

Abraham, 26, 36, 48, 66, 74, 144, 165, 201, 230, 237
Apollonius, 156
Archelaus, 142, 169, 239
Arian, 228
Augustine, 48, 50, 106, 173
Augustus, 50
Barabbas, 187, 189, 197, 198, 229
Bethlehem, xii, 24, 47, 61, 62, 63, 65, 67, 69, 77, 78, 99, 233, 247, 255
Book of Solomon, 35
Buddha, 46, 66, 68, 101
Caiaphas, 143, 186, 196, 198, 200, 240
Capernaum, 17, 35, 85, 92, 134, 247
Celsus, 48, 73, 84, 99, 107, 155, 184, 255
Christmas, 43, 58, 61, 255
Clement of Alexandria, 8, 9, 10, 59, 178
Clement of Rome, 7
Clopas, 86, 145
Constantine, 30, 242
David, 22, 26, 33, 48, 51, 63, 69, 71, 72, 73, 79, 83, 84, 142, 223, 224, 225, 229, 230, 231, 255
Dead Sea Scrolls, 38, 43, 80, 163, 171, 172, 255, 259
Dialogue with Trypho, 44, 64

Didache, 2, 199
Dionysius of Corinth, 9
Dionysus, 55, 70, 154, 202, 215
Docetism, 44, 241
Ebionites, 33, 72, 73
Egypt, 17, 18, 38, 53, 54, 98, 99, 100, 185, 237, 238, 244, 251
End Times, 97, 174, 238
Essenes, 32, 33, 58, 60, 69, 71, 79, 80, 90, 94, 95, 96, 97, 98, 111, 112, 118, 132, 146, 158, 163, 167, 170, 171, 174, 224, 238, 247
Essenes, 247
Eusebius, 9, 10, 38, 44, 72, 96, 189
Gnostic, 4, 120, 122, 173, 190, 192, 214, 216, 223, 256, 257
Golgotha, 197, 198
Gospel by Matthew, 5
Gospel of John, 2, 4, 7, 20, 22, 28, 63, 71, 72, 74, 75, 85, 88, 103, 104, 119, 121, 123, 124, 141, 142, 146, 159, 170, 178, 186, 187, 188, 195, 201, 208, 212, 216
Gospel of Judas, 135
Gospel of Luke, 7, 8, 9, 19, 32, 38, 58, 80, 84, 93, 106, 119, 142, 167, 227, 241

Gospel of Matthew, 2, 5, 7, 9, 16, 22, 24, 25, 30, 38, 58, 62, 64, 65, 67, 71, 74, 77, 79, 86, 91, 92, 99, 100, 105, 150, 167, 178, 187, 203, 216, 220, 229, 231
Gospel of Nicodemus, 189
Gospel of Peter, 125
Gospel of Philip, 192
Gospel of Thomas, 2, 38, 75, 85, 87, 94, 132, 136, 174, 175, 178, 180, 199
Hanina ben Dosa, 156, 159, 229
Herod, 46, 50, 57, 58, 61, 65, 67, 78, 80, 99, 141, 142, 169, 195, 196, 198, 224, 238, 239
Herod Antipas, 50, 142, 146, 239, 240
Herodians, 35
Herodias, 143, 240
Hippolytus, 59, 163, 192
Honi the Circledrawer, 45, 155, 229, 231
Horus, 23, 46, 51, 65, 68, 69, 142, 149
Ignatius, 5, 7, 36, 42, 45
India, 68, 100, 101, 102, 124, 191
Irenaeus, 8, 49, 72, 144, 201, 206, 241
Isaiah, 31, 64, 65, 66, 69, 77, 104, 127, 171, 223, 226, 227
Isis, 68, 69
James, Brother of Jesus, 11, 33, 52, 71, 72, 80, 85, 86, 87, 93, 126, 145, 165, 195, 199, 216, 218, 221, 240, 247, 259
Jesus ben Ananias, 54
Jesus ben Gamala, 54, 55
Jesus ben Saphat, 54
Jesus ben Sirach, 54
Jesus ben Stada, 54, 55
Jesus Seminar, 175, 176, 178
John the Baptist, xii, 22, 45, 84, 93, 95, 97, 98, 102, 112, 118, 132, 142, 143, 166, 167, 169, 170, 171, 173, 174, 184, 186, 190, 195, 200, 219, 222, 224, 234, 240, 247
Joseph, xii, 14, 38, 51, 52, 62, 70, 71, 72, 73, 75, 77, 78, 79, 80, 81, 82, 83, 85, 86, 87, 90, 91, 92, 98, 105, 145, 171, 221, 247, 255, 257
Joseph of Arimathea, 20, 27, 90, 145, 204, 206
Josephus, 5, 7, 38, 42, 51, 92, 93, 100, 106, 109, 111, 112, 113, 142, 143, 146, 155, 167, 186, 188, 200, 204, 221, 240, 241, 256
Judas Iscariot, 22, 36, 131, 147, 149, 186, 195, 217
Judas the Galilean, 112, 225, 239
Judas, Brother of Jesus, 80, 190
Justin Martyr, 8, 9, 44, 49, 64, 189, 241
Krishna, 46, 66, 68
Lazarus, 20, 90, 108, 117, 119, 121, 124, 125, 145, 186, 219
Magi, 37, 65, 66, 99, 258

Mamzer, 76, 78, 234
Mandaeans, 93, 102, 172, 190, 240
Marcion, 8, 9, 44, 72, 241
Mary Magdalene, 11, 83, 84, 85, 106, 117, 118, 119, 120, 121, 122, 123, 124, 125, 126, 127, 145, 147, 159, 216, 220, 243, 245, 247, 252, 255
Mary, Mother of James, 121, 147
Mary, Mother of Jesus, xii, 14, 22, 53, 60, 62, 64, 68, 69, 70, 71, 72, 73, 74, 75, 77, 78, 79, 80, 81, 83, 84, 85, 86, 99, 105, 145, 171, 216, 247
Mary, Sister of Martha, 83, 85, 119, 121, 145
Mary, Sister-in-law of Mary, 83, 86, 121
Mithra, 22, 23, 46, 47, 48, 55, 59, 60, 68, 215
Moses, 18, 36, 51, 99, 100, 106
Nag Hammadi, 32, 157, 191
Nasrani, 93, 155
Nazareth, xii, 14, 17, 38, 62, 83, 91, 92, 94, 233, 247
Nazarite, 17, 92, 93, 110
Nero, 37, 240
Octavian, 68, 238
Origen, 9, 64, 73, 81, 155, 178
Osiris, 46, 59, 68, 215, 217
Pandera, 46, 53, 73, 74, 99, 100, 244
Papias, 2, 5, 7, 8, 175, 206, 241

Passover, 80, 110, 131, 146, 166, 185, 195, 206, 217, 258
Paul, 6, 7, 9, 38, 45, 71, 72, 86, 87, 93, 104, 107, 126, 156, 158, 178, 206, 214, 216, 219, 220, 221, 226, 227, 240, 255, 258
Peter, 7, 9, 11, 17, 22, 30, 107, 108, 125, 147, 158, 165, 195, 196, 204, 207, 209, 212, 219, 222, 225, 240, 247, 254, 259
Pharisees, 17, 35, 53, 75, 98, 111, 112, 122, 135, 146, 186, 201, 224
Pilate, 18, 28, 50, 106, 142, 143, 147, 187, 189, 196, 197, 198, 200, 204, 206, 239, 240
Pistis Sophia, 125, 178
Polycarp, 5, 7, 36, 44, 188
Porphyry, 44
Protoevangelium of James, 64, 68, 77, 81, 84, 87, 241
Psalms, 36, 217
Pythagoras, 69, 98, 122, 155, 223
Q document, 2, 94, 132, 135, 175, 178
Quirinius, 57, 58
Qumran, 32, 64, 94, 95, 96, 97, 103, 113, 157, 170, 171, 205, 224, 234, 238, 239, 247
Qur'an, 100, 106, 167, 190
Sadducees, 17, 111, 112, 146
Sanhedrin, 17, 74, 185, 206, 217, 218
Scribes, 17, 63, 75, 111, 122, 196, 201

Secret Gospel of Mark, 10, 116, 117
Simon Bar Kochba, 50, 225, 241
Simon Magus, 120, 155, 184, 191, 192
Simon of Cyrene, 17, 188, 190, 191, 197, 198
Simon the leper, 145
Simon the Zealot, 22, 98, 149, 162, 186
Simon, Brother of Jesus, 80, 85
Sleb, 132
Sol Invictus, 59, 60, 108, 242
Son of God, 33, 47, 51, 116, 128, 129, 156, 167, 185, 210, 211, 222, 225, 228, 229, 230, 231, 254
Son of Man, 33, 212
Song of Solomon, 65, 124
Sons of Thunder, 27, 98, 119, 162
Suffering servant, 127, 211, 226, 227, 228
Talmud, 74, 84, 92, 97, 142, 184, 209, 242, 243
Tammuz, 46, 102, 215
Tatian, 8, 9
Tertullian, 9, 47, 48, 49, 59, 189
The Egyptian, 99, 100, 240
Therapeuts, 98, 153, 163
Theudas, 225, 240
Virgin birth, 67, 68, 69, 72, 73, 184
Wilderness, 95, 97, 134, 142, 156, 170, 224
Yahweh, 51, 251
Zealots, 98, 111, 112, 119, 162, 163, 186, 239

Interact with the Author

Come to our Internet site and interact with the author and other Jesus scholars from all over the world, and discuss important issues raised in this book.

Express yourself.

You can talk about:

- Movies (like The DaVinci Code)
- TV Specials (like the Gospel of Judas)
- Books (like The Jesus Papers)
- Magazines (like the recent Time issue on Mary Magdalene)
- Historical issues (like we discuss in the book)

http://www.JesusPolice.com

Printed in the United States
59167LVS00004B/6